Personality

Personality

Edited by ROM HARRÉ

BASIL BLACKWELL · OXFORD

British Library Cataloguing in Publication Data

Personality.
  Index.
  ISBN 0–631–17360–9
  1. Harré, Romano
  155.2′08   BF698
Personality – Addresses, essays, lectures

Printed in Great Britain
by Western Printing Services Limited, Bristol
and bound at The Pitman Press, Bath

Contents

Introduction

The study of social psychology, the attempt to understand the individual's relation to his social behaviour and social theories, has been transformed in recent years by the shift of attention from mere behaviour, to the genesis of action and the role of speech in the creation and maintenance of the social world. This has been reflected both in a radical change in theory and in an increasing shift away from naïve experimentation to more subtle methods of empirical investigation. As in most areas of social psychological study, the investigations of personality have been transformed. In this volume of essays and its companion, *The Self*, edited by T. Mischel, an attempt is made to bring together some recent strands of thought both as to theory and the empirical work associated with it, to weave the work of recent years into some sort of coherent whole.

Four main concepts are at work in our understanding of individual human beings as social actors. They are: the person, that is the embodied self, the social individual; the self, that is the individual considered as a psychic unity of sorts; the personality, the way a person's public presentation of himself is seen as invariant by those who interact with him in different situations; and finally the character, the supposed underlying qualities that are ascribed to a person in the course of his acquiring a public reputation. Character is sometimes thought to be the foundation not only of personality, that is not only of the self as presented, but also of the style and manner in which, and the kind of actions chosen by, a person in his daily interaction with others. In this volume, personality becomes the focus of our attention. We consider it in three stages. In the first section we examine various influences that bear upon the development of personality, seen both from the point of view of the person whose public reputation it is, and from the point of view of those in whose eyes he has a personality. We try to trace some, amongst the many influences that bear upon the growth and development of personality. In the second section we turn to critical and constructive accounts of the ways in which personality has been described, trying to combine an analysis of the language used by folk in their ascriptions of personality with a theoretical perspective in which this important but elusive aspect of human life can be adequately described. The third section is devoted to the consequences of the shifts in theory retailed in sections I and II for the methods we might use for the empirical study of personality, what one might not improperly call its assessment. We are well aware that none of the component studies of this volume presents a complete or finished treatment of the area investigated, but we hope that, taken together, the contributions to this volume have a certain unity of purpose and underlying conception of the social world and the proper methods of its investigation, on the basis of which the study freed from the cramps of its previous unsatisfactory theoretical state, can now go forward.

Several of the essays in this volume have already appeared in various places. We are grateful to the editor of *Support, Innovation and Autonomy*, and Tavistock Publications, and to the editors of *The Oxford Review of Education* for their permission to make use of material previously published by them. Chapters 2, 4 and 5 have appeared in *The Journal for the Theory of Social Behaviour*, edited by P. F. Secord and T. Mischel, and published by Basil Blackwell, Oxford.

Oxford, 1976   R. Harré
                                                                              Editor

PART I The Acquisition of Personality

1 The Self-Reliant Personality: Some Conditions that Promote it*

JOHN BOWLBY

The Concept of Secure Base

Evidence is accumulating that human beings of all ages are happiest and able to deploy their talents to best advantage when they are confident that, standing behind them, there are one or more trusted persons who will come to their aid should difficulties arise. The person trusted, also known as an attachment figure (Bowlby, 1969), can be considered as providing his (or her) companion with a secure base from which to operate.

The requirement of an attachment figure, a secure personal base, is by no means confined to children though, because of its urgency during the early years, it is during those years that it is most evident and has been most studied. There are good reasons for believing, however, that the requirement applies also to adolescents and to mature adults as well. In the latter, admittedly, the requirement is commonly less evident, and it probably differs both between the sexes and at different phases of life. For those reasons and also for reasons stemming from the values of western culture, the requirement of adults for a secure base tends often to be overlooked, or even denigrated.

In the picture of personality functioning that emerges there are two main sets of influences. The first concerns the presence or absence, partial or total, of a trustworthy figure willing and able to provide the kind of secure base required at each phase of the lifecycle. These constitute the external, or environmental, influences. The second set concerns the relative ability or inability of an in-

* Reprinted from Gosling, R., *Support, Innovation and Autonomy*, Tavistock, London, 1973.

dividual, first, to recognize when another person is both trustworthy and willing to provide a base and, secondly, when recognized, to collaborate with that person in such a way that a mutually rewarding relationship is initiated and maintained. These constitute the internal, or organismic, influences.

Throughout life the two sets of influences interact in complex and circular ways. In one direction the kinds of experience a person has, especially during childhood, greatly affect both whether he expects later to find a secure personal base, or not, and also the degree of competence he has to initiate and maintain a mutually rewarding relationship when opportunity offers. In the reverse direction the nature of the expectations a person has, and the degree of competence he brings, play a large part in determining both the kinds of person with whom he associates and how they then treat him. Because of these interactions, whatever pattern is first established tends to persist. This is a main reason why the pattern of family relationships a person experiences during childhood is of such crucial importance for the development of his personality.

Looked at in this light healthy personality functioning at every age reflects, first, an individual's ability to recognize suitable figures willing and able to provide him with a secure base and, secondly, his ability to collaborate with such figures in mutually rewarding relationships. By contrast, many forms of disturbed personality functioning reflect an individual's impaired ability to recognize suitable and willing figures and/or an impaired ability to collaborate in rewarding relationships with any such figure when found. Such impairment can be of every degree and take many forms: they include anxious clinging, demands excessive or over-intense for age and situation, aloof non-committal, and defiant independence.

Paradoxically, the healthy personality when viewed in this light proves by no means as independent as cultural stereotypes suppose. Essential ingredients are a capacity to rely trustingly on others when occasion demands and to know on whom it is appropriate to rely. A healthily functioning person is thus capable of exchanging roles when the situation changes. At one time he is providing a secure base from which his companion or companions can operate; at another he is glad to rely on one or another of his companions to provide him with just such a base in return.

A capacity to adopt either role as circumstances change is well-illustrated by many women during successive phases of their lives running from pregnancy through childbirth and on into mother-hood. A woman capable of coping successfully with these shifts is found by Wenner (1966) well able, during her pregnancy and puerperium, both to express her desire for support and help and also to do so in a direct and effective fashion to an appropriate figure. Her relationship with her husband is close and she is eager and content to rely on his support. In her turn she is able to give spontaneously to others, including her baby. By contrast, Wenner reports, a woman who experiences major emotional difficulties during pregnancy and puerperium is found to have great difficulty in relying on others. She is either unable to express her desire for support or else she does so in a demanding aggressive way, in either case reflecting her lack of confidence that it will be forthcoming. Commonly she is both dissatisfied with what she may be given and is herself unable to give spontaneously to others.

In order to provide the continuity of potential support that is the essence of a secure base, the relationships between the individuals concerned must persist over a period of time, measured in terms of years. Although, for clarity of exposition, theory is often best formu-lated in non-feeling terms, it must be borne constantly in mind that many of the most intense human emotions arise during the forma-tion, the maintenance, the disruption, and the renewal of those re-lationships in which one partner is providing a secure base for the other, or in which they alternate roles. Whereas the unchallenged maintenance of such relationships is experienced as a source of sec-urity, threat of loss gives rise to anxiety and often to anger, and actual loss to the turmoil of feeling that is grief.

The theoretical position proposed includes a number of concepts familiar in psychoanalytic object relations theory; for example, Fairbairn's concept of mature dependency and Winnicott's concept of the facilitating environment (Fairbairn, 1952; Winnicott, 1965). It differs, however, from traditional clinical theory at a number of points. One is the avoidance of the terms 'dependence' and 'depend-ency needs', which, it is held, are in part responsible for very serious confusion in existing theory. A second is to attribute importance for development to experiences during all the years of childhood and adolescence instead of almost exclusively to the earliest months or years. Others are that the schema proposed is cast in terms of control theory and that it draws not only on clinical data but also on the findings of a broad range of descriptive and experimental studies both of humans and of non-human primates.[1]

The aims of this paper are to indicate some of the evidence that supports the viewpoint sketched, to consider briefly what is known of the conditions that favour or impede the development of healthy personality as here conceived, and, if possible, to clarify theoretical issues that have proved troublesome.

Studies of Self-Reliant Men and Youths

During the past decade or two a number of clinicians have turned their attention to the study of individuals who, it is reasonable to believe, possess well-functioning and healthy personalities. Not only do these people show none of the usual signs of personality disturbance, either in the present or, as far as can be told, in their past, but they are plainly self-reliant and successful both in their human relationships and their work. Though each of the studies so far published is inadequate in a number of ways, findings are suggestive. First, these well-adapted personalities show a smoothly working balance of, on the one hand, initiative and self-reliance, and, on the other, a capacity both to seek help and to make use of help when occasion demands. Secondly, an examination of their development shows that they have grown up in closely knit families with parents who, it seems, have never failed to provide them with support and encouragement. Thirdly, though here evidence is less substantial, the family itself has been and still is part of a stable social network within which a growing child is welcome and can mix both with other adults and with peers, many of whom are familiar to him from his earliest years.

So far as it goes, each study gives the same picture, the picture of a stable family base from which first the child, then the adolescent and finally the young adult moves out in a series of ever-lengthening excursions. While autonomy is evidently encouraged in such families, it is not forced. Each step follows the previous one in a series of easy stages. Though home ties may be attenuated they are never broken.

[1] Both the theory itself and the evidence on which it rests are presented at greater length in the first and second volumes of *Attachment and Loss* (Bowlby, 1969 and 1973).

Astronauts rank high as self-reliant men capable of living and working effectively in conditions of great potential danger and stress. Their performance, their personalities and their histories have been studied by Korchin and Ruff. In two articles (Korchin and Ruff, 1964, Ruff and Korchin, 1967) they publish preliminary findings on a small sample of seven men.

Despite a high degree of self-reliance and a clear preference for independent action, all the men are reported to be 'comfortable when dependence on others is required' and to have a 'capacity to maintain *trust*, in what might seem conditions of *distrust*'. The performance of the crew of Apollo 13, which met with a mishap en route to the moon, is testimony to their capacity in this respect. Not only did they maintain their own efficiency in conditions of great danger but they continued to cooperate trustingly and effectively with their companions at the base on earth.

Turning to their life-histories we find that these men 'grew up in relatively small well-organized communities, with considerable family solidarity and strong identification with the father ... [They showed] a relatively smooth growth pattern in which they could meet available challenges, increase levels of aspiration, succeed and gain further confidence, and in this way grow in competence'.

Another study, this time of young men at college who appeared to their teachers to be of good general mental health and to promise well as youth leaders and community workers, is reported by Grinker (1962).

Among the sixty-five students interviewed Grinker regarded only a handful as showing neurotic character structure. The large majority seemed straightforward youths, honest and accurate in their self-evaluations, with a 'capacity for close and deep human relationships ... to members of their families, peers, teachers and to the interviewer'. Their reports of experiencing anxiety or sadness suggested that such feelings arose in appropriate situations and were neither severe nor prolonged.

As regards their experience of home life, the overall picture reported by the students is remarkably similar to that reported by the astronauts. In almost every case both parents were still alive. The typical picture presented was of a happy peaceful home in which both parents shared responsibilities and interests, and were regarded by the children as loving and giving. During childhood, they said, they had felt with mother above everything else secure. At the same time they had identified strongly with father. Grinker reports much further evidence in support of these conclusions.

The findings both of a developmental study, from age ten to seventeen years, of thirty-four adolescents of very different characters (Peck and Havighurst, 1960) and also of a small study of successful students during their transition from high school to first year in college (Murphey *et al.*, 1963) are very similar to Grinker's. Evidence presented suggests that both self-reliance and the capacity to rely on others are alike products of a family that provides strong support for its offspring combined with respect for their personal aspirations, their sense of responsibility and their ability to deal with the world. So far from sapping a child's self-reliance, it seems clear, strong family support can encourage it. Similar findings are reported from a more recent study of seventy-three teenage boys (Offer, 1969).

This same pattern of self-reliance resting on a secure attachment to a trusted figure, and developing from it, can be seen as early as a child's first birthday. Whether these early patterns are true forerunners of later ones, or not, must await further research. To those with experience of family psychiatry, however, it seems probable that they are.

Development during Infancy

Since Freud's earliest work a main tenet of psychoanalysis has been that the foundations of personality are laid during the early years of childhood. Opinion has differed, however, as to which years are the most important, what psychological processes are involved and what experiences are influential in determining outcome. So long as relevant empirical data were lacking it was inevitable that debate should reach deadlock. Now, however, thanks to the work of psychoanalysts, clinically oriented psychologists and ethologists, the position is changing. Though data are still woefully insufficient, enough are available to permit an attempt at a systematic articulation of data and theory. Thanks to developments in theoretical biology, moreover, theory can itself be reformulated in ways better suited to the data. Thus prospects for advance are now good.

Among those in the van of this movement is Mary Salter Ainsworth who, since working at the Tavistock between 1950 and 1954, has continued to study problems of attachment and separation.

Resulting from this she has published a naturalistic study of mother-infant interaction in Uganda (Ainsworth, 1967) and is now presenting results of a planned study of mother–infant interaction in white middle-class homes in Baltimore, Maryland.

During her study of infancy in Uganda Ainsworth noticed how infants, once mobile, commonly use mother as a base from which to explore. When conditions are favourable they move away from mother on exploratory excursions and return to her again from time to time. By eight months of age almost every infant observed who had had a stable mother-figure to whom to become attached showed this behaviour; but should mother be absent such organized excursions became much less evident or ceased. Subsequently Anderson (1972) has made similar observations of exploration from a base of children aged between fifteen months and two and a half years playing in a secluded part of a London park whilst mother sits quietly on a seat.

In her carefully planned project in Baltimore, Ainsworth is not only able to study this kind of behaviour more closely but has described many individual variations of it to be seen in a sample of twenty-three infants[2] at twelve months of age. Observations have been made of the infants' exploratory and attachment behaviour, and the balance between them, both when the infants are at home with mother and also when they are placed in a slightly strange test situation. In addition, having obtained data on the type of mothering each infant had been receiving throughout his first year of life (by means of prolonged observation sessions at three-weekly intervals in the child's home), Ainsworth is in a position to propose hypotheses linking certain types of behavioural organization at twelve months with certain types of preceding mothering experience. The project is described and preliminary findings reported in Ainsworth and Bell (1970); individual differences and their antecedents are discussed in Ainsworth, Bell and Stayton (1971, 1974).

The findings of the study show that, with only few exceptions, the way a particular infant of twelve months behaves with and without his mother at home and the way he behaves with and without her in a slightly strange test situation have much in common. Drawing on observations of behaviour in both types of situation it is then

[2] Although the total sample studied in the strange situation comprises fifty-six infants, only twenty-three of them have been observed also with mother at home.

possible to classify the infants into five main groups, according to two criteria: (a) how much or how little they explore when in different situations and (b) how they treat mother—when she is present, when she departs and when she returns.[3]

The five groups, with the number of infants classifiable into each, are as follows:

GROUP P: The exploratory behaviour of an infant in this group varies with the situation and is most evident in mother's presence. He uses mother as a base, keeps note of her whereabouts, and exchanges glances with her. From time to time he returns to her and enjoys contact with her. When she returns after a brief absence he greets her warmly. No ambivalence towards her is evident. N = 8.

GROUP Q: The behaviour of these infants is much like that of infants in Group P. Where it differs is, first, that infants in this group tend to explore more actively in the strange situation, and, secondly, they tend to be somewhat ambivalent towards mother. On the one hand, if ignored by her, an infant may become intensely demanding; on the other, he may ignore or avoid her in return. Yet at other times the pair are capable of happy exchanges together. N = 4.

GROUP R: An infant in this group explores very actively whether mother is present or absent, and whether the situation is familiar or strange. He tends, moreover, to have little to do with his mother, and is often not interested in being picked up by her. At other times, especially after his mother has left him alone in the strange situation, he behaves in a very contrary way, alternately seeking proximity to her and then avoiding it, or seeking contact and then wriggling away. N = 3.

[3] The classification presented here, based on behaviour in *both* types of situation, is a slightly modified version of one presented by Ainsworth *et al.* (1971) in which a child's behaviour in his own home is the *sole* source of data. Infants classified here into groups P, Q, and R are identical with the infants classified into Ainsworth's Groups I, II, and III. Those classified here into Group T are the same as those classified into Ainsworth's Group V, less one infant who, although passive at home, proved markedly independent in the strange situation test and is therefore transferred to Group S. The infants in Group S are the same as in Ainsworth's Group IV plus the one infant transferred. The classification presented here has Professor Salter Ainsworth's approval.

GROUP S: The behaviour of infants in this group is inconsistent. Sometimes they appear very independent, though usually for brief periods only; at others they seem markedly anxious regarding mother's whereabouts. They are distinctly ambivalent about contact with her, seeking it frequently yet not seeming to enjoy it when given, or even strongly resisting it. Oddly enough, in the strange situation they tend to ignore mother's presence and to avoid both proximity and contact with her. N = 5.

GROUP T: These infants tend to be passive both at home and in the strange situation. They show relatively little exploratory behaviour but much auto-erotic behaviour. They are conspicuously anxious about mother's whereabouts and cry much in her absence; yet they can be markedly ambivalent to her when she returns. N = 3.

When an attempt is made to evaluate these different patterns of behaviour as forerunners of future personality development the eight children in Group S and T seem the least likely to develop a stable self-reliance combined with trust in others. Some are passive in both situations; others explore but only briefly. Most of them seem anxious about mother's whereabouts, and relations with her tend to be extremely ambivalent.

The three children in Group R are most active in exploration and appear strongly independent. Yet their relations with mother are cautious, even slightly detached. To a clinician they give the impression of being unable to trust others, and to have developed a premature independence.

The four children in Group Q are more difficult to assess. They seem to lie half way between those in Group R and those in Group P.

If the perspective adopted in this paper proves correct, it would be the eight children in Group P who would be most likely in due course to develop a stable self-reliance combined with trust in others; for they move freely and confidently between a busy interest in exploring their environment, and the people and things in it, and keeping in intimate touch with mother. It is true that they often show less self-reliance than those in Groups Q and R, and that in the strange situation they are more affected than the latter by mother's brief absences. Yet their relations with mother seem always to be cheerful and confident, whether expressed in affectionate embraces or in the exchanging of glances and vocalizations at a distance, and this seems to promise well for their future.

When the type of mothering received by each of these infants is examined, using data obtained during the long visits the observers paid to the home every three weeks during the infant's first year of life, interesting differences appear between infants in each of the five groups.

In assessing a mother's behaviour towards her child Ainsworth uses four distinct nine-point rating scales. Ratings on these scales intercorrelate so highly, however, that in this paper the results of only one scale are drawn upon. This is a scale that measures the degree of sensitivity or insensitivity that a mother shows to her baby's signals and communications. Whereas a sensitive mother seems constantly to be 'tuned in' to receive her baby's signals, is likely to interpret them correctly and to respond to them both promptly and appropriately, an insensitive mother will often not notice her baby's signals, will misinterpret them when she does notice them, and will then respond tardily, inappropriately or not at all.

When the ratings on this scale for the mothers of infants in each of the five groups are examined, it is found that the mothers of the eight infants in Group P rate uniformly high (range 5.5 to 9.0), those of the eleven infants in Groups R, S, and T rate uniformly low (range 1.0 to 3.5), and those of the four in Group Q are in the middle (range 4.5 to 5.5). These differences are statistically significant (using the Mann-Whitney U test).

Differences between groups, in the same direction and of roughly the same order of magnitude, are found when mothers are rated on the other three scales. Thus mothers of infants in Group P are rated highly on an acceptance–rejection scale, a cooperation–interference scale and on an accessibility-ignoring scale. Conversely, mothers of infants in Groups R, S, and T are rated medium to low on each of these three scales. Mothers of infants in Group Q show ratings that lie roughly midway between the ratings for mothers of infants in Group P and those of infants in Groups R, S and T respectively.

Plainly a very great deal of further work will be required before it is possible to draw conclusions with any high degree of confidence. Nevertheless the overall patterns of personality development and of mother–child interaction visible at twelve months are sufficiently similar to what is seen of personality development and of parent-child interaction in later years for it to be plausible to believe that the one is the forerunner of the other. At the least, Ainsworth's findings show that an infant whose mother is sensitive, accessible and responsive to him, who accepts his behaviour and is cooperative in dealing with him, is far from being the demanding and unhappy child that some theories might suggest. Instead, mothering of this sort is evidently compatible with a child who is developing a limited measure of self-reliance by the time of his first birthday combined with a high degree of trust in his mother and enjoyment of her company.

Further strong evidence pointing in this direction is presented by Baumrind (1967) who made a very detailed study of thirty-two nursery school children, aged three and four years, and their mothers.

Thus, so far as the present all too meagre evidence goes, the hypothesis that a well-found self-reliance develops in parallel with reliance on a parent, who provides the child with a secure base from which to explore, is sustained.

Points of Difference to Current Theoretical Formulations

Although the theoretical schema presented here is not very different from that adopted implicitly by many practising clinicians, it differs at a number of points from much currently taught theory. Among these differences are the following:

(a) An emphasis in the present schema on the environmental parameter familiar-strange, which finds no place in traditional theory;
(b) Emphasis in the present schema on the many components of mother-infant interaction other than feeding, an over-emphasis on which, it is held, has greatly hindered our understanding of personality development and the conditions that influence it;
(c) The replacement of the concepts 'dependence' and 'independence' by the concepts of attachment, trust, reliance and self-reliance;
(d) The replacement of the orally derived theory of internal objects by a theory of working models of world and self that are conceived as being constructed by each individual as a result of his experience, that determine his expectations and on the basis of which he plans.

Let us consider in turn each of these differences, which are closely interrelated.

The immense importance in the lives of animals and men of the parameter familiar-strange has been fully recognized only during the past two decades, long after the various versions of clinical theory still taught had been formulated. In very many species, it is now known, whatever situation has become familiar to an individual is treated as though it provided safety, whereas any other situation is treated with reserve. Strangeness is responded to ambivalently; on the one hand it elicits fear and withdrawal, on the other it elicits curiosity and investigation. Which of these antithetic responses become dominant depends on many variables, the degree of strangeness of the situation, the presence or absence of a companion, and whether the individual responding is mature or immature, fit or fatigued, healthy or sick.

Why the properties of familiarity and strangeness should have come to have such powerful effects on behaviour is discussed in the final section of the paper, with special reference to their role in protection.

So long as the influence on man's behaviour of familiarity and strangeness was not appreciated, the conditions leading a child to become attached to his mother were little understood. The most plausible view, subscribed to by Freud and most other analysts and also by learning theorists, was that being fed by mother was the major variable. This theory, a theory of secondary drive, although never supported by systematic evidence or argument, soon became widely accepted and led naturally to two other views both of which have attracted a strong following. One is that what happens during the early months of life must be of very special importance for later development. The second is that, once a child has learned to feed himself, there is no further reason for him to be demanding of his mother's presence: he should therefore grow out of such 'dependency', which is thenceforward stigmatized as infantile or babyish.

The view taken here, and supported by much evidence (Bowlby, 1969), is that food plays only a marginal role in a child's attachment to his mother, that attachment behaviour is shown most strongly during the second and third years of life and persists at less intensity indefinitely, and that the function of attachment behaviour is protection. Corollaries of this view are that involuntary separation and loss are potentially traumatic over many years of infancy, childhood, and adolescence, and that, at appropriate degrees of intensity, the propensity to show attachment behaviour is a healthy characteristic and in no sense infantile.

From out of the same traditional assumption, that a child becomes attached to his mother because of his dependence upon her as the source of his physiological gratifications, come the concepts and terminology of 'dependence' and 'independence'. Once a child can provide for himself, say advocates of the theory of secondary drive, he should become independent. Henceforward, therefore, signs of dependency are to be regarded as regressive. Thus, once again, any strong desire for the presence of an attachment figure comes to be regarded as an expression of an 'infantile need', part of a 'baby' self that should have been left behind.

As terms and concepts in which to express the theory advanced here 'dependence' and 'independence' have a number of grave objections; they are therefore replaced by terms and concepts such as 'trust in', 'attached to', 'reliance on' and 'self-reliance'. First, dependence and independence are inevitably conceived as being mutually exclusive; whereas, as already emphasized, reliance on others and self-reliance are not only compatible but complementary to one another. Secondly, to describe someone as 'dependent' inevitably carries with it a pejorative flavour, whereas to describe someone as 'relying on another' does not. Thirdly, whereas the concept of attachment implies always attachment to one (or more) specially loved person(s), the concept of dependency entails no such relationship but instead tends to be anonymous.

Also much influenced by the special role given to feeding and orality in psychoanalytic theorizing is the concept of 'internal object', a concept that is in many ways ambiguous (Strachey, 1941). In its place can be put the concept, derived from cognitive psychology and control theory, of an individual developing within himself one or more working models representing principal features of the world about him and of himself as an agent in it. Such working models determine his expectations and forecasts and provide him with tools for constructing plans of action.

What in traditional theory is termed a 'good object' can be reformulated within this framework as a working model of an attachment figure who is conceived as accessible, trustworthy, and ready to help when called upon. Similarly, what in traditional theory is termed a 'bad object' can be reformulated as a working model of an attachment figure to whom are attributed such characteristics as uncertain accessibility, unwillingness to respond helpfully, or perhaps the likelihood of responding hostilely, In an analogous way an individual is thought to construct a working model of himself towards whom others will respond in certain predictable ways. The concept of a working model of the self comprehends data at present conceived in terms of self-image, self-esteem, etc.

The extent to which such working models are valid products of a child's actual experience over the years or are distorted versions of such experience is a matter of the greatest importance. Work in family psychiatry during the past twenty-five years has presented much data suggesting that the form models take is in fact far more strongly determined by a child's actual experiences throughout childhood than was formerly supposed. This is a field of vital interest and calls urgently for skilled investigation. A particular clinical and research problem is that disturbed individuals seem often to maintain within themselves more than one working model both of the world and of the self in it. Such multiple models, moreover, are frequently incompatible with each other and can be more or less unconscious.

Enough perhaps has been said to show that the concept of working models is central to the schema proposed. The concept can be elaborated to enable many aspects of personality structure and internal world to be described in ways that permit precision and rigorous research.

Thus the theory advanced here is not only couched in different language but contains a number of concepts distinct from those of traditional theory. Amongst many other things, these concepts enable a fresh approach to be made to the age-long problem of separation anxiety which, when excessive, is inimical to the development of self-reliance.

The Problem of Separation Anxiety

The many observations of the behaviour of young children when removed from their parents and placed in strange surroundings with strange people, described by James Robertson and others during the past twenty years, have still not been fully articulated into clinical theory. There is still no agreement on why the experience should be so distressing to a child at the time, nor why afterwards he should be so intensely apprehensive lest it happen again.

During recent years a number of experiments have been conducted on young monkeys in which they are separated from mother, usually for about one week. Whatever differences there may prove to be between the responses of monkeys and humans in such a situation, what is immediately striking is the similarity of response. In most species of monkey studied, protest at separation and depression during it are very pronounced, and, after reunion, clinging to mother is much increased. During the subsequent months, though individuals vary, the separated infants tend on average to explore less and to cling more; and they remain detectably more timid than young monkeys that have not had a separation. (For a review of these findings see Hinde and Spencer-Booth, 1971.)

These monkey studies are of great value in that:

(a) They provide clear evidence from planned experiments that hold stable many variables that in real life observations of humans make firm conclusions difficult to draw;
(b) They demonstrate that, even when all other variables are held constant, a period of separation from mother elicits protest and depression during the separation and much increased separation anxiety after it;
(c) They make it clear that the kinds of response to separation that are seen in humans can in other species be mediated at a primitive, and presumably infra-symbolic, level.

This last finding calls in question the various clinically derived theories that seek to explain separation anxiety, since most of them take it virtually for granted that involuntary separation from a mother-figure cannot of itself elicit anxiety or fear and that there must therefore be some other danger that is foreseen and feared. Many and diverse suggestions have been advanced of what this other danger might be. For example, Freud (1926), who from the first regarded separation anxiety as a key problem, suggested that for humans the ultimate 'danger-situation is a recognized, remembered, expected situation of helplessness'. Melanie Klein has advanced theories invoking a death instinct and fear of annihilation, and also theories deriving from her views about depressive and persecutory anxiety. Birth trauma is yet another suggestion. On reading the literature it is abundantly clear that many of the most strenuously debated issues in psychopathology and psychotherapy have turned, and still turn, on how we conceptualize the origin and nature of separation anxiety (Bowlby, 1960, 1961, 1973). Since the debate has been going on for so long and with so little progress the question is raised whether the wrong questions are being asked and/or the wrong initial assumptions made. Let us examine, therefore, what the initial assumptions have been.

Almost all theory about what arouses fear and anxiety in humans has started from the assumption that fear is aroused appropriately only in situations that are perceived as intrinsically painful or dangerous. Such perception is thought to derive either from previous experience of pain or else from some innate awareness of dangerous forces within. One or other of these assumptions is to be found in learning theory, in traditional psychiatry, as exemplified for example in a paper by Lewis (1967), and in all the various versions of psycho-analysis and its derivatives.

Anyone who adopts an assumption of this sort is, of course, very quickly faced with the fact that human beings frequently show fear in a number of common situations that do not seem inherently painful or dangerous. How many of us, it may be asked, would relish entering a completely strange house in the dark on our own? What a relief it would be were we to have a companion with us, or had a good light, or preferably both companion and light. Although it is during childhood that situations of this sort elicit fear most readily and intensely, it is idle to pretend that adults are above such things. To refer to fears of these kinds as 'infantile', as is often done, begs a lot of questions.

It is striking how few empirical studies there have been of the situations that commonly arouse fear in humans since Jersild's systematic work of the early thirties. The publications in which they are reported (e.g. Jersild and Holmes, 1935; Jersild, 1943) are mines of useful information.

In children between the second and fifth years of life, Jersild reports, there are a number of well-defined situations that commonly elicit fear. For example, records of 136 children over a three-week period show that not less than 40 per cent of them showed fear, on one occasion at least, when confronted with *each* of the following: (a) noise and events associated with noise, (b) height, (c) strange people, or familiar people in strange guise, (d) strange objects and situations, (e) animals, (f) pain or persons associated with pain.

There was also abundant evidence that children showed less fear when accompanied by an adult than when alone. To anyone familiar with children these findings are hardly revolutionary.

Yet it is not easy to square them with the assumptions from which most theorizing starts. Freud was keenly alive to the problem and confessed himself perplexed. Amongst the solutions he tried was his well-known attempt to distinguish between a real danger and an unknown danger. The argument he advances in *Inhibitions, Symptoms and Anxiety* (1926) can be put in a nutshell, using his own words. 'A real danger is a danger which threatens a person from an external object.' Whenever anxiety is 'about a known danger', therefore, it can be regarded as 'realistic anxiety'; whereas whenever it is 'about an unknown danger' it is to be regarded as 'neurotic anxiety'. Since fears of being alone in the dark or with strangers are, in Freud's view, about unknown dangers they are to be judged neurotic (*Standard Edition*, Vol. 20, pp. 165–7). Because all children experience such fears, moreover, all children are held to suffer from neurosis (pp. 147–8). There must be many who find themselves dissatisfied with this solution.

The difficulties Freud struggled with disappear when a comparative approach to human fear is adopted. For it becomes evident that man is by no means the only species to show fear in situations that are not intrinsically painful or dangerous (Hinde, 1970). Animals of very many species show fear behaviour in response to noise and other sudden changes of stimulation, to darkness, and also to strangers and strange events. The visual cliff and a stimulus that rapidly expands also regularly elicit fear in animals of a number of species.

When we ask how it has come about that situations of these sorts should so readily elicit fear in animals of so many species, it is not difficult to see that, whilst none of them is *intrinsically* dangerous, each is in some degree *potentially* dangerous. Put in another way, while none may carry a *high* risk of danger, each carries a slightly *increased* risk of danger, even if the risk is increased, say, only from 1 per cent to 5 per cent.

Looked at in this light each of these fear-arousing situations is seen to be a natural clue to an increased risk of danger. To respond with fear to all such situations is therefore to reduce risks. Because such behaviour has survival value, the argument runs, the genetic equipment of a species becomes such that each member of it at birth is biased to develop so that it usually comes to behave in these typical ways. Man is no exception.

A distinction that is invoked here that is a commonplace for ethologists but a source of much confusion and perplexity amongst psychologists, both experimental and clinical, is the distinction between causation and biological function—the distinction between, on the one hand, what conditions elicit behaviour and, on the other, what contribution to species survival such behaviour may make. In this theory strangeness and the other natural clues is each regarded as playing a causal role in eliciting fear behaviour; whilst the function of such behaviour is protection.

Perhaps the distinction between the cause and the function of a piece of behaviour can be clarified by reference to sexual behaviour in which the distinction is so patently obvious that it is usually taken for granted and virtually forgotten. Spelled out the distinction runs as follows: hormonal states of the organism and certain characteristics of the partner, together, lead to sexual interest and play causal roles in eliciting sexual behaviour. The biological function of that behaviour however is another matter; it is reproduction. Because causation and function are distinct, it is possible, by means of contraception, to intervene between the behaviour and the function it serves.

In animals of all non-human species behaviour is engaged in without the animal (presumably) having any insight whatever into function. The same is true also of most humans most of the time. Seen in this light there is nothing to surprise us that humans should habitually respond with fear behaviour in certain situations despite the fact that an external observer might know that in such situations risk to life is only marginally increased, or even not increased at all. What a person responds to initially is simply the situation— sudden change of noise or light level, a strange face or strange happening, sudden movement—not to any estimate of risk. Sober calculation of risk may or may not follow.

Unwilling separation of young from parent, or for that matter of adult from trusted companion, can be regarded simply as another situation of the same sort, although rather a special example of it. Even in civilized communities there are many circumstances in which the risk of danger is somewhat greater when one is alone than when one is with a companion. This is especially so during childhood. For example, risk of accidents in the home are obviously greater when a child is left alone than when his mother or father is around. The same is true of accidents in the streets. During 1968 in the London Borough of Southwark, 46 per cent of all traffic accidents happened to children under fifteen, with the highest incidence in the age-groups three to nine. More than 60 per cent of these children were entirely alone and two-thirds of the remainder in the company only of another child. For the elderly or sick, living alone is a notorious hazard. Even for healthy adult males to go hill-walking or climbing alone is materially to increase risk to life. In the environment in which man evolved the risks attendant on being alone are likely to have been much greater. Reflection shows therefore that, because being alone increases risk, there is good reason why man should have evolved behavioural systems that lead him to avoid it. For humans to respond with fear to loss of a trusted companion is thus no more puzzling than that he should respond with fear to any of the other natural clues to potential danger—strangeness, sudden movement, sudden change in noise or light level. In every case to respond so has survival value.

A very special feature of fear behaviour both in humans and other animals is the degree to which it is increased in situations characterized by the presence of two or more of the natural clues; for example, the stranger who suddenly approaches, the strange dog that barks, the unexpected noise heard in the dark. Commenting on the twenty-one-day observations made by parents of fear-arousing situations, Jersild and Holmes (1935) note that combinations of two or more of the following features were frequently reported to be present together: noise, strange people and situations, the dark, sudden and unexpected movement, and being alone. Whereas a situation characterized by a single one of these features might only alert, fear, more or less intense, may well be aroused when several are present together.

Because the response to a combination of factors is often so dramatically greater than, or different from, what it is to any one singly, it is convenient to refer to such situations as 'compound', a term chosen to echo the chemical analogue (Bowlby, 1973).

In keeping with other findings on the effects of compound situations, experiments both with human children and with rhesus monkeys (Rowell and Hinde, 1963) show what a tremendous difference to the intensity of fear responses is made by the presence or absence of a trusted companion. For example, Jersild and Holmes (1935) found that, when children in their third and fourth years were asked to go alone to find a ball that had gone down a dark passage, half refused to do so despite encouragement from the experimenter. When the experimenter accompanied them, however, almost all were ready to do it. Differences of a similar kind were seen in a number of other slightly frightening situations, for example, when a child was asked to approach and pat a large dog brought in on a lead.

These findings are so much in keeping with common experience that it may seem absurd to labour them. Yet, it is evident that, when psychologists and psychiatrists come to theorize about fear and anxiety, the significance of these phenomena is gravely underestimated. For example, when due attention is paid to these findings it ceases to be a mystery that, in all but very familiar situations, fear and anxiety are greatly reduced by the mere presence of a trusted companion. These findings enable us to understand also why the accessibility of parents and their willingness to respond provides an infant, a child, an adolescent and a young adult with conditions in which he feels secure and with a base from which he feels confident to explore. They cast light too on the way that, from adolescence onwards, other trusted figures can come to provide similar services.

This brings the argument full circle and helps to explain how it comes about that strong and consistent support from parents, combined with encouragement and respect for a child's autonomy, so far from sapping self-reliance, provide the conditions in which it can best grow. It helps to explain, too, why, conversely, an experience of separation or loss, or threats of separation or loss, especially when used by parents as sanctions for good behaviour, can undermine a child's trust both in others and in himself, and so lead to one or another deviation from optimum development—to lack of self-confidence, to chronic anxiety or depression, to aloof noncommittal, or to defiant independence that has a hollow ring.

A well-based self-reliance, we may conclude, is usually the product of slow and unchecked growth from infancy into maturity during which, through interaction with trustworthy and encouraging others, a person learns how to combine trust in others with trust in himself.

REFERENCES

AINSWORTH, M. D. S. *Infancy in Uganda: Infant Care and the Growth of Attachment.* Baltimore, Md: The Johns Hopkins Press, 1967.

AINSWORTH, M. D. S. & BELL, S. M. Attachment, Exploration and Separation: Illustrated by the Behaviour of One-Year-Olds in a Strange Situation. *Child Development,* 1970, 41, 49–67.

AINSWORTH, M. D. S., BELL, S. M. W. & STAYTON, D. J. Individual Differences in Strange-Situation Behaviour of One-Year-Olds. In H. R. Schaffer (ed.), *The Origins of Human Social Relations.* London: Academic Press, 1971.

AINSWORTH, M. D. S., BELL, S. M. W. & STAYTON, D. J. Infant-Mother Attachment and Social Development: 'Socialization' as a Product of Reciprocal Responsiveness to Signals. In M. P. M. Richards (ed.), *The integration of a Child into a Social World.* Cambridge: Cambridge University Press, 1974.

ANDERSON, J. W. Attachment Behaviour Out of Doors. In N. Blurton-Jones (ed.), *Ethological Studies of Human Behaviour.* Cambridge: Cambridge University Press, 1972.

BAUMRIND, D. Child Care Practices Anteceding Three Patterns of Preschool Behaviour. *Genetic Psychology Monographs,* 1967, 75, 43–88.

BOWLBY, J. Separation Anxiety. *International Journal of Psycho-Analysis,* 1960, 41, 89–113.

BOWLBY, J. Separation Anxiety: a Critical Review of the Literature. *Journal of Child Psychology and Psychiatry,* 1961, 1, 251–269.

BOWLBY, J. *Attachment and Loss.* Vol. 1: *Attachment.* London: Hogarth Press, 1969; Harmondsworth: Penguin Books, 1971.

BOWLBY, J. *Attachment and Loss.* Vol. 2: *Separation: Anxiety and Anger.* London: Hogarth Press, 1973; Harmondsworth: Penguin Books, 1975.

FAIRBAIRN, W. R. D. *Psychoanalytic Studies of the Personality.* London: Tavistock/Routledge, 1952.

FREUD, S. *Inhibitions, Symptoms and Anxiety.* Standard Edition, Vol. 20. London: Hogarth Press, 1926.

GRINKER, R. R. Sr. 'Mentally Healthy' Young Males (Homoclites). *Archives of General Psychiatry* 1962, 6, 405–53.

HINDE, R. A. *Animal Behaviour: A synthesis of Ethology and Comparative Psychology*. 2nd ed. New York: McGraw-Hill, 1970.

HINDE, R. A. & SPENCER-BOOTH, Y. Effects of Brief Separation from Mother on Rhesus Monkeys. *Science* 1970, 173, 111–18.

JERSILD, A. T. Studies of Children's Fears. In R. G. Barker, J. S. Kounin & H. F. Wright (eds.), *Child Behaviour and Development*. New York and London: McGraw-Hill, 1943.

JERSILD, A. T. & HOLMES, F. B. *Children's Fears*. Teachers College, Columbia University Child Development Monograph No. 20, 1935.

KORCHIN, S. J. & RUFF, G. E. Personality Characteristics of the Mercury Astronauts. In C. H. Grosser, H. Wechsler and M. Greenblatt (eds), *The Threat of Impending Disaster: Contributions to the Psychology of Stress*, Cambridge, Mass.: M.I.T., 1964.

LEWIS, A. Problems Presented by the Ambiguous Word 'Anxiety' as Used in Psychopathology. *Israel Annals of Psychiatry and Related Disciplines*, 1967, 5, 105–21.

MURPHEY, E. B., SILBER, E., COELHO, G. V., HAMBURG, D. A. & GREENBERG, I. Development of Autonomy and Parent-Child Interaction in Late Adolescence. *American Journal of Orthopsychiatry*, 1963, 33, 643–52.

OFFER, D. *The Psychological World of the Teenager*. New York: Basic Books, 1969.

PECK, R. F. & HAVIGHURST, R. J. *The Psychology of Character Development*. New York: John Wiley, 1960.

ROWELL, T. E. & HINDE, R. A. Responses of Rhesus Monkeys to Mildly Stressful Situations. *Animal Behaviour*, 1963, 11, 235–43.

RUFF, G. E. & KORCHIN, S. J. Adaptive Stress Behaviour. In M. H. Appley & R. Trumbull (eds), *Psychological Stress*. New York: Appleton-Century-Crofts, 1967.

STRACHEY, A. A Note on the Use of the Word 'Internal'. *International Journal of Psycho-Analysis*, 1941, 22, 37.

WENNER, N. K. Dependency Patterns in Pregnancy. In J. H. Masserman (ed), *Sexuality of Woman*. New York: Grune and Stratton, 1966.

WINNICOTT, D. W. *The Family and Individual Development*. London Tavistock Publications, 1965.

2 Acquired Powers: The Transformation of Natural into Personal Powers

JOHN SHOTTER

In an earlier paper (Shotter, 1973) I distinguished between people as *individual personalities* possessing *personal powers* and as *natural agents* possessing *natural powers* on the grounds that people can distinguish in their behaviour between what they as individual personalities do, and what they just find happening to or within them. They are prepared to take responsibility for the former but not the latter, for it is not within their personal power to control it. This latter activity seems to spring from two distinguishable sources: from obvious agencies outside the person and from sources within him, an expression of his natural powers over which he, as an individual personality, has no direct control. In my earlier paper, I suggested that personal powers were derived in some way from natural powers. Now, I want to discuss the possible details of such a process. Specifically, I want to discuss what goes on between and within a child and his mother during that part of his early development which results in him being transformed from a natural agent, a child of Nature so to speak, into an individual personality, a child of Culture. If he is ever to act *responsibly* he must learn to *use* different *forms* of behaviour in ways which make sense to other people; he has to acquire personal powers. But personal powers are not things which, it seems, can be acquired at first on one's own; the help of one who already possesses them is required, and usually that help is supplied by one's mother.

Are Personal Powers Acquired or Innate?

Let me begin by putting this issue in a larger perspective. Harré and Secord (1972, p. 207) characterize human beings by *the fact* that

B

they possess the power to control their performances in accordance with rules. I shall reject that characterization as not sufficiently inclusive: it excludes young children of quite advanced age, who do not (Piaget, 1951, p. 142) play games according to rules until about the age of 4–7 years, never mind conducting their everyday affairs according to rules. I shall propose instead that we characterize human beings by *the fact* that they possess a natural power to construct or create in interaction with other human beings a personal power to control their performances in accordance with rules. Harré's and Secord's characterization (along with Chomsky's) would necessitate assuming (as does Chomsky) that powers exercised according to rules are present in human beings, albeit in a generic form, at birth. Which suggests that such powers should not be thought of as emerging during the course of social interaction, but as underlying it. And, if they undergo any development at all, they are merely differentiated in the course of their exercise. Chomsky states the position with which he aligns himself thus:

> ... rationalist speculation has assumed that the general form of a system of knowledge is fixed in advance as a disposition of the mind, and the function of experience is to cause this general schematic structure to be realized and more fully differentiated (Chomsky, 1965, p. 60).

I believe that this is a fundamentally misleading hypothesis about the basis of human action and its development. It leads one, mistakenly I think, to consider human beings only as *individual personalities* and to concentrate one's attention only upon what they do deliberately, in relation to objective criteria rather than criteria made 'logically adequate' for a purpose (negotiated criteria), and to miss entirely the apparently vague, chaotic, and spontaneous exchanges which go on between people as *natural agents*, and which are unrelated to any objective criteria at all. It is clearly a version of this hypothesis that leads people studying social interaction and language acquisition to search for the rules or rule-systems said to be underlying observed performances when such a search may be wholly misguided. For, while the observed behaviour may indeed be *regulated* it may not be *rule*-regulated at all. *Regulation* is a characteristic of all processes in 'open systems' maintained in a 'steady state' according to 'system parameters' (v. Bertalanffy, 1968); that is, it is a characteristic of all organic systems, human beings included. And, after all, strictly, rules involve agreements between people. Thus rule-regulated processes, strictly, are processes regulated in a particular kind of way; namely, by the individuals involved in them all *agreeing* to perform their activities within certain acknowledged constraints or a system of interlocking constraints.[1]

Now, assuming that rule-regulated personal powers are acquired, means that we cannot use Chomsky's method of investigation solely, i.e. his method of deriving a characterization of a power from records of its past manifestations. That will provide us only with what our powers are *now*; it gives us no indication of what they might *become*. We need to combine Chomsky's method with both a deeper conceptual analysis of what personal powers are, and with a detailed consideration of certain empirical matters. For only if we can understand how rule-regulated powers are developed can we understand how what is now their nature might be changed.

These, then, in broad outline are the methods I shall try to employ. And within the general framework of thought provided by the

---

[1] I am adopting in this paper a position similar to Richards (1974, p. 85), who says '...I do not regard the infant as a social creature. He has the potentiality of a social being but this requires development in a social world for its expression. As Becker (1972) has said, socialization "means the formation of *human beings* out of helplessness, dependent *animal matter*...".' But I cannot now agree with this view. Infants must be treated both practically *and* theoretically in a personal manner from birth; mothers must treat their activity, not in organic terms as merely reaction to a stimulus, but in *personal* terms. While she may act to elicit from her infant certain forms of no doubt innately organized activity, a mother may do very much more. She may, by her continual adjustment of the eliciting circumstances, influence the long-term, temporal structure of her child's activity in ways which would otherwise remain unexpressed at this early stage—e.g. simply by noting the direction of his gaze, she may make *and maintain* something as a visual object for him for a long period. But as well as 'motivating' some characteristically human activity, she may also reply to it in terms of the meaning she interprets it as having—e.g. having got her baby to look at her she might then smile at it and say 'Hello'. Thus she begins straight away to school him in what, practically, it means to look at other people, the ways that personal recognition is expressed and what happens when the other person 'takes it up'.

Thus the position I would try to defend now it that *all* human interaction relies upon interpretation, and we must look to achievements in our history rather than to our biological structure for the source of the patterning to be observed in our social exchanges.

concept of powers, I shall try to elucidate the nature of acquired personal powers. So it is to the details of that process I now turn.

The Beginnings of 'Psychological Symbiosis' in the Very Young Child

Very young babies do very little, but around the end of the first week of life they do begin to respond to some cues. One such cue is a change of *equilibrium*. If, after the eighth day, a breast-fed baby is lifted from the crib and held in a nursing position, he turns his head towards the breast. In contrast, if he is held in a *vertical* position he does not (Spitz, 1965). In general, however, for the first two months of life the child could not be said to 'perceive' his surroundings at all. But after that time, an approaching adult begins to acquire a unique place in the child's environment. At this stage, a hungry, crying child begins to perceive, in his sense of the term, an approaching adult visually: he will become quiet, and open his mouth or make sucking movements. But this only takes place when the child is hungry; the response is to a totality of both internal and external factors. Two or three weeks later there is further progress: when the infant 'perceives' a human face, he follows it with concentrated attention. Later, at 6–12 weeks, he will *smile*, and this smile is, Spitz maintains, the first manifestation of active, directed, and intentional behaviour on the child's part.[2] This is the end of what Spitz calls the 'objectless stage' the stage of no active relationship with the mother) and the beginning of what he calls 'psychological symbiosis'. This is

[2] But actually the child smiles much earlier (see Macfarlane, 1974). Macfarlane also provides evidence for the position taken in note 1. Whether the child intends them or not, from the moment of birth he does things capable of being given a personal attribution by his mother. And, as Macfarlane remarks, "To the mother some of these abilities will simply be included in the humanness of her infant. For instance, the one-month-old's ability to appreciate a three-dimensional object might be noticed by the mother as the baby reaching out when a bottle is put to its lips.' And he continues, 'Mothers are good observers of their infants, though they tend to negate their findings in the face of vicariously acquired information.' So, although they may or may not *account* for their own behaviour in personal terms, mothers do not in fact act like animal trainers for the first six months trying to *condition* their children, and then only later turn to treat them in a personal manner, they begin as they mean to go on treating them as one term in a personal relationship.

a very interesting and important stage. Clearly, at first, a child does not exist in the world as an autonomous, self-directing, self-actualizing and self-transforming agency, but he can become one. How does it come about? I shall suggest that the formative processes operating in him, which culminate in his emergence as an individual personality, have their *source* in his mother. These processes seem to be controlled in part by influences transmitted in the course of *affective* exchanges between the mother and her child during this period of 'psychological symbiosis'. That is, they are transmitted in the course of exchanges in which one individual responds in an immediate and unconsidered manner as a result of the way he perceives or apprehends the immediate and unconsidered reaction of the other individual to him. This sort of perception, the perception of feeling or affect, is very primitive, and all writers on the child's early development (Schaffer, 1971; Spitz, 1965; Koffka, 1921) note that distinctive reactions to different forms of human expression appear a few months before a child's reactions to 'things' or 'thing-qualities'. As affective exchanges are central to my whole thesis, I must begin with a short discussion of this form of perception.

Inner and Outer Perception: Objective and Negotiated Criteria

Harré and Secord (1972, ch. 6) distinguish between bodily and mental predicates, or perhaps better, between the non-mentalistic and the mentalistic uses of predicates, and point out the necessity in psychology of using both. In the past, both philosophers and psychologists have supposed that mental predicates involved reference only to privately satisfiable criteria.

But this Harré and Secord (1972, p. 121) point out is mistaken; both criteria are necessary and *are* available for scrutiny. 'There are always some situations for any state-of-mind predicate where others have some degree of access to that state of mind, even in another person,' they say. Our feelings, moods, beliefs, intentions, etc., are *shown* in our actions, and although they may not involve reference to objective criteria, they do involve readily observable criteria which can be made 'logically adequate' (Harré and Secord, 1972, pp. 114–23) as required, i.e. *they are negotiable*. What has misled philosophers and psychologists, Harré and Secord maintain, is their failure to distinguish between *access* and *authority*: although a person is often (but not always) the best authority on what he is doing—he is, after all, his own closest observer—*he is not the only one to have access to the relevant data.* One way or another that is made available in the temporal sequencing of his behaviour for all to grasp, and indeed, when it comes to assessing the nature of his own behaviour he is in no better position than anyone else. Only as his intentions are realized in performance is he able to tell whether he is successfully executing them or not—a point I shall take up later when I discuss monitoring our speech for its meanings. While he usually (but not always) knows what he intends, he must judge the adequacy of his own performances as others do, as they occur in time and space—it being the temporal sequencing of spatial possibilities which reveals the person's choice and thus manifests his intention. Learning how to judge his own performances so is a skill he must learn in the course of his early social exchanges.

Now if the criteria involved in the assessment of psychological states are not private, and people do show their states of mind in the temporal organization of their behaviour, how do we determine the character of these states? Consider for the moment our own psychological states. We distinguish, for instance, a joyful person *outside* us from the feelings (of joy, or otherwise) which he occasions *within* us. Accepting that all our experiences are derived from outside us, this distinction can only be a function of the way in which we determine these categories: one aspect of our experience is determined as *outer* and ascribed to an object (in space), the other is determined as *inner* and ascribed to ourselves as feeling (in time)—space and time being respectively the forms of outer and inner perception (Kant). Returning now to our problem of understanding the feelings of others, I want to suggest that when confronted by another person it is open to us to determine the temporal and spatial aspects of his behaviour similarly: it is in *time* that a person reveals his feelings to us.

Now when investigating a real object in order to determine its nature it does not, so to speak, answer back; it neither acts nor reacts. Thus, in this case, the categories of outer perception can be made as determinate as an investigator pleases (and his categories of inner perception are idiosyncratic and irrelevant to all except himself). However, a non-object, a source of expression cannot be determined as one pleases for it does answer back. So there is an essential indeterminacy associated with the categories of perception in this case which can only be resolved *via negotiation and agreement with the source being investigated*—to approach a point about negotiation made by Harré and Secord (1972, p. 161) from another direction.

So the essential difference between the processes involved in the perception of expression and the perception of things seems more to do with *the way in which we make these categories determinate* than anything to do with the perceptual process itself. The criteria of inner perception involve negotiation and agreement with the source (or are otherwise left indeterminate, for people do not always exactly know either their own or other people's feelings), while those of outer perception, at least in their objective paradigm form, do not involve such negotiation.

Now if processes of inner perception work on 'expressions' and interpret them *irrespective of whose expressions they are*, the classical theories of our experience of other minds are unnecessary. The idea that we first experience other peoples' beliefs, intentions, etc., indirectly via some process of deduction or 'unconscious inference' from sequences of behavioural events objectively perceived in outer perception may be quite mistaken. We might be able to perceive or apprehend mental activity directly in our inner perception. If what in actuality happens is that in our interactions with other people there is a continuous flux of activity within us, *undifferentiated as to theirs or ours*, the problem becomes one, not of appreciating the nature of mental activity in others, but of distinguishing which has its *source* in us and which in them. This, I think, is the young child's problem in this period of 'psychological symbiosis'.

The Continuation of 'Psychological Symbiosis'

As Spitz said, the smile is the first directed and intentional expression of affect on the child's part. At first (at 3 months), the individuals to whom the infant responds with a smile are freely interchangeable. This is because the three-month-old does not perceive the human face as such at all, as Spitz has established experimentally, he perceives only a sign Gestalt: a specific configuration within the face as a totality, consisting of just the forehead-eyes-nose sector, triggers the infant's smile response after the manner of an 'innate releaser mechanism' (an IRM—Tinbergen, 1951). But as Spitz (p. 95) remarks:

... this sounds quite mechanical: sign Gestalten, releaser mechanisms triggering innate responses. The reader may well ask: couldn't a mechanical doll, fitted with the sign Gestalt rear our children just as well? No, it could not. ... Only a reciprocal relation can provide the experiential factor in the infant's development, consisting as it does of an ongoing circular exchange, in which affects play the major role. When the infant experiences a need, it will provoke in him an affect that will lead to behavioural changes, which in their turn provoke an affective response and its concomitant attitude in the mother; she behaves 'as if she understood' what particular need of the infant causes his affective manifestation.

Although the relationship between a mother and her child is clearly an unequal one, they do have the power in some sense to complete or fulfil one another's intentions. To the extent that a mother can appreciate the mental content or intentional structure in her baby's behaviour, she can complete their intention and in some manner satisfy his needs for him. But the mother pursues intentions within the interactive scheme also, she wants her baby to suck, to stop crying, to acknowledge her by looking into her eyes, to grasp her finger, etc. And she discovers strategies and tactics via which she can elicit these responses from her child. Thus, both gain a great deal of idiosyncratic knowledge about one another as individuals, knowledge which at this stage is very important.

Now within the totality of the child and his mother, she constitutes a 'mechanism' or 'set of mechanisms' via which he can execute actions in the world. (That even very young children (4–18 weeks) will execute intentional actions if given access to the appropriate mechanisms has been strikingly demonstrated by Bruner (1969).) It is only via her instrumentality that he comes to differentiate the forehead-eyes-nose sign Gestalt as a meaningful entity. She appreciates in his movements, his manifestations of affect, the nature of his mental state and responds to them in such a way that she presents him with the characteristic Gestalt just at the time she is gratifying his needs. It thus only appears and functions within the ongoing circular affective exchange which has its source and its terminus in the child, but which is mediated via the 'mechanisms' the mother provides. The child could not have distinguished the sign Gestalt entirely by his own devices. Currently, he can only act because his mother acts 'as if she understood' him, and it is in this sense that the child of 3 months is in 'psychological symbiosis' with his mother. He can only differentiate himself from her by constituting within himself some of the 'mechanisms' the mother now provides.

The Constitution of Mental Totalities

Now, about the processes going on within the child responsible for his constitution of the forehead-eyes-nose sign Gestalt we can only surmise, but there is no doubt at all that we must postulate the existence of something like, to use Chomsky's (1972) terms, *intrinsic processes of mental organization*. For clearly, there are processes within us which take sensory data and organize them in such a way that subsequent data are not regarded *de novo* but are responded to in a characteristic way preconditioned by past data.

What this characteristic way is has been elucidated recently by some experiments of Garner (1966). He gave people experience with (incomplete) families of visual and auditory patterns constructed according to definite principles. But, as he remarks, '... a single stimulus can have no real meaning without reference to a set of stimuli, because the attributes which define it cannot be specified without knowing what the alternatives are.' And he did find, in fact, that people seemed to 'infer', as he put it, from their limited experience, what the appropriate family of alternatives might be. But they did not do this consciously, they did not do it, we would say, as individual personalities, they did it as natural agents, using their natural powers of mental organization or construction in such a way that the principles of construction used to match the encountered situations could be used to construct others not yet encountered in the same style. In other words, the person augments a natural power in such a task.

The perception of such totalities seems to be an active process at every level, and Bohm (1965) has elucidated other aspects of it. He points out that nothing is seen without movements and variations on the retina of the eye, and the characteristics of these variations must play some part in determining the structure of what is seen. The relevant data must be extracted from the *relations* between the outgoing movements and their incoming consequences. So we do not at any level perceive just what is in front of our eyes, we do not just perceive any stimulus for what it is in itself, what we perceive contains 'structural features which are not even on the retina of the eye at a given moment, but which are detected with the aid of relationships observed over some period of time' (Bohm, 1965, p. 203). In fact, Bohm goes on to argue, the attempt to base our idea of perceptual process upon some physical time-order of events can only lead to confusion for 'the order of signals is not essentially related to the order of time' (p. 210)—it is not, for instance, in the constitution of a television picture. It is the way a person *relates* his actions and their consequences that matters, and to some extent, that is up to him. Perceiving is a skill:

> ... a person must actively meet his environment in such a way that he coordinates his outgoing nervous impulses with those that are coming in. As a result the structure of his environment is, as it were, gradually incorporated into his outgoing impulses, so that he learns how to meet his environment with the right kind of response (Bohm, 1965, p. 211).

As Garner says, the perceiver actively participates in the process of perceptual organization, but if Bohm is right, in realms way beyond those Garner has so far investigated experimentally.

Garner's work suggests why the forehead-eyes-nose sign Gestalt only functions within the totality of the human face: stimulus configurations only have their significance in relation to some mentally constituted totality of possible configurations. Bohm's arguments suggest that the sign Gestalt (and later the mother herself, personally) is singled out because the mother coordinates her activities closely with her child's. She is the only one who can be incorporated in the circuit of activities which has its source and terminus in the child. It is via his own actions *and* her instrumentality in them that he singles out the sign Gestalt (and will later single out her); and it is via his own activities that he will eventually differentiate himself from her, and end the period of 'psychological symbiosis'.

The End of the Period of 'Psychological Symbiosis'

The child thus begins to do things on his own, and as a natural agent he may manifest powers in an apparently directed and regulated way. But it is not behaviour in which he *knows what he is doing*. It is not, as Harré and Secord would say, *monitored* behaviour. There is some way to go before that.

The end of the period of psychological symbiosis is indicated by the development of the child's ability (around 15 months) to actively deny his mother the option of influencing him, in other words, by him learning effectively to say 'No'. The child begins to move around. Until now it was the mother's task to gratify or not the needs and wishes of her infant, now she has to curb and prevent some of his initiatives. And apparently, when acting as an agent in his own right, he will not easily tolerate being forced back into the position of a puppet; he attempts to sever the links via which she exerts her control over him. The period of social games can now begin. For, if one is to play one's part in a game properly, it can only be done if one can cut oneself off from the influences of others while doing it, however, only if one is open to the influences of others does one know when to play it. Knowing how to open and close the social link at will must be the first social skill a child acquires if he is to play social games and acquire personal powers.

The Exercise of Natural Powers in Play and their Regulation according to Rules in Social Exchanges

The three-year-old still reacts to adults affectively, but in contrast to early childhood these affective reactions are directed and regulated in a generalized manner, e.g. the child acts as if he senses in general an adult's authority, etc. His behaviour manifests the influences of his past exchanges with adults and the physical world and is, presumably, regulated by some internally constituted structures.

Now, in Vygotsky's (1966) view, the child's play at this stage is essentially a generalized expression of affect: an expression of his basic needs and desires, structured as a result of his earlier action exchanges with adults and the world. Thus the child when he plays does not understand *what* he plays, he simply plays in accord with some internal structure, what Vygotsky calls an 'imaginary situation'. It would be wrong, then, to say that he plays 'according to rules', he does not. He simply seems to be attempting to play out the possibilities inherent in his internally constituted mental totalities. The establishment of rules or rule-systems is, as we shall see, *a final, negotiated consequence of this process, not an essential part of it.* So, although the child's play may seem to be regulated by rules, and someone may extract rules from it and use them to re-enact his play, to extract the rules is not to reconstitute their original basis in the 'imaginary situation'. The rules would only characterize the possibilities realized in that situation, not necessarily the whole field of both realizable *and unrealizable* tendencies in it—rules, after all, have nothing to say about mistakes. Any rules there might be in the child's play are not formulated in advance, but issue in the course of playing with others in a coordinated way, i.e. they issue in the invention of something like a game.

Now, most importantly, playing in accord with an 'imaginary situation' involves *meanings*. Usually, the 'things' in a young child's environment dictate what he must do, but in play in an 'imaginary situation' they do not. Here, he is regulating his own behaviour not by reference to the 'things' actually present in his own environment at all. In a sense, he is detached from it, and is acting in a cognitive or mental realm. The 'things' in his environment may be incorporated into his play, not for what they are in themselves, but for their meanings. That is, they may be incorporated to the extent that they fall in with or offer no resistance to those aspects of his play regulated by his 'ideas'. (And in this sense, of course, a child's mother is the best play 'thing' he has.) And the most unlikely things may enter into his play in all sorts of guises. All that matters is that whatever 'thing' is used it must allow for the execution of at least some of the same actions as an imaginary thing in the imaginary situation. Now we are not at the stage of symbolism involving *rules* yet, such play still essentially operates in affective terms, but now the affective meaning he assigns to 'things' dominates and determines his behaviour towards them. But if any 'thing' can mean almost anything in play, as long as it is used as an *enactive* representation (Bruner, 1966), how can meanings and 'things' ever become linked in any determinate fashion? The role of other people seems to be crucial in this process.

Vygotsky (1966, p. 9) discusses a situation in which two sisters (5 and 7 years) play at being 'sisters'. The vital difference between simply being sisters and playing at it is that, in play, they try to be sisters and are conscious of one another's aim. They thus distinguish and discuss what it is to be a sister; they enact whatever emphasizes their relationship as sisters *vis-à-vis* other people: They are dressed

alike, they walk about holding hands, the elder keeps telling the
younger about other people—'That is theirs not ours'. Everything
associated with the children's intuitions of what it is to be a sister is
expressed in one way or another and emphasized, and presumably
on occasions, discussed amongst themselves and accepted, modified
or rejected accordingly. So that, as Vygotsky says, 'what passes
unnoticed by the child in real life becomes a rule of behaviour in
play'. Now this situation is most interesting for the sisters are, in
fact, playing at reality. They are interacting with one another not in
terms of what they are to one another in any immediate sense, but
in terms of how they imagine one another to be; they are interacting
in terms of what they *mean* to one another in their *roles* as sisters.
Each is playing their proper part in a social game. Clear criteria have
been adduced, some in action others in discussion, and what it is to
be a sister has, for the moment at least, been decided between them.
They have laid down the rules for their 'sisters-game'. Thus they
know what criteria they must meet to be sisters; they can thus now
be self-directing in sisterly activities. 'Play gives the child', Vygotsky
says (1966, p. 14), 'new forms of desire, i.e. it teaches him to
desire by relating his desires to a fictitious "I"—his role in the game
defined by its rules.'

But the function one sister performs for the other in the game
described above is the function a child's mother continually performs
for him: in her play with him she gets him to coordinate his activity
with hers in relation to definite criteria which are important to her
in some way. She cannot in this situation instigate his activities for
him, but she can exert nonetheless a powerful controlling influence.
She can do this because she is still the means of his gratification, and
because she and her child know one another personally from their
earlier inarticulate and affective relationship. She makes use of this
relationship time and again to draw him into involvements which,
if left to his own devices, he would never otherwise undertake.

It is thus, in the course of these informal involvements, that 'language games' (Wittgenstein 1953) are established; there is nothing
absolute about the rules or criteria functioning as the reference
points in such exchanges. As Wittgenstein (1958) remarks '... re-
member that in general we don't use language according to strict
rules—it hasn't been taught us by means of strict rules, either ... We
are unable to clearly circumscribe the concepts we use; not because
we don't know their real definition, but because there is no real

"definition" to them. To suppose that there *must* be would be like supposing that whenever children play with a ball they play a game according to strict rules.' Clearly, they do not. What they do do is to make the rules definite as required. And clearly, one skill the child acquires in the course of all his 'games' with his mother, as the sisters manifest in their 'sisters game', is the skill to make the *meanings* of their actions determinate as required by coordinating their behaviour with others, by making implicit or explicit agreements with them in one way or another.

Natural Agents Construct Forms: Individual Personalities Monitor Meanings

We shall begin now to touch on the nature of personal powers, those powers whose exercise is monitored by the individual exercising them. It will be convenient to concentrate our attention on the activity of speaking in discussing their development.

No explicit agreements making meanings determinate are possible until the child has learnt the skill of making agreements verbally; he first learns 'language games' and the agreements they involve implicitly by participating in 'forms of life' (Wittgenstein, 1953). Via action exchanges, he coordinates his activities, including their *vocal* aspect, with the activities of others. The processes discussed above suggest how this might be done, thus there is no necessity and indeed no warrant to assume that, at first, he vocalizes, presumably according to internally constituted mental structures in both an immediated and unconsidered fashion. His vocalizations are not, of course, always intelligible; the constitution of his natural powers of vocalization allow for the expression of a whole field of possibilities appropriate in some tenuous way to the current situation. His vocalizations are thus regulated but not yet rule-regulated.

While it may be correct to assume that he is aiming at definite articulatory targets in his *construction* of word-forms, and definite syntactic criteria in his *construction* of sentence-forms, it is not necessary to assume that he is *using* words and especially sentences according to any definite criteria at all. To suppose that there must be strict rules for using words and sentences 'would be like supposing that whenever children play with a ball they play a game according to strict rules'. A sentence is something one *uses* to express one's meaning, and it is not an expression of a meaning itself; its meaning is a logical construction to be completed both by oneself and one's listener out of the influences exerted by one's utterance. And one may find, just as one's listener does, that the sentence just uttered was inadequate to the purpose intended; one may find even in the course of uttering it that it is inadequate, hesitate, and begin again.

The construction of a sentence (as an instrument) is thus to be distinguished from the uses to which it can be put. And, although sentences are clearly constructed for precise and special functions, it would still be a mistake to think that its use was completely specified by its construction. Rather than specifying a single actual use, its construction seems to specify a field of possible uses. And as I said earlier, only if necessary, for particular practical purposes, are the criteria making its use determinate negotiated and agreed upon, and there are all sorts of strategies for doing that, some drawing on negotiations before the use of the sentence, some during, and some after its use.

What then is the relation between personal powers and rules? Do we speak in accordance with rules? While speaking we obviously remain sensitive to our listener's nods of comprehension and grimaces of bafflement, and modify our talk accordingly. It is just not the case, empirically, that we turn our eyes inward, shut ourselves off from our environment, and refer to some pre-established inner plan to determine what we say. We can in some cases, but we do not usually. Face-to-face conversations are not mediated solely by linguistic 'rules'. Rather what seems to be the case is that we continually monitor the construction of our expressions in relation to our intended purpose. And we do this by constructing as we utter them their meanings, in just the same way as our listener must construct them. We can say that our natural powers present us with possible forms of expression and regulate their forms, while our personal powers allow us to select among them the expressions whose meanings are appropriate to our purpose.[3]

[3] Here I take a position like that described in Mead (1934, p. 347) in which the expression of our 'biologic inheritance from lower life' is channelled through so-called 'cognitive structures' acquired in the course of the instructive exchanges that I have been discussing. This surely is to make the mistake of which Anscombe (1957, p. 57) complains, that of taking 'an incorrigibly contemplative conception of knowledge'. If such knowledge is to be used to inform practical activities, 'a very queer and special sort of seeing eye in the middle of the acting' is required to make use of it, she points out. Thus now

So while the vocalizing of linguistic forms is not *rule*-regulated but simply regulated, speaking to other people in a purposeful manner is, potentially at least, rule-regulated—I say, *potentially*, because it may very well be that the agreements which will actually make the meanings of one's utterances determinate may only be reached *after* one's utterance in the course of subsequent exchanges. So what people seem to be aware of while they talk are not the regulations determining the possible *forms* of their talk, but the possible criteria (and thus the possible operations) for determining what is *meant* by their talk. And these rules are in no way fundamental. They reflect just as much aspects of one's circumstances as 'the general character of one's capacity to acquire knowledge'. They are human constructions involving human agreements. Thus I think it is fanciful of Harré and Secord (1972, p. 123) to take seriously the idea of seeking the 'grammars of the social order, and perhaps even for the deep structure or social universals that may lie behind all human communities'. All we can seek, I feel, are the strategies and techniques via which we realize our natural powers and bring them under control of our personal powers, the process via which we negotiate the restraints on our social expressions thus determining their form.

Natural Agents cannot become Individual Personalities on their Own

In what has gone before then, I have suggested that human beings have no personal powers at birth at all; they only gain them in negotiated interaction with those who already possess them. To possess personal powers and to become a reasonable person is to manifest not just directed but *self*-directed activity; one has to do more than just direct one's activities in an ordered manner, one has to express *meanings* in one's actions. Reasonable people are expected to show not just awareness (i.e., consciousness) of their circumstances but *self*-consciousness; that is, they are expected not just to act in

I would follow Anscombe and attempt to develop an account of *practical knowledge*, noting that while the concept of *rule* may be needed in constructing *accounts* of practices, orderly performances of such practices need not be informed by knowledge of rules at all. In general, 'Efficient practice precedes the theory of it' (Ryle, 1949, p. 31).

some sense appropriately to their circumstances, but to act in a socially intelligible manner, and to be *responsible* for what they do by being able to indicate when required what they intend or mean by their actions. Only as individual personalities, as selves, can we act reasonably; as natural agents we can only act as we must in relation to our own bodily states. To act responsibly people must be able to monitor their own actions; they must be able to assess the value or significance of their own performances in relation to needs, goals, and interests other than their own immediate and idiosyncratic ones. In order to do this, they must be able to order their own activities in relation to some internally constituted totalities, both interpreting and operating on the physical world and coordinating their actions with those of other people in relation to such totalities. Only in this way can one's actions be said to be rule-regulated and one be said to know what one is doing, thus meeting the fundamental requirements for what it is to be an individual personality.

In this paper, then, I have attempted to elucidate the processess going on between and within a child and his mother as he gains his personal powers. Concerning the processes within the child: Garner has shown that we seem to mentally constitute a whole *family of related alternatives* from a limited experience of some of its possible members, and Bohm has argued that such a construction is only possible if one can find a *relation* between what one does and what happens as a result. Concerning the processes between mother and child: What begins as a physiological contact, moves through a period of purely idiosyncratic exchanges mediated via affect in which the mother is instrumental in bringing the child's vague intentions to fruition, and finally ends with a period of social games. It is on acquiring the skill to conduct games with others that the child embarks on the path to true personal powers. In playing with others he will ultimately acquire the skill to play all the parts of the game himself, and in his dialogues with himself conduct reflective thought. At first, it was his mother who reflected him back to himself, but ultimately he will be able to do everything without her help at all, and even, in the invention of new games, go beyond her personal grasp of the world to the realization of new and unimagined powers, relying always, though, on forms of expression negotiated with others.

REFERENCES

Anscombe, G. E. M. *Intention*. Oxford: Blackwell, 1957.

Becker, E. *The Birth and Death of Meaning*. 2nd ed. Harmondsworth: Penguin, 1972.

Bertalanffy, L. V. *General System Theory*. New York: George Braziller, 1968.

Bohm, D. Relativity and Perception. Appendix to *Relativity*. New York: Benjamin, 1965.

Bruner, J. S. *Toward a Theory of Instruction*. New York: Norton, 1966.

Bruner, J. S. On voluntary action and its hierarchical structure. In A. Koestler & J. R. Symthies (eds.), *Beyond Reductionism*. London: Hutchinson, 1969.

Chomsky, N. *Aspects of the Theory of Syntax*. Cambridge, Mass: M.I.T., 1965.

Chomsky, N. *Problems of Knowledge and Freedom*. London: Fontana, 1972.

Garner, R. To perceive is to know. *American Psychologist*, 1966, 21, 11–19.

Harré, R. & Secord, P. *The explanation of Social Behaviour*. Oxford: Blackwell, 1972.

Koffka, K. Die Grundlagen der psychischen Entwicklung Osterwieck am Harz. Quoted in E. Cassirer, *The Philosophy of Symbolic Forms*, Vol. 3. New Haven: Yale University Press 1921, pp. 64–5.

Macfarlane, A. If a smile is so important. *New Scientist*, 24 April 1974.

Mead, G. H. *Mind, Self, and Society*. Chicago: University of Chicago Press, 1934.

Piaget, J. *Play, Dreams and Imitation in Children*. London: Routledge & Kegan Paul, 1951.

Ryle, G. *The Concept of Mind*. 1949. Harmondsworth: Penguin, 1963.

Schaffer, H. R. *The Growth of Sociability*. Harmondsworth: Penguin, 1971.

Shotter, J. Prolegomena to an understanding of play. *J. for the Theory of Social Behaviour*, 1973, 3, 47–89.

Spitz, R. *The First Year of Life*. New York: International Universities Press, 1965.

Tinbergen, N. *The Study of Instinct*. Oxford: Oxford University Press, 1951.

Wittgenstein, L. *Philosophical Investigations*. Oxford: Blackwell, 1953.

Wittgenstein, L. *Blue & Brown Books*. New York: Harper Torchbook, 1958.

Vygotsky, L. S. Play and its role in the mental development of the child. *Soviet Psychology*, 1966, 12, 6–18.

3 Living up to a Name*

ROM HARRÉ

1. *Introduction*

Common-sense reflection on the influences which are likely to determine personality would suggest that a person's name and the various appellations which he acquires through life would be likely to have a considerable influence upon the kind of person he takes himself to be. A name would not perhaps be a *determining* feature of someone's personality, that is of the public version of himself, but it seems reasonable to suppose that it is a basic datum to be managed by a person in his presentation system. In this respect it is a given, like one's physique and other physical characteristics, such as colour, facial form, and so on. Unlike these more static characters, names, though they have an intransigent existence as objects determined by social practices outside an individual's control, such as, for example, christening and registering the name, their remedy can lie within a person's sphere of influence since, at least in some countries, he is legally entitled to style himself anything he likes. Or, if his given name is sufficiently complex he can choose which aspect of it to emphasize when he gives his name to other people. But given, official names are not the only names one acquires. There are also the names generated by the elaborate system by which other kinds of names are generated, acquired, managed, denied and so on, in the processes of the management of the social images of oneself. The obviousness of these reflections ought not to suggest that no further empirical work than mere social intuition is required. I shall be indicating in what follows those points at which further work could be done, as well as those matters about which empirical information has recently been accumulated.

*I am grateful to the editors of the *Oxford Review of Education* for their permission to reprint some material from Vol.1, No. 2 of their journal.

The investigation of the way in which a name is effective in influencing personality is a good example of a form of social psychological process which could not be subjected to the naïve experimentalist approach. How could one proceed to test 'hypotheses' about the effect of names by manipulating the independent variable? The impossibility of such a form of investigation has led to the almost complete neglect, in the literature, of the study of the influence of names on personality. For example, in Hollander and Hunt (1972) there is no entry for Names in the subject index and so far as I am aware the subject is not adverted to in the text. Even in the more up-to-date survey by Secord and Bachman (1972) naming as a determinant of personality is not discussed.

The first general observation to make is to draw attention to the peculiarly intimate sense in which one's name is oneself, in that the ambiguity of the question, 'Who are you?' allows both for a name and a description to be offered as an answer. Usually the name stands in for the description. The potency of this answer is well enough illustrated by the feelings of pride, shame, etc. which cluster around the name. Very little work has been done on these name emotions, but it needs to be undertaken in a non-experimental style in that the relationship between names and name emotions must be elicited from the accounts of people who have experienced them.

Anthropologists have investigated names and naming systems in much more detail than have psychologists. There are important investigations of the systems in which the 'real' name is concealed for fear of the control which might be obtained over a person should an enemy obtain his real name (surely indicative of the degree to which, amongst human beings, one's name is peculiarly oneself). I shall be using an important anthropological distinction in the work which follows, namely that between internal and external influences on a naming system, what has been called by Barley (1974) external and internal motivation. Anthropologists have noticed that the choice of a name is determined partly by descriptive or empirical features of the object or individual named, partly by systematic features of the naming system itself. For example, in Barley (1974) this distinction allows him to explicate the Anglo-Saxon naming system, which is determined in part by an internal property, namely the alliterative properties of the names related to the Anglo-Saxon rules of poetic composition, introduced into naming for mnemonic purposes, and external properties of the person named, such as, for example, whether that person is of the male or the female sex. We shall find that the distinction between external and internal motivation in naming runs through the empirical material upon which this chapter is based.

Finally, by way of introduction, it is important to grasp the fatefulness of names, whether they be given names in the official sense of the name chosen for an individual by those responsible for such matters and officially ratified and recorded, or the fatefulness of nicknames, the effect of which may last a lifetime. A very striking example of this is to be found in the account by Remedios Reyes in Fraser (1973) on the fatefulness of nicknaming in a small Spanish town.

> The people are very witty. They invent nicknames in a flash. Everyone has one and they're often passed down from generation to generation. Usually people don't know a family by their real name but by the nickname. There are whole generations of Satans, Little Stars, Bad Feet. I imagine a woman looking at her new-born and saying 'Ay, what a tiny prick he's got,' because the poor man has been 'Tiny prick' for the rest of his life.

2. Social Aspects of Given Names

I shall distinguish throughout this chapter between given names, those that a person acquires through the official machinery of naming, and which in general he has little choice in deciding. There are some exceptions to this in that it is possible in some legal systems for a person to change his name officially and ceremonially to a name of his own choice. It is also possible nowadays for a woman, on marriage, to choose to adopt her husband's name or to continue to be referred to by her maiden name. Finally, in the British system of peerages, the title taken by a man on elevation to the peerage is a name of his own choice. In general, though, I shall assume that given names are acquired by an individual at, or shortly after, birth and that he or she has little or no say in what they will be. In contrast to these are what I shall generally call nicknames, which will be discussed in the next section.

In order to identify properly the areas in which research could usefully be done on the social aspects of given names, I shall sketch

out two main areas of influence that the name bears upon personality
and the person upon his name, where I hope to indicate possibilities
of various pieces of empirical work. The first of these concerns the
discovery of one's name. So far as I can ascertain, it is unknown
when one discovers one's names, in what order, and how attitudes
to these names develop, change, and are initiated in the first place.
One might assume, in the absence of empirical work, that one's
personal name and one's family name were acquired by oneself as
social knowledge at different times in the course of one's development. This may or may not be so. There are various curious features
about the early naming practices of parents to infants that I shall
discuss in another section, summarizing empirical work that has
been done on that matter, which leads one to think that at least in
same cases, family name and personal name are both available to
an infant at about the same age. Having discovered one's name, one
then, bit by bit, one supposes, comes to understand its significance,
quite apart from its role as an indexical and referential expression.

There must come a time at which some unfortunate children
realize that their names are in themselves stigmata. There seem to be
at least two possibilities for kinds of name stigma. Some names have,
for a variety of reasons, become absurd, ridiculous, the object of
derision. A recent example of such a name stigma is that attached
to the name 'Horace', which, so far as I can trace this matter, seems
to have had its origin in the use of the name by the cartoonist Walt
Disney for a particularly absurd horse, the popularity of the cartoon
spreading the stigma attached to the name. Again, there are names
which in one way or another seem to be ridiculous in themselves.
The name 'Longbottom' was an object of derision in my schooldays
and, consequently, so was its bearer.

But name stigma may be of other kinds. There are, for example,
in those societies where there are stigmata attached to ethnicities,
ethnically-revealing names, so that the name itself begins to acquire
an emotional or attitudinal load in proportion to the stigma attached
to the ethnicity. It would be invidious of me, in the absence of
empirical work, to introduce examples of this, but the reader can
supply them from his own experience, experiences which will be
different according to the time at which he acquired his attitudes
to varying ethnicities and to the local situation.

Stigmata are managed successfully, more or less, by the people
who suffer them and we have, from Goffman, a discussion of the

systematic methods by which stigmata are managed. It remains a question for empirical investigation as to how far Goffman's rules are employed in the management of stigmatizing names.

The first step to management is related to an observation of Goffman's (1963): 'Shame becomes a central possibility arising from the individual's perception of one of his own attributes as a defiling thing to possess and one he can readily see himself as not possessing.' It is the poignancy of the person's realization that his name is something that might very well have been other that makes name-stigma both so strikingly damaging and so apparently remediable. Goffman identifies three different techniques by which stigmata can be managed.

1. It may be that those who cannot support 'a norm' by reason of their stigma nevertheless become passionate supporters of that very norm. It is hard to see how this technique could be applied generally in the case of names, though it might have been an element in the Anglicization of names in nineteenth-century America.

2. A stigmatized individual may simply alienate himself from the community in which his peculiar name or other property would be stigmatizing. Again, it seems hard to conceive of a social practice which would be an example of an adult person managing a damaging name by such a move. We have reason to think children do resort to this technique.

3. However, Goffman identifies another technique which appears in various forms in impression management. In so far as a person's name is implicated in generating the views others have of him, then change of name is itself an example of impression management. Changes may be subtle, such as alterations in spelling, which can modulate a name from one ethnicity to another, or seem to change the etymology of a name, e.g. 'Rosenberg' becomes 'Montrose'. Again, it may be possible to shift from one part of one's given name to another, altering in that way the projected personality, as, for example, 'Lizzie' may become 'Beth'. The management of nicknames is, of course, a much more difficult affair, since they lie not so much within the personal power of the nicknamed as within the social practices of his peers. He can do little to cope with that, other than adopting Goffman's second strategy, namely leaving that social milieu altogether. It seems, then, that it is not unreasonable to see unfortunate names as falling within the general category of stigma as Goffman defines them, and involving techniques of management

which fall within the general categories that Goffman recognizes, but the instances I have cited are quite anecdotal and systematic exploratory empirical work remains to be done.

Complementary to the influence of name-stigmata are the effects of the acquisition of names of which one might justly be proud. For example, one may have a name that connects one in some way with an honoured person, family, or ethnic group. However, the positive effects of names have, among some communities, not been left simply to chance. That is, parents have chosen virtue and good-quality names for their children. This was common practice in Victorian England, in which names like 'Faith', 'Hope', and 'Charity', were not unusual, and it is presently still the custom amongst many Chinese families. An empirical investigation on the Chinese practices is presently being conducted to try to ascertain how far it is that Chinese parents who choose a virtue or quality name hope (and/or believe) that this will affect the character of their children, and complementary to this, an investigation of how far those who bear such names are able to identify in their psychological autobiographies any influences and occasions on which virtue followed a name.

There seems also to be a very widespread phenomenon about which little systematic knowledge has been obtained, namely the wish amongst adolescents to change their names. Of course, common-sense understanding suggests that nicknames and identities are as closely bound up as, I believe, a disparity between actual and envisaged personality. A disparity likely to become particularly prominent in the self-reflections of adolescence could be managed by a shift of name in the direction of that taken to reflect a more desirable personality. This has a second aspect, which could also be the subject of an empirical investigation, namely, the practice, still quite prevalent, of the adoption of stage names, such as, for example, when Norma Jeane Baker[1] becomes 'Marilyn Monroe', or Jerry Dorsey becomes 'Engelbert Humperdinck'. There must be, in the tacit understandings of impresarios, some, possibly systematic, conceptions of what *sort* of name goes with what sort of personality. Such understandings might well be usefully tapped by some empirical investigations. One would expect these to be both culture specific and changing over time. Investigations on a cross-

---

[1] Or Mortenson.

cultural and a historical basis might prove illuminating in revealing whether there were any universal principles that could be discerned in these cases, as, for example, the appearance of alliteration.

Complementary to the discovery of one's own name, and its fateful consequentiality, there is the reading of one's name by others, that is the public understandings of the personality etc. implications of this or that name. I have already pointed out that parental choice of names should reflect to some extent the local understandings of these personality implications, so that the empirical study of the Chinese naming practices will perhaps reveal some aspects of how other people's names are read. Similarly, the annual league tables of names published by the newspapers in England ought to reveal, via the differential choices made in different parts of the country and in areas dominated by different kinds of professions and jobs, something of the social implications of certain names. There do seem to be some pointers in this direction, though systematic work remains to be done. The *Sunday Times* of 11 January 1976 reported a survey they had themselves conducted in a somewhat jocular spirit, comparing four areas in Britain. There were distinct regional variations which could be perhaps associated to some extent with class. There is a distinct difference between the degree to which Victorian girls' names are currently being used between the South and the North of England, so that a name like Emma is found in the South more frequently than in the North. But what is often erroneously called class differences seemed much more potent than geographical distinctions, in that in an area where manual labour was the most common form of work, a somewhat more elaborate form of naming was apparent and the names seemed to have been influenced to some extent by American naming practices, whereas in those areas of London where the predominantly professional workers live, the standard, traditional and simple names predominated. A further complication, which runs counter to the simple versus elaborated names, is to be found by a recent trend to classical, i.e. Greek and Roman names, particularly for girls, as e.g. Olympian, the name of Alexander's mother.

Such work as reported in newspapers is, of course, rudimentary. What lies behind it is a so far unexplored feature of tacit social knowledge, namely, the social and personality associations of names. This is the kind of thing which 'everybody knows', but which has scarcely been systematically explored. There is, for example, a kind of parlour game played in some families on guessing the sort of person who is likely to be the bearer of a particular kind of name. Sometimes this turns out to be an idiosyncratic product of meeting this or that person who had the name, but I am inclined to think that careful empirical research is likely to reveal a name culture in which these associations will have some local generality.

The social aspects of given names, then, seem, from our common sense intuitions and unreflective experience, to be associated in various ways with matters of personalities, that is, with the self as presented to others, with the public version of oneself. It is also clear, I hope, that a considerable amount of empirical work could usefully be done to extend our knowledge of this hitherto unconsidered matter. Much of this research is already being undertaken in a systematic project, the results of which will be published from time to time.

3. The Genesis of Nicknames

Considerable work has already been done on nicknaming practices amongst children, by myself and associates. It is clear that nicknaming is a most important feature of children's social worlds and is perhaps the more striking for its independence of influences stemming in any direct way from adults. Nicknames are invented by children, for children, and show, as we shall see, an elaborate and subtle systematicity. However, before I turn to an exposition of the results of our investigations to date into the social naming practices of children, I should like to discuss very briefly what we have so far been able to discover about the practices of pet naming, the names that parents give infants before those infants can speak.

Nothing is yet known about how an infant acquires the ability to receive the name as his and in particular, as a young child, to receive from parents, friends, siblings and others his first nicknames. Empirical studies have shown that, seemingly independent of a particular culture, an infant is bombarded with a variety of names, none of which is his official name, and any one of which may be used by his parent, or parents, to refer to him. He seems to know how to cope with this multiplicity of referring expressions long before he can talk. The names employed by husband and wife for an infant are systematically different with a certain overlap. Each may use anywhere between five and eight names for the child and to the child, none of which is the name they chose for purposes of official registration, though some of these names are, of course, related to it, one example of such official name-related cognomen being a contraction, as, for example, 'Benjamin' becoming 'Benjos'. Similarly, it seems to be a practice for fathers to use a very formal mode of address, referring to their daughters as 'Miss So-and-so' and sons as 'Mr. So-and-so', or whatever might be the appropriate formal title. Work done so far has found no evidence of this practice by mothers. Finally, there is a use of descriptive phrases like 'Baby man', or '*Nañe*' for a referential term, which has the force of a nickname. Much more work requires to be done to understand this practice more thoroughly, but it has two striking characteristics.

(i) the child is subjected to a multiplicity of referring expressions and seems to be capable of realizing that it is he or she that is meant by whichever name they happen to be addressed;

(ii) there is a distinct difference in the naming practices between mothers and fathers, each using a multiplicity of names, but so far in our investigations we seem to see a very different list appearing from each of them.

The names that are created for people by those who know them, involve the use of a quite distinct methodology by which the names are created. One way of classifying methods follows the anthropological distinction between externally and internally motivated names. Extensive empirical work amongst children has shown that there are four basic principles at work in the genesis of nicknames.

1. The recognition of qualities: physical, intellectual and characterlogical attributes can be the basis of the created name. An excellent account, which one must suppose to be based upon some life experience of this process in the course of action, can be found in a recent novel (Le Carré, 1976).

In the course of that same summer term, the boys paid Jim the compliment of a nickname. They had several shots before they were happy. They tried Trooper, which caught the bit of military in him, his occasional, quite harmless cursing and his solitary rambles in the Quantocks. All the same Trooper didn't stick, so they tried Pirate and for a while Goulash. Goulash because of his taste for hot food, the smell of curries and onions and paprika that

greeted them in warm puffs as they filed past the Dip on their
way to Evensong. Goulash for his perfect French which was held
to have a slushy quality. Spikely of Five B could imitate it to a
hair: 'You heard the question, Berger. What is Emile looking
at?'—a convulsive jerk of the right hand—'Don't gawp at me,
old boy, I'm not a juju man. *Qu'est-ce qu'il regarde, Emile, dans
le tableau tu as sous le nez? Mon cher Berger*, if you do not very
soon summon one lucid sentence of French, *je te mettrai tout de
suite à la porte, tu comprend*s, you beastly toad?'

But these terrible threats were never carried out, neither in
French nor English. In a quaint way, they actually added to the
aura of gentleness which quickly surrounded him, a gentleness
only possible in big men seen through the eyes of boys.

Yet Goulash didn't satisfy them either. It lacked the hint of
strength contained. It took no account of Jim's passionate
Englishness, which was the only subject where he could be relied
on to waste time. Toad Spikely had only to venture one
disparaging comment on the monarchy, extol the joys of some
foreign country, preferably a hot one, for Jim to colour sharply
and snap out a good three minutes' worth on the privilege of
being born an Englishman. He knew they were teasing him but
he was unable not to rise. . . .

Finally they hit on Rhino.

Partly that was a play on Prideaux, partly a reference to his
taste for living off the land and his appetite for physical exercise
which they noted constantly. Shivering in the shower queue first
thing in the morning they would see the Rhino pounding down
Combe Lane with a rucksack on his crooked back as he returned
from his morning march. Going to bed they could glimpse his
lonely shadow through the perspex roof of the fives court as the
Rhino tirelessly attacked the concrete wall. . . .

Some elaboration on this will be seen in the final section, when I
shall discuss the relationship between naming and the social order
that comes to exist amongst children.

2. Incidents: Lévi-Strauss has remarked how famous or striking
incidents, in a culture, may be marked in various ways. Amongst
children the marking may be achieved by the derivation of a name.
For example, during a French lesson one child, in reading from the
set book, found herself, every time it was her turn, with the phrase,

'*J'aime*'. Her previously anonymous status was remedied and from then on she became 'Jam'. A boy, at the awkward, adolescent stage for voice control, reading his French set book, was embarrassed by his voice breaking on the word '*Coupable*', and from then on bore the mysterious name 'Coop'.

Names based on qualities and names based on incidents in biography are, in the anthropologist's terminology, externally motivated. That is, the name does not derive from its place in a naming system.

3. However, another main category of naming methods is of an internally motivated character, where the naming depends upon a verbal analogy. There are two main categories, the first where an alliterative connection exists between the given name and the nickname. An alliterative sequence begins with the name 'Jackie Amos' to 'A Mosquito' and then, by another process, also internal, to 'Flea'. Similarly, 'Stephen Hill' becomes 'Chill', becomes 'Charlie'. Also to be treated as internally motivated, I believe, are what one might describe as cultural analogue names, as for example, where someone called 'Donald' becomes 'Duck', for obvious reasons. Closely connected with the cultural analogue case and a variant on it is a method of deriving a name which combines both internal and external motivation, as, for example, a teacher who was known to the children as 'Kiki', because she looked like a frog puppet who appeared on television.

4. Finally, there are the traditional names, both those associated with names internally motivated, such as 'Nobby' for 'Clarke', 'Dusty' for 'Miller', 'Flash' for 'Gordon', and those associated with social place, based upon some discernible physical tendency, such as 'Porky', 'Streak', and so on. Again, I shall elaborate upon the role of these names in the section to come. They must be regarded as externally motivated.

Our empirical studies of naming practices have provided a very rich collection of empirical data and we are currently in the process of providing a detailed analysis of the methodology under these four main headings. It is worth noticing in passing that the techniques of name-giving are one of the few areas of language use open to children where free creativity within a rule system can be enjoyed. We hope to show, in the final product of our investigations, just how elaborate and sophisticated the detailed structuring of the methodology turns out to be.

4. *Nicknames in the Society of Childhood*

The nicknaming system is powerfully influential in generating and maintaining the social order that children create for themselves, their own autonomous society. In general, the naming system seems to effect three main divisions. First, it marks those who are rejected from the society at large in that particular children's group. Secondly, it seems also to be used to mark a well-knit group who have the privilege of using each other's names. For example, amongst thirteen-year old girls, a tightly knit group uses the names 'Phlea',[2] 'Jam', 'Chocky', 'Felix', and 'Porky'. Moving in and out of the group seems to involve slipping between these and the formal or given name. Finally, there is the process by which the offices of the micro-society are filled, the process we have called 'slotting'.

There are two issues of importance we must address to understand the inwardness of all this verbal activity. How far do other attributes in the dimension of the nickname cluster around one of these names, and are required of someone with the nickname? And how far do attributes in other dimensions cluster round the central attribute from which the use of the name originally derived? For example, how far is 'Fatty' as much a role, that of *fat boy*, as a description?

We know from ethnographers that there is a tendency for those who originally find themselves in the Eagle totem purely as a representation of the logical relation between them and some other endogamous group, say the Bears, after a time, as one might say, 'to make like Eagles'. A participant ethnographer of tender age but sharp eyes reports from an Oxford school of the slow development of a florid display of feline characteristics of behaviour by one who originally acquired the nickname 'Pussy' from the shape of her eyes alone. Thus on analogy with the totem-name case one might expect the attribution of a nickname to prompt a behaviour style that would tend to fill out its implications thus showing the holder to be worthy of the name.

But what of time-honoured nicknames like 'Fatty', 'Flea-bag', 'Tombstone' and the like? They repeat themselves generation after generation, and are part of the fixed resources of the child's autonomous culture as much as wart-cures and marble games. I want to

[2] This curious spelling of 'Flea' is explained by Phlea, as follows: 'I don't want to be associated with the nasty little bugs!'

argue that the traditional nicknames are very much more than descriptions of physical characteristics, and that their attribution to someone carries him or her into what I shall call a 'slot'. A slot is a place in the social fabric having fairly well-defined social demands, rather as an 'office' in the generalized sense has well-articulated social demands put upon it.

This suggests the possibility that slot or office and the behaviour and attitudes appropriate to it may be a more prominent attribute of the holder than the physical property which is the nickname's apparently prime attribution. Thus we may be prompted to ask how fat must 'Fatty' be, or how dirty must 'Flea-bag' stay. So far as I can ascertain no adequate studies of these matters have been made.

Since the ethnography of this strange tribe 'the children' so often at our very feet but so often not *seen*, is still far from adequate, we must, until empirical findings are to hand, fall back upon its representation in fiction, from whence I would like to draw two clear, and I think ethnographically plausible, *fat boy* slots, to illustrate the elaboration of the demands of the slot over purely fulfilling the physical description. Billy Bunter is the greedy, bullying fat boy, using his weight to push others around, but likely to turn tearful in a crisis. He can be found in an earthier version in the character of Greedy Greg in *Whizzer and Chips*. He is inclined to fill his stomach by stealthy and sneaky grabbing and greedy stuffing of food. Piggy is the knowledgeable fat boy, for ever in Fourth Remove, the only one with a chemistry set who really did the experiments. He has thick-lensed glasses, and he runs like a girl, and always in some mysterious way is unfit for games. I would like to claim that these character complexes are socially, and not physiologically determined, for these are the only two ways that the *fat boy* slot can be filled. I believe that in any class or group of children, of roughly this culture, that slot can be filled in each way *only once*. Regardless of adiposity, each class can have only one Billy Bunter and only one Piggy. To explain the existence of these slots and their role in the social life of the tribe will require a great deal more research than the little that has been done so far.

Let us look a little more closely at the 'Piggy' slot, for we have the inestimable advantage of a portrait of one of the occupants of this slot by a writer of genius, since he is a central character in Golding's *The Lord of the Flies*. Piggy is the archetypal henchman, a descendant of Falstaff and Sancho Panza. In Golding's story his Prince Hal is Ralph, tall, fair, and athletic. Piggy, by contrast, was 'shorter than the fair boy and very fat'. Archetypally he is 'excused games'. '"My auntie told me not to run," he explained. "on account of me asthma"' He is marked out by this physical handicap as 'the only boy in the school who had asthma', and his spectacles, the necessary accoutrement of the special sort of henchman that Piggy is, are a proud possession. As he says to Ralph, 'I've been wearing specs since I was three.'

In the story Piggy is not only Ralph's squire, lugging his clothes about, but is his intellectual superior, the one who thinks, who makes plans and who values order above all. Indeed his death at the hands of Jack's gang is in defence of the one symbol of civilized order the boys possess, the conch. The boys on the island laugh at Piggy, as the children of our schools laugh at their Piggies, but it is to them they must turn when technical mastery is required.

Why are such boys so frequently fat? Until the Opies can provide us with a definitive ethnography of these names I would like to venture the hypothesis that it is *tradition* that demands it. The resistance to change of the ethogenics of the autonomous childhood world, amply demonstrated by the Opies, includes, I believe, such standard slots as *fat boy* $1 \equiv$ Billy Bunter, and *fat boy* $2 \equiv$ Piggy. And that moderately suitable children are squeezed into them. Thus those that are merely plump, but not endowed with the rest of the attributes, are just among the undistinguished citizenry of the private republics of childhood.

It seems clear that the Billy Bunter role has something of the force of a scapegoat in that he is licensed to stuff himself greedily and then to bear all the opprobrium that would have accrued to his classmates had they done that. The same sort of distinction seems to be available as an explanation of why there are two slots for intellect —'Thinker and 'Tombstone'. 'Thinker' is the walking dictionary, the solver of people's problems, the intellect conceived as admirable, whereas 'Tombstone', though intelligent, is required to play the role of a dunce and to be mocked and to some extent denigrated. Thus he is in polar opposition to 'Dimmy' or 'Twit', who is really thick. The remaining traditional slots, 'Flea-bag' or 'Sewage' and 'Titch', are also, I think, fairly readily explicable on microsociological lines. 'Flea-bag' is like Fatty, No. 1, in that he bears the opprobrium of being dirty for everyone. 'Titch', on the other hand, is allowed a kind of waspish licence, something of the order of a joker, and his

C

size is ritually allowed to protect him from the consequences of his sharp tongue.

But why have the rest of the citizenry got nicknames? The answer, we think, has been revealed by a detailed study of the nicknaming techniques at a local school. When the standard nicknames, 'Fatty', 'Podgy', 'Titch', 'Twit', 'Sewage', are deleted, there remain a rich collection. The etymology of the remaining names is fairly straightforward. There are certain standard names, such as 'Carrots', there are alliterative names such as 'Hot Dog' for someone whose name begins with 'Ot'. There is 'Sherlock' for a 'Holmes', 'Flash' for a 'Gordon' and so on, and there are style names, such as 'Snail' and 'Flash' in the 'Flash Harry' sense. But the role of these names is not revealed by their etymology, rather by the sad plight of the seven members of that class who had no nicknames. It was apparent to the investigator that the lack of a nickname went with a peripheral position in the social order of the group, and was in general a fairly good indicator of friendlessness. Disproportionately many West Indian children were in the nameless group. The two West Indians who were popular had nicknames. Thus, nicknaming seems to be connected in some way or another with membership and social recognition. As yet, we are unable to distinguish the chicken and the egg in this matter.[3]

It is fairly clear, too, that at the break between eleven and twelve years of age, or thereabouts, a difference is discernible in the nicknaming system. Indeed, there is evidence to suggest that the nicknames used for individuals up to about that time are abandoned at the onset of adolescence and a new system is introduced, children characteristically changing their nicknames at about this time. Empirical studies have so far shown that the newly acquired nicknames do not contain the traditional slots and are very much more related to personal appearance and behavioural properties which are idiosyncratic. At this point a difference is revealed between school classes in professional areas and manual-worker areas, because the lists of nicknames in the higher classes in the manual-worker areas tend to be much more conservative than amongst the children of professional people. This conservatism is not only shown in the

---

[3] A younger group of children in a near-by junior school had few nick-names, but a strongly marked 'in' and 'out' boundary, those who were 'in' being addressed by first name and surname, and those who were 'out' by obscene names, like 'wanker'.

names themselves, but in their etymology. There is, for example, a much greater persistence of names which are derived by some kind of contraction or joke rhyming from surname. For instance, 'Carrot' from 'Barrett' in a working-class area, contrasts with 'Choc-ice' for someone in a professional-class area who acquires the name from eating habits.

Who gives the nicknames? What little evidence we have so far accumulated suggests that there is someone who is, as it were, licensed name-giver in any given group of children. It may sometimes be a teacher, but it seems usually not to be so. Efforts by others to promote nicknames are generally unsuccessful. We have noted the pathetic efforts by a West Indian out group to sell their nicknames for the unnamed members of their group, which proved quite unsuccessful.

The solidarity function of naming is emphasized by the discovery of the role of multiple nicknames. Many people have several nicknames and each seems to be related to a particular group. Two friends, or perhaps a small group of friends, may have special names for each other, which no one else is allowed to use, while when mixing with a wider group a different nickname is employed and proper to that occasion. As in many social matters, the nickname system seems to be not only a source of solidarity but a resource for other kinds of social activity, such as, for example, teasing and put-downs. The very same nickname can be the mark of affection in one mood and a source of insult and denigration in another, though, of course, it is clear that to be insulted and denigrated is a way of being noticed and those twenty per cent, on average, who had no names, were noticed in no way.

The assimilation of West Indians into the child's precursor world society is easily mapped, using the nickname system. Popular, noisy, West Indian children with strong personalities, have nicknames derived from the usual stock of Anglo-Saxon techniques, Their nicknames are, as one might say, ordinary. But if they are disliked, and as we remarked, that itself is a way of being noticed, they get disagreeable names, such as 'Nigger', 'Blackie', 'Blackcurrant' etc.

Finally, it was worth remarking that up until the age of fourteen at least, there was no discernible difference between the treatment of boys and girls.

REFERENCES

BARLEY, N. F. Perspectives on Anglo-Saxon Names. *Semiotica*, 1974, 11, 1–31.

FRASER, R. *The Pueblo*. London: Allen Lane, 1973, p. 134.

GOFFMAN, E. *Stigma*, Harmondsworth: Penguin Books 1963, p. 18.

HOLLANDER, E. P. & HUNT, R. G. *Classic Contributions to Social Psychology*, New York: Oxford University Press, 1972.

LE CARRÉ, J. *Tinker, Tailor, Soldier, Spy*, London: Pan Books, 1976, pp. 16–17.

SECORD, P. F. & BACKMAN, C. W. *Social Psychology*, New York: McGraw-Hill, 1972.

PART II   The Description of Personality

4 Traits, Consistency and Conceptual Alternatives for Personality Theory

WILLIAM P. ALSTON

The trait approach to personality has been under heavy attack of late. Palpable hits have been scored. Traits would seem to be on the run. However, even if we accept the critics' assessment of the results, it is not sufficiently clear exactly what has been shown, nor indeed exactly what they take themselves to have shown. In particular the literature leaves relatively indeterminate:

A. The exact target of the attack. In just what sense of 'trait' are traits being criticized? What variables are to be put under this rubric?

B. Just what defects are traits claimed to have? What *desiderata* is it they are said not to satisfy?

Until we have rendered the position sufficiently determinate on these points we will not be in a position to determine whether any of the arguments deployed by the critics give adequate support to their contentions. Nor, assuming that the arguments do the job, will it be sufficiently clear just *what* has been shown defective in *what* way. As a result we will be exposed to the twin dangers of dismissing concepts that do not fall under the ban, and of reintroducing concepts that do. In scientific, as in political matters, it is all too easy to win the war and lose the peace.

This paper is an attempt to provide the needed clarification by invoking some fundamental conceptual and methodological distinctions. I should make it explicit at the outset that my interest is by no means confined to removing ambiguities in the existing literature, or to determining exactly what certain authors 'really mean' (or ought to mean). My primary interest is in making a contribution of my own to the enterprise of choosing between basic conceptual alternatives for personality description. However, that contribution being of a conceptual and theoretical rather than an empirical sort, a useful springboard will be provided by the identification and resolution of indeterminacies in the recent controversies over traits,[1] and an assessment of the argumentation in that literature.[2]

By way of preview the most important conclusions of this essay will be:

1. Although the attack on traits has primarily focused on their generality (lack of situational specificity), there is a more basic issue of conceptual type that has been masked by the former concern.

2. The 'utility' of trait-attributions, another focus of attention, is both multi-faceted and complexly determined, and it is important to separate out the simpler components and consider them separately.

3. Empirical consistency data have little bearing on the choice of a basic conceptual framework.

4. The crucial considerations for that choice lie in the theory of motivation.

I shall direct my remarks specifically to the leading opponent of traits on the contemporary scene, Professor Walter Mischel. I choose Mischel for this purpose not because his writings are especially rich in ambiguities. On the contrary, just because he is the most careful and incisive of the critics, any clarification called for by his writings is genuinely needed to advance the discussion.

I. *What is the target of the criticism? Traits and other personality characteristics*

In the most recent statement of his position (Mischel, 1973) Mischel opposes the 'fundamental assumption' of 'traditional trait approaches', that 'personality comprises broad underlying dispositions

---

[1] In some instances where the critic is precise and unambiguous my point will be rather that there are other possibilities that should also be considered and that are sometimes much more important.

[2] I should also counter any impression I might already have created that I will be arriving at a single resolution of the indeterminacies mentioned, e.g. a single specification of the target of the attack. Rather I will often display a spread of alternatives, between which it may or may not be necessary to choose.

which pervasively influence the individual's behaviour across many situations and lead to consistency in his behaviour' (p. 253). In other passages he specifies his target in similar terms: 'global traits that manifest themselves pervasively' (p. 253), 'global personality disposition' (p. 253), 'widely generalized dispositions' (p. 256), 'global underlying traits and dispositions' (p. 262). Thus it is clear that Mischel conceives the object of his criticism as 'broad dispositions'. But in order to pinpoint the target more narrowly, we need to know whether 'broad dispositions' are opposed just because of their breadth, just because of their dispositionality, or because of both. If because of both, is one or the other also objectionable by itself? And if being a disposition at least contributes to the deficiency, is *any* kind of disposition objectionable, or only some sub-type thereof?

A full budget of questions. Fortunately one of them is quickly answered. Clearly Mischel objects to the *breadth* of traditional trait concepts. Most of his critical arguments concern that point. The only difficult questions are whether he objects to other features as well, and, if so, just what they are.

I fear we will not get much help on these points from Mischel's explicit statements, which leave it quite unclear whether he opposes dispositions generally or only the 'broad' kind. Indeed we are given no guidance as to just what Mischel means by 'disposition' and so to what does and does not fall under this term. On the whole one gets the impression that he is using the term to cover all personality characteristics, including those he himself advocates,[3] in which case he could not be objecting to dispositions as such. But there are also hints that he means to be using the term in some narrower sense in which it would not range over all personality characteristics.[4] If we are to determine whether the attack on traits is (or could be or should be) at least in part an attack on 'dispositions' in some sense of that

---

[3] Thus he seems to take the disposition–situation relation as equivalent to the personal variable–situation relation (1973, pp. 253, 256). Again almost all his negative remarks about dispositions (e.g. that inferences to them have little predictive utility) use a qualification like 'broad' or 'global'; he never explicitly objects to dispositions without qualification.

[4] For example, in introducing his own positive proposals he says, 'The focus shifts from attempting to compare and generalize about what different individuals "are like" to an assessment of what they *do*—behaviorally and cognitively—in relation to the psychological conditions in which they do it' (1973, p. 265). This makes it sound as if on his approach we are not dealing with dispositions of any sort.

term, we shall have to give explicit consideration to the concept of a disposition and the varieties thereof.

A. T-CONCEPTS: S-R FREQUENCY DISPOSITIONS

To say that x has a certain *disposition* is to assert a certain hypotheticap proposition, a proposition that if x is in a certain type of situation (S),[5] x will emit a certain type of reponse (R). It is better to speak of dispositional *concepts* (alternatively, 'dispositional *terms*'), rather than of dispositions as a kind of state or attribute; for one and the same state or condition can often (perhaps always in principle) be conceptualized both in dispositional and non-dispositional terms. Thus fragility is construed dispositionally when we think of x's being fragile simply as the truth of the hypothetical proposition, 'If x is struck sharply x will break.' But if we can discover what microstructure of x is responsible for the truth of that hypothetical proposition, we can think of the same attribute in non-dispositional terms. This ambiguity does not affect concepts, which are unequivocally either dispositional or not, depending on whether in attributing the concept to x we are committing ourselves to some proposition of the form 'If x is in S, then x will R'. The content of a particular dispositional concept is given by such a hypothetical proposition: a dispositional concept is made up of an S-category and an R-category put together in an if-then structure. Thus a dispositional concept 'embodies' an $S–R$ regularity, differing from a mere report of that regularity only by way of also embodying the claim that there is something more or less stable in x's constitution that is responsible for the regularity (but without specifying what that is).

Dispositional concepts are familiar in personality description. Thus in attributing sociability to x, we are saying that if (when) x is (S) presented with an opportunity for social contact, x will (R) take advantage of it. Some other familiar concepts of this sort, each with its distinctive S- and R-categories are:

Cooperativeness —(R) complies with (S) (reasonable) requests.
Persistence   —(R) continues an activity (S) in the face of
                                difficulties.
Domineeringness—(R) takes advantage of (S) opportunities to
                                exercise control over others.

[5] Note that I am *not* using S to abbreviate *stimulus*.

To be sure, in attributing, e.g. sociability, to x we are not claiming that x takes advantage of *every* opportunity for social contact; we are in no position to attribute *absolute* or *unqualified* dispositions to persons. The S- and R- categories with which we work are not invariably connected. Rather we work with *frequency* dispositions: sociability is a matter of *frequently* (relative to some norm for the S–R pair) taking advantage of opportunities for social contact. To be somewhat more precise, we think of different persons having different degrees of the disposition, where the degree is a function of the frequency of R's in a representative set of S's, along with the average magnitude of the R's. The term 'trait' has often been defined along these lines.[6] But since 'trait' if often in fact used more widely I shall use the more schematic term 'T-concept' for concepts that fit the S–R frequency disposition model.

If one is to work out a wholly explicit and unambiguous model for T-concepts[7] he will have to deal with some rather thorny issues. Here I shall mention only two.

(A) S- and R-categories of various sorts can be put into the T-form. The above examples all involve overt, publicly observable R's: but there are familiar T-concepts with 'private' R-categories that range over cognitive or affective responses. Consider, e.g., 'introspective' where the R-category is something like 'paying attention to or dwelling on one's own thoughts, feelings, and characteristics'; or 'analytical' where the R-category is something like 'thinking about problems in an analytical way'. Again the above examples feature S-categories that are stated in terms of objective features of the situation, e.g. whether there *is* an opportunity for social contact or whether a request *has* been made. But it may be more useful in personality description to construe the S-categories as having to do with how the person perceives the situation; a failure to comply with a request of which one was unaware should not count against one's cooperativeness.

(B) T-concepts differ in the extent to which distinctive S-categories are involved, i.e. in the extent to which R's will count in favour of the trait attribution only in certain kinds of situations. Where there are such situational restrictions, this may be because the restriction is built into the very meaning of the R-category (it makes no sense

---

[6] See Allport (1937), p. 295 and (1961), p. 337; Vernon (1933), p. 542; Cattell (1965), p. 28; Cronbach (1960), p. 499.

[7] For a detailed discussion see Alston (1970).

to speak of 'complying' unless one is responding to something like a request) or it may be that although R's of that category are possible in other situations they do not count as manifesting this trait unless the appropriate S-category is exemplified. (Thus 'continuing an activity' does not count as manifesting persistence unless it is 'in the presence of difficulties'.) However, there are traits which appear to involve no situational restrictions at all; this is most obviously true with respect to 'stylistic' traits, the R-categories of which have to do with the manner in which something is done—*methodical* or *energetic*. It would seem that one may proceed in a methodical or energetic manner in any situation in which one is doing *anything*; and that doing so will count towards possession of the trait, whatever the situation.

B. PC (PURPOSIVE–COGNITIVE) CONCEPTS

Although many psychologists are given to using the term 'trait' (defined as an S–R frequency disposition) to cover all concepts employed in personality description, the fact remains that not all of them fit the T-model. This can be shown by applying a basic test for the applicability of the model. When we attribute a high degree of a T to x, it is part of what we are asserting (what we mean) that, given a representative set of S's, x will emit a large number of R's (relative to the norm for that disposition). The concepts listed above, and many others, pass this test. To say that x is very cooperative is to *say* that if x is confronted with a representative spread of reasonable requests, he will comply in a large proportion of the cases. That is what we mean by 'cooperative': it is constitutive of our *concept* of cooperativeness. But concepts of needs, motives, interests, values, attitudes, and abilities, among other, do not pass the test. In these cases there is no empirically accessible R-category such that a high degree of the attribute necessarily involves a frequency of such R's. To be sure, these attributes *do* often have typical R-manifestations. Thus an ability is typically manifested in its exercise, a need in efforts to satisfy it, a favourable attitude in actions directed to promoting or benefiting its object. Nevertheless it is not part of what we *mean* in attributing (even a strong degree) of some ability, need, or attitude, that such manifestations will frequently occur. A person may have abilities that he rarely exercises. Thus a man may be a crack pistol shot, but, because he doesn't have a pistol or because of lack of interest, rarely exercises this ability. A person may have a strong need for close relationships, but because of fear of rejection rarely or never seeks to satisfy it.

The point I am making is a conceptual rather than an empirical or factual one. I am not saying that there really are factors that can prevent even highly developed abilities from being exercised and that can inhibit attempts to satisfy even very strong needs, although I believe this to be the case. My contention has to do with the structure of concepts. I am saying that it is part of what we *mean* when we attribute a *T* that *R*'s of the appropriate category will be frequently emitted; whereas nothing of the sort is part of what we *mean* when we attribute a need, ability, or attitude. It would be self-contradictory to say 'he is very cooperative but he rarely complies with (reasonable) requests'; but it would not be at all self-contradictory to say 'he has a strong need for close relationships, but he rarely does anything to foster them'. The contrast is most striking when we take *T* and *PC* concepts with the same 'filling'. If one agrees that *S* rarely takes advantage of opportunities for social contact, one is thereby debarred (conceptually) from going on to say that *S* is very sociable (a *T*-concept), but one *can* go on to say without contradiction that *S* has a strong *need* for social contact. One would be contradicting himself if he said '*S* is very methodical (a *T*-concept), but rarely proceeds in a methodical fashion'; but it is intelligible to say '*S* is *very good at* methodical organization but he rarely takes the trouble to do things methodically'.

Thus needs, abilities, attitudes and the like cannot be construed as *S–R* frequency dispositions. How then? To put the matter in wider perspective, let us note with Mischel that the characteristics we attribute in personality description are not themselves observable but are inferred from observation.[8] One way in which a concept of something non-observable may be formed in a scientifically respectable fashion (so as to permit empirical testing of its applications) is to put observable characteristics into an if–then form, thereby yielding a dispositional concept. Here though the filling of the concept is observational, the hypothetical form prevents the attribute conceptualized from being itself observable. But most philosophers of science recognize another way in which non-observable concepts

---

[8] Actually he makes this point explicitly (1973, p. 253) only for 'broad underlying dispositions', but it patently applies to any sort of personality characteristics, including those he favours (see below, pp. 31–2, and footnote p. 29).

may be formed, a way which yields concepts that do not even have an observational filling but still preserve sufficient links to the observable. This other way involves constructing a theory of the unobservable 'fine structure' of an object or system with a view to explaining its observable behaviour. The various terms of that theory will then get their meaning from their place in the theory, understanding 'place in the theory' to include the functioning of the theory in the explanation of empirical data, as well as its internal structure. 'Theoretical' terms are thus related to observable data more indirectly than dispositional terms. An application of a dispositional term, as we have seen, has definite implications all by itself for patterns of observable occurrences. But an application of a theoretical term will have such implications only in conjunction with other premises. In applying the dispositional term 'magnetic' to x I *thereby* imply that certain observable movements will occur under certain observable circumstances. But an application of a theoretical term like 'has a free electron in the outer shell' to x does not, by itself, imply anything about observables. To get such implications we have to put that particular attribution in the context of a complicated theory as to how being in that state will be manifested in certain observable phenomena. Theoretical terms relate to observable phenomena only in systematic interrelations, while dispositional terms are hooked up to the data one by one.[9]

My suggestion is that the non-T items among concepts of personality characteristics, at least the more interesting and prevalent of them, are theoretical concepts. Of course each theory constitutes a spawning ground for theoretical concepts; there are as many distinctive sets of such concepts as there are distinctively different theories. In principle concepts for personality description might be drawn from various neurophysiological theories, information processing theory, and so on. However I would suggest that virtually all the interesting theoretical concepts in personality theory spring from one or another form of a theory of motivation that I shall call Purposive–Cognitive Theory. According to this way of thinking, which in its gross outlines is familiar to all of us from early childhood, intentional action is undertaken in order to reach certain goals, the particular means employed being a function of the agent's beliefs as to what, in the current situation, is most likely to attain that goal. Sam is

[9] For a classic presentation of the theoretical–dispositional distinction see Carnap (1956).

starting his car because the dominant goal for him at present is to arrive at his office at 9.00 a.m. and he believes that the best way of ensuring this is to drive his car to a certain parking lot, and that in order to do so he has to start the car. In stark outline this model features three basic types of inner psychological determinants, *desires*, which, so to speak, mark out certain states as 'to be striven for', beliefs, which provide bases for selecting lines of action as the most promising ways of reaching those goals, and *abilities*, which delineate the response repertoire from which the desire–belief combinations make their selection.

Typically more than one desire (including aversions under that heading) is activated at a given moment; and for any given goal, typically more than one means is envisaged. This means that usually there is conflict as to which of several alternative lines of action is most promising *vis-à-vis* a given goal; and, since the various desires and aversions activated at a given moment can rarely all be satisfied simultaneously there is conflict as to which goal is to be actively pursued. These facts force us to complicate the theory by inserting a 'field' of tendencies between the activated desires and beliefs on the one end, and the actual responses on the other. An appropriate desire–belief pair would, in the absence of contemporaneous competition, give rise to the actual deployment of the means in question (assuming they are within the power of the person). Where there is competition, we may think of *each* desire–belief pair as giving rise to a *tendency* to a certain response, where to say that P has a 'tendency' to R at a time k, is to say that in the absence of interference (and assuming that R is within his power) P emits R at k. Thus we get a field of such tendencies, and out of the interaction within that field, some particular actual R emerges, its character being determined by such factors as the relative strength of the various tendencies and their compatibility or incompatibility. The desire to go to a party, plus knowledge concerning its location and available means of transportation, gives rise to a tendency to walk toward the garage, while the contemporaneous desire to finish a paper, plus relevant beliefs concerning location of materials and suitability of work spaces, gives rise to a tendency to walk to the study. Since these R's are clearly incompatible and since a compromise direction would have no chance of even partially satisfying either desire, the issue will be determined by the relative strength of the two tendencies. This theoretical approach has been elaborated in different ways by Freud, Lewin, Tolman, and more recently by e.g. Atkinson and Birch (1970) and by 'cognitive social learning' theorists, such as Bandura (1969) and Mischel (1968, 1973).

To return to our conceptual concerns, a desire or belief, I would suggest, is conceived as what occupies a certain position in motivational processes as depicted by the *PC* theory. A desire for a goal, *G*, is that psychological state which, together with a belief that doing *A* is likely to contribute to the realization of *G*, will give rise to a tendency to *A*: that state which, together with a belief that *G* has been attained, gives rise to a tendency to feel elated, and so on. A complementary statement can be given as to what a belief is. Let us use the term '*PC* concept' for the concepts that are spawned by *PC* theory.[10]

We can now see *why* it is conceptually possible to have even a strong desire without frequent manifestations. Whether the tendencies to which a desire is a disposition are actually carried out depends not just on *their* character, but also on the competition they encounter in the current psychological field. A strong desire will (given suitable beliefs) necessarily give rise to one or more strong *tendencies*, and its strength *is* a function of the strength of those tendencies. But whether those tendencies will frequently, or even ever, be carried out is not a function of their strength alone. Thus even a strong desire may fail to be frequently manifested if frequently confronted by even stronger contrary desires.

However we are not yet at the level of personality characteristics. What I have just presented under the heading of 'desire' is what we may term an 'activated' desire, an internal state that exercises an active influence on thought, behaviour, and feeling. A person has an activated desire for food or for recognition during those periods in which there is some internal pressure on him to seek food or recognition, some tendency to feel disappointed if he fails to secure it, and so on. Activated desires are typically rather short-lived; they dissipate upon satiation, continued frustration, or the onset of more pressing concerns. Desire for food is notoriously cyclical, and even with a more 'psychogenic' desire like that for dominance or recognition, it is rare to find a person so single-minded as not to be sometimes wholly preoccupied with other matters. But when we set out to describe *S*'s personality, we mean to be attributing to him

[10] Alston (1970), (1973) present a more detailed contrast of *T*- and *PC*-concepts (the latter called *D*'s rather than *PC*'s).

relatively stable characteristics, each of which he possesses uninter-ruptedly for a considerable period of time.

Of course there is controversy as to how stable something needs to be to count as a component of personality. Mischel, along with other opponents of traits, is given to inveighing against the idea that personality should be described in terms of 'relatively stable, highly consistent attributes that exert widely *generalized* causal effects on behaviour'[11] (1973, p. 253). One gets the impression from such statements that Mischel wants personality theory to restrict itself to studying particular person–situation interactions, and to abjure any attempt to describe what it is a person carries around with him from one situation to another. However, this impression is countered both by the next paragraph in which Mischel indicates that persono-logy should be concerned with 'the psychological products within the individual of cognitive development and social learning experi-ences', and by scrutiny of his proposed variables. One of these is 'encoding strategies and person constructs,' which is explained as 'the perceiver's ways of encoding and grouping information from stimulus inputs' (1973, p. 267). By this is meant not the way a person does this on some particular occasion but the way he generally or habitually does it (when in the presence of certain kinds of inputs). Another of the variables is 'behaviour–outcome and stimulus–out-come expectancies'. Suppose we determine how Mr. *A* expects Mr. *B* to react to him in a particular situation. Surely no one would take that to be even part of a description of *A*'s personality. For that expectation might be quite atypical, due to some constellation of circumstances that rarely if ever recurs. What we need for a characterization of *the person* is an account of what he usually

---

[11] Consider also the following passages, in which he is working up to the introduction of his own favoured variables:

... it seems reasonable in the search for person variables to look more specifically at what the person *constructs* in particular conditions, rather than trying to infer what broad traits he generally *has* ... (1973, p. 265). ... The proposed cognitive social learning approach to personality shifts the unit of study from global traits inferred from behavioral signs to the individual's cognitive activities and behavior patterns, studied in relation to the specific conditions that evoke, maintain, and modify them and which they, in turn, change. The focus shifts from attempting to compare and generalize about what different individuals 'are like' to an assessment of what they *do*—behaviorally and cognitively—in relation to the psychological conditions in which they do it (*loc. cit.*).

expects to result from doing so-and-so in a certain kind of situation. However specific we make the so-and-so and the kind of situation, they will still be general categories that can have many particular instantiations. There is an ineluctable generality in personality characteristics, even in the hands of one who emphasizes specificity as much as Mischel.

Hence a report of the activated desires or beliefs that are operative in a person during a minute, an hour, or a day, would not count as part of a description of his personality. When we say, as part of a personality description, that x has a strong desire to dominate others (or in Mischel's lingo, that domination of others has a 'high subjective stimulus value' for x) what we are ascribing to him is rather a general liability to frequently acquire activated desires for domination; this liability is something he *can* possess uninterruptedly for considerable periods of time. Similarly when we say, in the context of personality description, that x expects to be rejected by new acquaintances, we are not reporting a particular activated expectancy he has at some particular time, but rather a general tendency for expectancies of that sort to be activated in situations of that sort. Let's call these higher level liabilities *latent* desires (expectancies, etc.).[12]

It follows from the preceding paragraph that latent desires are conceived as dispositions in a sense, i.e., dispositions to undergo the formation of activated desires for the object in question. For that matter activated desires themselves can be thought of as a sort of disposition. Recur to our characterization of an activated desire on page 25. One part of it reads: 'A desire for a goal, G, is that psychological state which, together with a belief that doing A is likely to contribute to the realization of G, will give rise to a tendency to A.' Another way of putting that is to say that a desire for G is a disposition to R if S, where R is the arousal of a tendency to do A and S is the activation of the belief that doing A is likely to contribute to the realization of G. But if both active and latent desires are construed as dispositions, how can we say they are distinguished from T's in being theoretical rather than dispositional?

---

[12] It is worthy of note that not all *PC*-concepts exhibit this two-level structure, with a distinction between the activated factor that is operative in motivation, and the general liability thereto that characterizes personality. With abilities, e.g., it seems to be the same ability to fly an airplane that characterizes the person and that is one necessary condition of flying behaviour in a particular situation.

A way out of this dilemma is found by considering the fact that a great variety of materials can be put into the dispositional form. Put most generally, to attribute a disposition to x is to say that under conditions of a certain kind, C, x will do or undergo some kind of happening, H. In this most general sense dispositions are by no means limited to cases in which C and H are directly observable. But in characterizing T's as S–R frequency dispositions, we were implicitly limiting our S- and R-categories to what is directly observable either by sense perception or by introspection,[13] and neither active nor latent PC's are dispositions of this kind. An activated desire is a disposition *to* a postulated, non-observable state (a tendency) and a latent desire, being a disposition to a disposition, also lacks an observational R-category. The basic contrast between dispositional and theoretical concepts concerns how they relate to the observational level; this difference remains firm even after we recognize the sense in which PC's are dispositional.

So far the discussion of PC-concepts has been restricted to desires, beliefs, and abilities, which I take to be basic because of the role of their active forms in motivation as depicted by PC theory. Other PC personality characteristics can be shown to derive from abilities, latent desires and latent beliefs. An expectation is a certain kind of belief; a need (in the psychological, not the biological sense) is a desire the non-satisfaction of which has particularly aversive consequences; an interest in music is (primarily) a complex of latent desires for goal-states connected with, e.g. music, an attitude is made up of such items as latent desires for the weal or woe of its object and evaluatively toned beliefs about that object. The detailed mapping of this conceptual field is, I believe, of the utmost importance for the psychology of personality, but I shall have to reserve that task for another occasion.

Personologists have not taken proper account of the T–PC distinction.[14] They typically speak in a blanket fashion of the various

---

[13] This restriction captures the positivistic, anti-theoretical orientation that has dominated the trait approach to personology. Much of the attractiveness of the T-model has stemmed from its promise of avoiding anything more occult than a disposition to observable responses, given observable conditions.

[14] Mischel is no exception. He does note that in psychodynamic theory 'diverse behavioural patterns serve the same enduring and generalized underlying dynamic or motivational dispositions' (1973, p. 253). That is tantamount to recognizing that, as we have put it, a given desire is not necessarily manifested in any one particular pattern of behaviour. But he seems to suppose that this is only because of the defensive distortions postulated by psychodynamic

'indicators', 'behavioural referents', and 'measures' of an attribute without distinguishing the crucially different ways in which an attribute may be related to its 'indicators'. Thus they miss the point that whereas it is part of the *meaning* of a T-term like 'domineering' (part of the concept of domineeringness) that if one is very domineering, 'indicators' like attempts to control others will happen frequently, it is not part of the meaning of a PC term like 'need for dominance' that if a person has a strong need of this sort, such attempts will frequently occur. Although we may have good (independent) reasons for supposing that they will, that does not follow just from what is meant by 'x has a strong need for dominance'. The neglect of this point is only one example of a general lack of concern for the precise boundaries of one's concepts, a failing by no means restricted to personality theory but especially prominent there.[15]

Let's recall that we entered onto this extended conceptual investigation in the context of considering whether the criticism of 'traits' like aggressiveness is directed only at their generality, or also at their being 'dispositions' in some sense. What has emerged from our conceptual contrast is the point that the basic conceptual alternatives confronting the personality theorist include 'T or PC (or both)' as well as 'more or less general'. Mischel, along with most other critics of traits, does not explicitly raise the former issue, but it is there under the surface none the less. This is apparent from the fact that Mischel's own variables differ from (most of) those he explicitly criticizes not only in being more specific, but also in being PC-rather than T-concepts.[16] Clearly the switch from very general T's to

theory. He fails to see that the same is true of all PC-concepts, whether or not they are used within the version of PC theory that features defences. Hence he includes, e.g., attitudes and motives among the 'global traits' he is attacking. And he fails to note that his own variables may also be manifested in 'diverse behavioural patterns'.

[15] For a similar complaint see Fiske (1971). The particular conceptual unclarity under discussion here is no doubt encouraged by operationalism, which encourages its devotees to lump all measures and indicators indiscriminately into the content of the concept. A more respectable reason for failure to notice the T–PC distinction is the fact that it cross-cuts some more salient distinctions. We find PC theorists, e.g., on both sides of the learning theory–psychodynamics distinction and the nomothetic–idiographic distinction, which have been so central in thinking about personality.

[16] A concise summary of these variables is on p. 275. Briefly, his 'construction competencies' are particular kinds of *abilities*; the 'encoding strategies

Mischel-type variables is not sufficiently motivated just by a concern for specificity. If over-generality were the only defect of T's like aggressiveness (construed as a disposition to behave equally aggressively in any interpersonal situation) the most obvious remedy would be to transform them into more specific T-concepts (like a disposition to act aggressively when in the presence of one's parents), rather than move to a radically different type of concept. Therefore in proposing that *his* list of variables be substituted for very general T's, Mischel is implicitly raising the T–PC issue as well as the specificity issue. No doubt he is not plumping for *any* PC concepts but for a distinctive sub-type. Nevertheless the general T–PC contrast is very much involved in the contrast between what he rejects and what he favours.

And quite apart from what Mischel and other current trait-critics do and think, I am prepared to argue that the T–PC distinction is the most fundamental conceptual alternative for personality description. Which of these conceptual types we use (or which we stress if we use both) reflects, as we shall see pervasive theoretical allegiances in psychology. And many issues will take on quite different forms depending on which sort of concept is involved among them, choice and validation of measures, hypotheses relating personality to behaviour, and the structure of personality.[17] By comparison, questions concerning degree of generality are matters of empirical detail rather than of basic theoretical orientation.

II. *What negative thesis about traits are the critics asserting?*

Just what is Mischel's conclusion concerning traits? Again there is some uncertainty. In his most explicit statements he stresses that he is not denying that traits exist (in fact he is avoiding that question)

and personal constructs' have to do with the conceptual resources available for *belief* formation, and predilections for using some of these rather than others in certain kinds of situations. 'Behaviour-outcome and stimulus-outcome expectancies' are particular kinds of *beliefs*. 'Subjective-stimulus values' represent an alternative way of talking about what I have been calling *desires*. 'Self-regulatory systems and plans' constitute a certain kind of *internalized rules*, which are found at a higher level of the PC motivation theory, discussion of which is prevented by lack of space.

[17] These points are discussed in Alston (1973).

but only that there is less utility than traditionally supposed in 'inferring broad dispositions from behavioural signs' (1973, p. 262). Utility for what purposes? The emphasis is on prediction and guidance of therapeutic intervention (the latter being based on prediction) (*loc. cit.*). Explanation is also mentioned but is not discussed as such. Mischel is also at pains to emphasize that trait attributions can still be of value in other connections, e.g., in everyday non-scientific dealings with people and even for (rough) predictions, especially provided further factors are taken into account (1973, pp. 262–3).

However, some of Mischel's arguments seem to point to the conclusion that people are simply not generally characterized by very unspecific traits, like acting dependent in *any* interpersonal situation. The studies he cites in Mischel (1968) demonstrating a lack of correlation of R's across situational differences show, if they show anything, that people do not generally *have* a stable disposition to emit R with a certain frequency. And his theoretical considerations concerning discrimination learning (1973, pp. 258–9) point to the same conclusion.

Whatever the correct interpretation of Mischel, the issues can be clarified by becoming more explicit about (various) questions of existence and utility and their interrelations.

First, it seems that Mischel eschews the question of existence because he thinks of it as 'metaphysical' (1973, p. 263). Is it? The question whether a given characteristic 'exists' (at least the question that is of interest in the present connection) is the question of whether anything *has* that characteristic or perhaps whether every member, or a certain proportion of members, of a given class have it. Now why should we deny that it is an empirical question whether a given person has a given trait? Because traits (like other personality characteristics) are unobservable? But in order to use empirical evidence to settle the question of whether x has characteristic C it is not necessary that we be able to observe C (or observe that x has C), but only that some thing(s) we observe will confirm or disconfirm the hypothesis that x has C. So the question of whether the 'existence' of traits is an empirical issue boils down to the question of whether it is possible to use empirical data to confirm or disconfirm trait attributions. And, granting the adequacy of the above analysis of trait concepts, the answer to that is clearly in the affirmative. Ideally we would observe a person, P, in each of a considerable number of sets of S's and determine the frequency of R's in each set. We would then determine how stable this frequency is over the different sets of S's. If we get a reasonable stability we have strong empirical support for the hypothesis that S is characterized by a reasonably stable disposition to emit R in S with a frequency that falls within certain limits. If we find no such stability, we have strong support that S is not characterized by any such stable disposition.[18]

No doubt T-concepts are imprecise in various ways and this will introduce some indeterminacy in the outcome of empirical tests. For example, there is no definite answer to the question, 'How stable a frequency of R's over different sets of S's must we have in order to be justified in attributing the corresponding T?'. And it would undoubtedly be unwise to tighten-up T-concepts by making a precise requirement. But if we were to rule out of science all questions infected with this kind of indeterminacy, what would be left standing? T-concepts are certainly precise enough to permit an empirical determination of their applicability that satifies any reasonable requirements.

Of course psychologists are interested not just in whether some particular individual has a given trait but also in whether everyone has traits, and with whether there are certain traits that everyone, or most people, have. But if it is possible to determine empirically whether a given person has a given trait, it will thereby be possible to answer these further questions on empirical grounds.

Not only can the question of existence be raised in a scientifically legitimate fashion; it is more fundamental than questions of utility. The former must receive an affirmative answer before the latter can usefully be raised. We can hardly expect that trait attributions will be useful for prediction or explanation unless people really do have the traits in question. How could we expect to predict academic performance from degree of conscientiousness (except by luck) unless people *are* conscientious to various degrees. And a person's inability to maintain friendships cannot be explained by certain of his traits unless he does have those traits: it is intrinsic to the concept of

---

[18] No doubt we are rarely if ever in a position to gather empirical data of this maximally conclusive sort: we have to content ourselves with more indirect indications that such an ideal investigation would have one or another outcome. However the present point is only that trait concepts leave open the possibility of this sort of empirical test.

explanation that a phenomenon can be explained only by what is really there.

These truisms may be obscured by talk of 'useful fictions' and 'models' that can be used without supposing them to literally represent the actual state of affairs. But we have recourse to such devices only when we are unable to determine empirically, in some more direct fashion, just what the state of affairs is.[19] When we are using concepts the applicability of which can be determined empirically the only sensible course is to settle that question first and then, if the answer is affirmative, go on to use the concepts in prediction and explanation.

Though applicability of trait concepts is a necessary condition of their scientific utility it is hardly sufficient. A concept, e.g. nose length or liking for Dover sole, can be applicable to persons without being of any great utility in the prediction or explanation of behaviour. As the discussion progresses we shall see what else is required.

One final point about utility. We should not assume in advance that different utilities are perfectly correlated. The trait of methodicalness may be very useful for predicting success in library work and other occupations, but not be of much value for basic theory or for explaining any wide range of behaviour. And unconscious conflicts may be efficacious in explaining neurotic compulsions, but, because of the difficulty of antecedent diagnosis and because of the complexity of other factors, not give us much leverage on the prediction of neurotic disorders.

III.   *The bearing of empirical evidence on the conceptual issue*

Against the background of these distinctions let us consider what empirical evidence might conceivably show about the suitability of *T*- and *PC*- concepts for personality description.

The first point to make is that the most a particular study can show by itself is that the particular concept under investigation is deficient in some respect; any more general conclusions will be based

---

[19] Indeed I should suppose that to the extent that a 'fiction' or a model does help us to predict or explain, we thereby have reason to suppose that it does, to some extent, accurately represent the subject matter.

on an induction from a number of such studies. Thus the first order of business is to determine what a certain kind of investigation can show about the particular concept investigated; this will set a ceiling on what we can hope for in the way of general conclusions.

The empirical studies most often cited by Mischel in his attack on traits are those indicating poor predictions from trait measures and those indicating a lack of 'consistency'. We shall consider them in turn.

Suppose we gather measures on one or more traits, for a certain population, and then try using this information to predict some outcome, such as academic success in college or diagnosis as neurotic. And suppose the results are disappointing. Does this show, or tend to show, either that the traits in question do not 'exist' generally in that population, or that they are not useful for prediction? No such conclusion can be drawn just from these data. The point is that there are at least three factors that would be responsible for the failure, alone or in combination. (To simplify the exposition I shall suppose that only one putative trait was involved.) (1) Most of the population simply does not have the trait. (2) The instruments used do not give accurate measures of that trait. (3) The trait is not tightly enough connected with that outcome to afford a basis for predicting *it*. If (2) could produce the results all by itself, then the results leave wide open the possibility that the trait does 'exist' and that it is closely enough connected with that outcome to be a good predictor if we could just find a way of getting at *it*. If (3) is the culprit, then though the existence of the trait is not cast in doubt, it does follow that the trait is not usable to predict that sort of event. But of course it remains possible that the trait can be used to predict other outcomes, or even, when combined with other variables, to predict this one.

Thus in order to use these results to show non-existence we have to be able to rule out the possibility that (2) or (3) could be responsible; to show lack of predictive utility, even for this particular dependent variable, we have to rule out (2). And the point is that we are rarely, if ever, in a position to do so. As for (2), with the exception of behaviour sampling all of the commonly employed trait measures are of dubious validity. As for (3), if we know anything about 'outcomes' like academic success and onset of neurosis, it is that they can be influenced by a great variety of factors. We are rarely, if ever, in a position to say that *if* a person does have a high position on trait dimension T_1, $T_2 \ldots$, then (it is reasonably certain that) he will get high grades in college.[20] Hence lack of predictive success generally *could* be due just to the fact that the trait in question is not lawfully connected with what we are trying to predict.

Of course when a prediction from trait measures does consistently pan out, that is good evidence we have hold of something real and useful. But because of the above considerations negative results are highly ambiguous.

'Consistency studies' can usefully be divided into three types:

(1) Studies showing a low correlation between measures of the same trait.

(2) Studies showing a low correlation between different sub-classes of the appropriate *R*-category for a given trait.

(3) Studies showing a low correlation between responses of the appropriate *R*-category in different sub-classes of the appropriate *S*. (1) would be exemplified by a study showing the absence of high correlations between measures of 'dependency' by self-report questionnaire ratings, direct observation of behaviour, Rorschach, and TAT. (2) would be exemplified by a study showing an absence of high-correlation between a number of sub-classes of 'dependency behaviour' in children, e.g. 'negative attention seeking' 'positive attention seeking', 'seeking reassurance', 'touching and holding', and 'being near'.[21] (3) would be exemplified by a study showing lack of high correlation between frequency of dependency behaviour in different kinds of situations, e.g. classroom, home, and playground, or in the presence of different persons or type of persons, e.g. parents, siblings, peers, teachers. Of course one and the same study may exemplify more than one type.[22]

---

[20] Of course this itself constitutes a reason for regarding traits as low in predictive utility, a reason based on much more general considerations than those we are presently considering.

[21] See Sears, (1963).

[21] The difference between the first type and the other two is often slighted, for reasons similar to those responsible for the neglect of the *T–PC* distinction. If one lumps together all 'indicators' of an attribute, he will see no difference between those that are implied by the very concept of that attribute (the *R*'s studied in the second and third types) and the 'measures' that are *believed* to be correlated with it. But they are fundamentally different. It is part of the concept of rigidity, as a *T*-concept, that the rigid person will relatively frequently cling to a solution, concept, or attitude, even in the face of reasons

All that we can conclude from the first kind of study is that not all the measures studied are (good) measures of the same thing. If there is no basis for picking any one measure as sufficiently reliable[23] we can further conclude that we are not presently in a position to determine whether or to what degree the concept applies to a given case and, *ipso facto*, are in no position to use the concept in prediction or explanation. But nothing follows from this concerning the place of the characteristic in the structure of personality or its potentialities for personality theory. Even if we are not *now* able to find a valid measure of T, it still may be that T actually characterizes people and that it is central enough to be important for the explanation and prediction of behaviour. No doubt failure after many and varied attempts is some augury of continued failure. But it is always difficult to estimate how skilful and determined have been the attempts to date. And in any event there are well-known pitfalls in predicting future scientific developments.

What about the second kind of study? What further implications can be drawn from the lack of a high correlation between sub-classes of R? Before tackling that question, let us note that this kind of 'inconsistency' seems to be an ineradicable feature of any $S-R$ disposition, no matter how specific. The point is simply this. The R-category in an $S-R$ disposition is general, ranging over an indefinite number of instances. Indeed this is involved in the very

---

to think it no longer appropriate. Hence, data about the frequency of such responses have a direct and unambiguous bearing on the concept and its application. But it is *not* part of what is meant by 'rigidity' that the rigid person will give certain sorts of responses on the Rorschach or TAT or self-descriptive questionnaire, or that he will be rated as rigid by his acquaintances. (If one of these measures were to become firmly entrenched in scientific practice and theorizing, the concept of rigidity might undergo such an accretion. But clearly that is not the present state of affairs.) Hence if a person gets a low rigidity score on one of these measures that does not decisively and unquestionably show that he is not rigid, and if these measures of rigidity are uncorrelated, that does not in itself discredit the concept.

[23] It would seem to follow from our analysis of T-concepts that there is always a reliable measure that is in principle available to us, *viz.*, behaviour sampling. If we have found a reasonably stable frequency of R's in a number of largish sets of S's, then by the very definition of the T-term, this constitutes good reason for ascribing a certain degree of that trait. Of course this procedure is rarely a practicable alternative. And PC concepts, as well as many other sorts of psychological concepts, do *not* carry with them any such built-in guarantee of the reliability of a particular measure.

notion of a *disposition* as a liability to emit an *R of a certain sort* whenever in an *S of a certain sort*. Furthermore, even if it is possible to construct an *R*-category so specific that it admits of no sub-categories, and this is debatable, it is clear that any interesting *R* will admit of sub-categorization. One can be aggressive either physically or verbally: one can be sociable by engaging someone in conversation, issuing invitations to a party, showing up for communal lunches, and so on. The same point holds at more specific levels. Consider one of the sub-categories of dependency behaviour distinguished in Sears (1963), 'seeking reassurance'. One can seek reassurance by explicitly asking someone what he thinks of one, or by indirectly steering the conversation in that direction; one can seek reassurance concerning one's appearance, one's competence, and so on. Even if we make the category much too specific to be of any interest for personality description, there will still be many alternative modes of realization. Consider the category, *asking some-one whether I am attractive*. This can be done by using a variety of different sentences, even in the same language; it can be done in speech or in writing; in many different tones of voice, inflection patterns, and degrees of loudness. All these matters and many others would have to be precisely determined before we arrived at a maximally specific category that permits no sub-categorization.

Now it would be enormously surprising if the frequency with which a person exemplifies one sub-category of a given *R* were closely matched with his frequency on all the others. Among the various ways of exemplifying a category a given person will generally have a style that limits him to some sub-set of those ways most of the time. It would be a fantastic virtuoso who would use the various possible dynamic intensities, intonation patterns, and accents, in about the same proportions over the occasions on which he asked a certain question. Again it would be a veritable chameleon who would use equally often all the various modes of seeking dominance. This is not to say that *some* sub-categories may not be highly correlated. For example, it could have been the case that 'positive attention seeking' and 'seeking reassurance' (as sub-categories of 'dependency behaviour') are highly correlated; it is a contribution of Sears to have shown otherwise. However I do believe that considerations of the above sort strongly support the thesis that for any *R*-category likely to be of interest to a psychologist, there will be some sub-categories that are not highly correlated with each other.

To return to the question at issue. Clearly a lack of high correlation between sub-classes of R can do nothing to show an inapplicability of the concept, for no such correlation is required by a T-concept. A T-concept is at a level of generality defined by its embedded R-concept. It does not 'purport' to encapsulate information about more specific response types; it is irrelevant to its applicability how those more specific types are distributed. So long as Jones' frequency of dependency behaviour is fairly stable over different sets of situations he can unambiguously be credited with a certain degree of the trait of dependency, whether or not he seeks succourance in some ways much more than others. It may well be interesting to determine the pattern of these sub-types, but that is a *further* question: it cannot affect the truth of the more general trait attribution.

Essentially the same point is to be made concerning the bearing of these studies on predictive or explanatory utility. The fact that one does not seek succourance in all possible ways to the same extent has no implications whatever as to the scientific utility of information about one's degree of dependency. We *may* be able to predict and explain many differences between Jones and Smith just by knowing that whereas the former frequently seeks succourance in some way or other, the latter infrequently seeks succourance in any way. Think of a trait like *creativity*, sub-categories of which no one would ever have expected to be highly correlated. It would be absurd to suppose that highly creative persons are equally creative in music, painting, literature, science, institutional innovation, and personal relationships. Obviously people specialize in their creative endeavours. Nevertheless it is useful to distinguish persons who are highly creative in some way or other from those who are not highly creative in any way. No doubt it is *also* useful to classify people in terms of more specific attributes, like 'creative in music', and 'creative in science'. But this by no means implies that it is *not* useful to employ the more general concept. The third kind of consistency study is more to the point. We have pointed out that in attributing a T to a person we imply that he will produce something like the same frequency of R's in every large set of S's. And the results of this third sort of study seem to directly contradict that implication. If S frequently seeks succourance at home but infrequently at school, that shows he does not have a stable disposition to seek succourance with about the same frequency in any kind of interpersonal situation.

But we must proceed with caution. The implication of even approximately equal frequencies of R's in any large set of S's is obviously false for any interesting R- and S-categories. We can always devise variations on the appropriate S-category so as to produce a marked deviation from the average R-frequency. No matter how dependent a person is, so long as he is in control of his behaviour he will seek succourance less often than usual where severe penalties are attached to doing so. No matter how cooperative a person, he will cooperate less than usual when under severe emotional strain. No matter how creative, a person will act less creatively at some times and in some moods than others: Mozart did not produce a masterpiece every day. But this is to make trait psychology too easily refutable. A sober conception of traits will allow for variations in mood, for satiation effects, and for effects of abnormal situations. The stability condition will rather be that there is a fairly stable frequency over 'normal' situations in which the subject is in a 'normal' condition. These are rough qualifications, and so there will be no sharp line between satisfaction and non-satisfaction of the condition. But in a typical 'consistency' study of the third sort we take a large number of subjects and compute the average correlation between frequency of aggressive behaviour over several different kinds of interpersonal situations. Because of the number of subjects oscillation in mood and other temporary conditions will presumably cancel each other out, and we take care to make the situations 'normal'. Hence if the average correlation turns out to be very low, insignificant, or negative, we *can* conclude that people in general[24] simply do not have any such general trait as aggressiveness in interpersonal situations. For the data do indicate that even if we held the relevant emotional and motivational condition of the subject constant and avoided unusual features in the situations, people would not generally act aggressively to about the same extent in any interpersonal situation. These data do show that the R- and S-categories for that trait are not suitably matched, that S's of that sort (at that level of generality) cannot be depended on to consistently produce any particular frequency of R's of the specified category.

[24] Clearly the fact that aggression at home and at school are not generally highly correlated does nothing to show that *some* people may not have a stable disposition to be aggressive to about the same degree in any interpersonal situation.

It is interesting that the only type of consistency study with direct bearing on the status of trait concepts, should bear directly on their existence rather than their utility. No doubt it follows from a successful study of this sort that the T-concept studied is not to be recommended for explanation and prediction. But that is because what the study directly shows is that the concept is not applicable in the population at large and *therefore* is incapable of advancing our general understanding of behaviour.

At this point we may digress briefly to consider what bearing empirical studies of these sorts might have on the status of PC-concepts. Predictive studies and the first kind of consistency study (correlation between different putative measures) can yield the same conclusions as with T-concepts. The differences between T's and PC's are not relevant here. Where the differences obtrude themselves is in the second and third types of consistency studies. We cannot (properly) do those studies for PC-concepts just because there is no R- and S-category for a PC. This is not to say that psychologists have not tried to do this sort of thing for PC-concepts, but in doing so they have betrayed a lack of understanding of the concepts with which they are dealing. With respect to the third kind of study in particular, since in attributing a PC we are not committing ourselves to a stable frequency of R's of some particular category in sets of S's of a certain category, correlations or lack of correlations of R-s over sub-types of some S can have no direct bearing on the status of the concept.[25] While showing that the incidence of aggressive acts differs sharply between home and playground undermines the general T-concept of aggressiveness, it leaves the concept of a need for aggression untouched, for that concept by itself has no implications concerning the frequency of aggressive acts. In fact there is good reason to suppose that a strong need for aggression would *not* give rise to similar frequencies of aggressive acts in all situations, for different situations will often present contrary motivation to different degrees, which means the inhibitory forces will often be of different strength in different situations.

[25] This is not to say that PC concepts are invulnerable to any empirical data (and a good thing, too). But to show their inapplicability is a much more complicated task. Because of their systemic embeddedness in a theory, what is required is to show that the theory from which they spring does not (or, much more conclusively, cannot) adequately perform its allotted task *vis-à-vis* empirical data. And that is a notoriously difficult matter to settle for any interesting theory.

This point is often missed for just the reasons we cited earlier in explaining the failure to notice the T–PC distinction.

Let us return to T's. We have seen that of the sorts of empirical investigation cited by Mischel, only the third type of consistency study has a strong bearing on the viability of the T-concept under investigation. Can any conclusions be drawn from this for the status of T-concepts in general? Clearly nothing can be concluded about T-concepts generally from the deficiencies of a single concept. But suppose that all T-concepts investigated have been shown defective. Can't more general conclusions be drawn in that case? Well, if the concepts investigated all have quite general R- and S-categories such results may show that we are unlikely[26] to find stable S–R dispositions *at that level of generality*. Thus data like these can have a bearing on one of our conceptual alternatives—degree of generality. But it is not helpful with respect to the more basic T–PC alternative. More specifically, it cannot show that *no* T-concepts can pass the test. In fact the data suggest a way of removing *this* defect from any given T-concept: viz. make the S-category more specific.[27] If there is low correlation between aggression at home and aggression in play situations, separate the general concept of aggressiveness into aggressiveness at home and aggressiveness at play, and see whether we get stable frequencies of aggressive behaviour across different home samplings and different play samplings. If degree of yielding to social influence differs markedly with different role relationships, try some new T-concepts with the same R, but where the S in each case embodies some specification of role relationship.[28] These are still T-concepts; they have the basic T-structure we outlined earlier. It is simply a matter of the *degree* of specificity of the S-category. Of course there is no guarantee that these or any other more specific T's will turn out to be consistent across sub-types of their S-categories. It may well turn out, e.g. that frequency of aggressive behaviour is uncorrelated over different kinds of home situations. It

---

[26] Whether this is just an unlikelihood, rather than an impossibility, will have to be settled by a determined search for exceptions, or else by theoretical considerations.

[27] Note that the S- and R-categories provide two independent dimensions along which T-concepts can vary in generality. It seems plausible to suppose that consistency will vary inversely with generality of S, but directly with generality of R. If the R-category is general enough (doing something) its frequency will be guaranteed to be the same in all situations.

[28] Cf. Argyle and Little (1972).

may even be that no matter how specific we make the S- and R-categories we still fall short of consistency. But the studies we are now considering, which all deal with very general S-categories, are insufficient to yield that conclusion.[29] Indeed it is dubious that any empirical data could show that no consistent T-concepts *could* be constructed. For consistent T-concepts might be produced not only by making our categories more specific, but also by finding more felicitous ways of constructing S- and R-categories (more felicitous in that the S-concept captures more fully the determinants of the R). And one can hardly expect to have any real basis for supposing that a given kind of conceptual breakthrough will *not* occur in science.

IV. *A theoretical basis for the choice of concepts*

The preceding discussion has revealed the powers and limits of consistency data. A consistency study can show that a particular T-concept is not generally applicable; from a number of such results we can conclude, more generally, that T-concepts above a certain level of generality are unlikely to be applicable. But consistency data will do nothing to show that no T-concepts are applicable nor, assuming that is the case, that it is PC-concepts, either in general or of the sort favoured by Mischel, that should be put in their place. Consistency data will not support the claim that T-concepts should be replaced by concepts of a radically different type. For this more fundamental considerations are needed.

A. METHODOLOGICAL CONSIDERATIONS

One may be tempted to exclude T's on purely methodological grounds. We have seen that the T-concepts actually in use are, at most, frequency dispositions; none of them specify S- and R-categories that are invariably associated. That being the case, we need invoke nothing more specific than the general principle of determinism to show that even if such concepts are applicable, they cannot represent *fundamental* features of persons. Consider sociability. Not even the most gregarious of men takes advantage of every opportun-

[29] Of course it may be that in order to get cross-situational stability of R-frequencies we have to make the S so specific as to render the concept useless for personality description. But again further investigation would be required to show *that*.

D

ity for social contact. At best people differ only in the *average frequency* of doing so. But if all behaviour is causally determined there must be some thing(s) that makes the difference between the occasions on which the person does and those on which he does not act sociably. So long as that is unspecified we cannot claim to have given an adequate account of (this aspect) of the person. Frequency dispositions are at best a first stab at describing a person.[30]

Unfortunately this argument has exactly the same limitations as the consistency argument. It shows a defect in the *T*-concepts currently employed, but it does nothing to show that *any T*-concept must display those defects, and hence it fails to show that *T*-concepts as such are defective. It leaves open the possibility that *S–R* dispositions can be found that are invariable and hence (on this count) are suitable for describing what a person is fundamentally like.[31]

---

[30] Note that this argument is quite independent of the consistency argument. Even if the relative frequency of sociable responses is quite stable across situations (so that the concept *does* apply), sociability would still fail to qualify as a fundamental feature of personality just by virtue of being a frequency disposition.

[31] It is worth noting that if we are sufficiently liberal with our *S*-categories, there is a strong argument for the conclusion that there *must* be invariable *S–R* dispositions. If we add to the general principle of determinism the assumption that only what exists now can produce an effect now, we get the result that for any actual response, there must be some set of present conditions that casually determine it to occur just as it does occur. But that means that a set of conditions of that sort will invariably be followed by a response of that sort. So that if we could embody these sorts in *S*- and *R*-categories, we would be in a position to formulate an invariable *S–R* disposition.

The hooker in this argument is that it depends on putting no restriction on what can be included in the set of antecedent conditions. In particular it allows that set to include unobservable states of the person; it does not follow just from the general principle of determinism that every *R* is causally determined by *observable* factors. Hence this argument does not show that persons possess absolute *S–R* dispositions, where the *S*- and *R*-categories are restricted to directly observable variables. And that restriction is largely responsible for the attractiveness of *T*-concepts. Moreover even if every *R* is causally determined by a set of observable factors, there is no guarantee that the associated *S–R* dispositions will be simple enough, or general enough, to be usable in personality description. Suppose that we can find obserable causal determinants for an *R* only by giving descriptions of both *R* and determining factors which are so specific that the constellation will rarely occur, and so specific that an enormous number of such dispositions would be possessed by a given person. In that case, the existence of absolute S–R dispositions would be of no significance for psychology.

B. THEORY OF MOTIVATION

We have not succeeded in determining the fate of T-concepts by appeal to general methodological principles. The next place, in the order of decreasing abstractness to look for 'fundamental considerations', is basic psychological theory. Here, I believe, we shall find the crux of the matter. I would suggest that the question of what *sort* of description of personality is *theoretically* preferable is to be decided by determining the most adequate theoretical account of that range of phenomena to the explanation of which personality is supposed to contribute. Now it is generally agreed that personality, whatever else it is, is that which is contributed by the person to the determination of behaviour. But then the question of how to conceptualize personality *is* the question of how to conceptualize what contribution the person makes to the determination of behaviour. And how we answer that question will depend on our general theory of motivation.[32]

On what theory of motivation would one or the other of our basic conceptual types be preferred? That question has already been answered for PC-concepts. For we saw that those concepts derive their content from their place in a certain theory of behaviour. But what about T-concepts? My suggestion is that personality could be adequately described by T-concepts only if an $S-R$ theory were adequate for the explanation of behaviour. This whole matter can be best set out by a parallel comparison of the two sorts of theories and the two sorts of concepts.

On both $S-R$ and PC theories, stimuli from the environment and from the organism play a role in response determination.[33] But what is contributed by more stable features of the person, features that could properly be mentioned in a description of personality? Here too there is at least one common element—abilities. On both approaches it will be acknowledged that response evocation is limited by the response repertoire of the person, what he is capable of. But as for what determines the selection from the repertoire the accounts

[32] I am using the term 'theory of motivation' to cover any theory of the contemporaneous determinants of behaviour. It has to do with what Tolman called 'principles of performance' in contrast to 'principles of learning'.

[33] The current state of the organism may contribute in other ways too, as in a theory that gives a prominent place to current drive level.

diverge. On an *S–R* approach the further contribution of the person is in the form of a (very large) number of '*S–R* bonds', each of which consists of a disposition to emit a response of a certain type upon the presentation of a stimulus of a certain type, these dispositions conceived as varying in strength. The stimuli presented to the organism at a given moment 'activate' all its dispositions that involve stimulus categories to which any of the current stimuli belong. As a result of this activation, instances of the response categories of each of these dispositions will be produced, except where (as is normally the case) two or more such categories are incompatible; in this latter case the response from the strongest of the competing tendencies will be emitted.[34]

In *PC* theory, on the other hand, selection from the response repertoire is determined by which tendency is strongest in the current 'tendency field'; and this in turn is determined by the relative strength of various desires and beliefs, which combine in various ways to produce response-tendencies, as we saw in our earlier sketch of the theory. Here stimuli function both to produce new beliefs (concerning the present state of the environment and organism) and to activate various standing beliefs and desires. (The details of the latter process must be enormously complicated and are still very little explored.)

Thus on *S–R* theory the motivational resources deposited in the individual by past learning[35] consist of an enormous number of (more or less specific)[36] 'habits', dispositions to react to a certain kind of stimulus with a certain kind of response. And behaviour is generated through the 'automatic' elicitation of these by current

[34] It goes without saying that each of our theory-types exists in many different versions, which will differ among themselves on more or less crucial points, e.g. how competition between simultaneously activated tendencies is resolved. Furthermore my general rubrics, especially '*S–R* theory', are sometimes used with different boundaries from those I am drawing. Hence even my highly schematic characterization cannot claim to be completely neutral as between rival versions. However I feel sure that this partiality does not compromise the generality of the points I am concerned to make in this paper.

[35] Again it is controversial just what is learned and what is innate. And again the contentions of this paper would be unaffected by where that line is drawn.

[36] It is often assumed that the bonds postulated by *S–R* theory must involve highly specific *S*- and *R*-categories. But no matter how general the categories, an *S–R* approach is sharply differentiated from a *PC* approach in the ways we are emphasizing.

stimulation. Whereas in *PC* theory motivation involves the individual's utilization of what he has 'learned' about the world in an ordinary sense of 'learn' (acquisition of information), in relation to his desires and other orientations towards goals. These, together with current information from the environment, enter into what is much more like a process of *computing* what responses are most likely to arrive at certain goals. Indeed in the more explicit and sophisticated cases of response-generation it can become a literal conscious computation.[37]

Thus on an *S–R* theory of motivation personality (what the person contributes to the determination of behaviour) consists of *S–R* dispositions:[38] while on a *PC* theory personality consists of such facts as latent desires and beliefs. Hence whether personality should be described in *T* or *PC* terms depends on what theory of motivation is most adequate. Whatever reasons we have for supposing that behaviour can be adequately explained without invoking anything more conceptually complicated than the activation of dispositions by current stimuli, are also reasons for choosing *T*-concepts for the description of personality. And whatever reasons we have for sup-

---

[37] The stark outlines of this contrast inevitably become softened as each approach tries to take account of the points emphasized by the other. In that process one contestant may take on features of the other to the extent that discrimination becomes problematic. As things have worked out, it is *S–R* theory that has increasingly taken on features of *PC* theory, rather than vice versa. To be sure in the work of Tolman *PC* theory was dressed out in a quasi-*SR* garb. But with unanticipated reinforcement from computer modelling and information theory *PC* theory has exhibited a new-found determination to stick to its guns. *S–R* theory, on the other hand, has been forced by the stubborn pressure of the facts to recognize that a wholly peripheralist version is untenable. Behaviour is not solely a function of the objective features of current physical stimulation; it makes all the difference in the world how this is perceived by the person, and how this engages his goal-hierarchy. *S–R* theorists have attempted to take account of this, without using *PC* concepts, by inserting *S–R* links between the external stimulation and overt behaviour. They seek to preserve the basic conceptual shape of the approach, while complicating the details and abandoning the Puritanical restriction to publicly observable factors.

[38] Just what filling is allowed in these dispositions depends on how liberal the *S–R* theory is. If and only if it countenances internal 'responses' can the *S–R* theorist allow his *S*-categories to range over how the situation is perceived, as well as its objective character. But in either case he will want his description of personality to feature units that can be 'automatically' activated by current stimulation.

posing that behaviour cannot be adequately explained without considering the beliefs and goal-orientations of the behaver, are *ipso
facto* reasons for choosing *PC*-concepts for personality theory.

Recalling the distinctions of section II, let us make explicit just
what negative conclusions about *T*'s (and positive conclusions about
PC's) could be established by an argument from the theory of
motivation. Like the methodological argument described in section
IV.A, this argument will *not* show that *T*'s do not exist. A *PC*
theory of motivation is compatible with the existence in a given
individual *and* in the population at large, of any number of *S–R*
connections of any degree of consistency, provided these *S–R* regularities are themselves to be explained by the operation of desires and
beliefs, rather than taken as ultimate features of the personality.
Suppose that *x* tries to dominate others whenever he is in a social
situation. Suppose further that each such attempt is due to a strong
desire for reassurance of his own worth (and a belief that dominating
others provides a good chance of securing that reassurance). The
consistency of the domineering behaviour would then be explained
by the fact that this desire–belief pair is consistently activated in
sufficient strength in any interpersonal situation. Or it may be that
some attempts at domination are to be given that *PC* explanation
and others are due to some other desire–belief pair, e.g. one involving fear of what might happen if someone else were in control. In
that case the consistency of attempts at domination would be explained by the fact that in any interpersonal situation, *some* desire–
belief pair that will yield domineering behaviour is activated in
sufficient strength. Thus a *PC* theory of motivation does not imply
that there are no generally shared consistent *T*'s. What it does
imply is something about their lack of utility; not (primarily) predictive utility, but *theoretical* utility, usability in a theoretically
fundamental description of personality.[39] On a *PC* theory of motivation, if there are consistent *S–R* connections they are explainable by
features of the person's desire–belief structure. In that case the most
fundamental description of personality would specify not the surface

[39] Of course if *PC*'s are theoretically fundamental, they are *in principle* more
powerful predictors, for other features of personality are derivative from them.
However, since actual success in prediction requires not only that we have
identified the right type of variable, but also that we have accurate measures
of particular instances, there is no guarantee that we can actually make correct
predictions from *PC* descriptions, however fundamental they are.

$S-R$ consistencies, but the desire–belief structure that is responsible for it.[40] What the theoretical argument, if successful, will show is that PC's rather than T's are the basic constituents of personality.

We must keep in mind the possibility that both a pure T and a pure PC theory of motivation are inferior to a mixed theory, according to which some behaviour occurs in order to reach certain goals, whereas in other cases one acts 'just out of habit', regardless of one's current beliefs and desires. For example, even if I am typing at this moment (rather than, e.g. driving my car) because I want to finish this paper and believe that using the typewriter is the best way to do it, it may still be that various features of my current behaviour, e.g. stroking my beard between bursts of typing, results from the activation of $S-R$ bonds rather than from any belief, even unconscious, that stroking my beard is likely to contribute to the attainment of some desired goal. On a mixed theory of motivation we would need both T- and PC-concepts for a theoretically basic description of personality.

The theoretical argument and the current controversy

Conflict over fundamental issues makes strange bedfellows. Despite the controversy between 'social learning' theorists like Mischel and 'psychodynamic' theorists, they are clearly on the same side of the $T-PC$ alternative.[41] In insisting on the importance of the latter issue I do not in the least want to play down the importance of the issues separating different PC theorists. To justify his own 'social learning' brand of PC personality description, as against the psychodynamic brand, Mischel quite properly deploys different theoretical

---

[40] This means that the theoretical argument, like the methodological one, is independent of the consistency argument. Whether or not there are consistent T's, theoretical considerations may show that they are not fundamental.

[41] It would seem that Mischel, and other 'cognitive social learning' theorists, like Bandura, are not aware of this. They tend to present their theory as one form of 'liberalized' $S-R$ theory. Of course, in view of the protean shapes and transformation assumed by $S-R$ theory one cannot deny them the right to the label; and no doubt their sort of PC theory is one that has been tightened up empirically in ways heavily influenced by the $S-R$ tradition. Nevertheless the fact remains that the issues would be considerably clarified if it were recognized on all hands that the variables stressed by Mischel are fundamentally PC in their conceptual type.

considerations from those I have brought to the T–PC alternative.[42] I would only insist that unless we keep the various issues straight one may not know who his opponents and his allies are in a given struggle. And since the considerations needed to support 'cognitive social learning theory' variables against S–R dispositions, and against other kinds of PC variables are so radically different, it is important to disentangle these different issues and appreciate the distinctive character of each.

I do not wish to make a secret of my conviction that a PC theory offers the only real hope of understanding the springs of motivation and hence the only hope of understanding personality. Even if there are *some* pure S–R connections (so that a mixed theory is required) I still believe that desire–belief structures are responsible for the most interesting aspects of human behaviour. However, I cannot defend that conviction in this paper, but must content myself with the humbler job of pointing to the field on which the decisive battle will be fought.

REFERENCES

ALLPORT, G. W. *Personality: A Psychological Interpretation*. New York: Henry Holt, 1937.

ALLPORT, G. W. *Pattern and Growth in Personality*. New York: Holt, Rinehart, and Winston, 1961.

ALSTON, W. P. Toward a Logical Geography of Personality: Traits and Deeper Lying Personality Characteristics. In M. K. Munitz (ed.), *Mind, Science, and History*. Albany, New York: State University of New York Press, 1970.

ALSTON, W. P. A Conceptual Divide in Personality Description. Invited address to the Personality and Social Psychology Division of the American Psychological Association, September, 1973.

ARGYLE, MICHAEL & LITTLE, BRIAN R. Do Personality Traits Apply to Social Behaviour? *Journal for the Theory of Social Behaviour*, vol. 2, no. 1, April, 1972, pp. 1–33.

ATKINSON, J. W. & BIRCH, D. *The Dynamics of Action*. New York: John Wiley & Sons, 1970.

[42] It is also worthy of note that Mischel relies on theoretical considerations only to support his positive proposals, not (or hardly ever) to argue *against* traits.

BANDURA, A. *Principles of Behaviour Modification*. New York: Holt, Rinehart, & Winston, 1969.

CARNAP, R. The Methodological Character of Theoretical Concepts. In H. Feigl & M. Scriven (eds.), *Minnesota Studies in the Philosophy of Science*, vol. I. Minneapolis: University of Minnesota Press, 1956.

CATTELL, R. B. *The Scientific Analysis of Personality*. Chicago: Aldine Pub. Co., 1965.

CRONBACH, L. J. *Essentials of Psychological Testing*, 2nd ed. New York: Harper & Row, 1960.

FISKE, D. W. *Measuring the Concepts of Personality*. Chicago: Aldine Pub. Co., 1971.

MISCHEL, W. *Personality and Assessment*. New York: Wiley, 1968.

MISCHEL, W. Toward a Cognitive Social Learning Reconceptualization of Personality, *Psych. Rev.*, 1973, vol. 80, no. 4.

SEARS, R. R. Dependency Motivation. In M. R. Jones, (ed.), *Nebraska Symposium on Motivation*, Lincoln: University of Nebraska Press, 1963.

VERNON, P. E. The Biosocial Nature of the Personality Trait, *Psych. Rev.*, vol. 40, 1933.

5 A Helical Theory of Personal Change*

ROBERT C. ZILLER

Individual and social change is inherent, yet stability or at least predictability is often the preferred state (Lecky, 1945). Under these circumstances, the human compromise must involve the monitoring of social change and the adaptation of group and individual processes in an effort to maintain control over the changing system. Social scientists' investigations of the control of individual and social change have been fractionated. Social psychologists in departments of psychology have focused on attitude change (see McGuire, 1968). Social psychologists in departments of sociology have examined the problem of personal change in relation to role and self concept under the rubric of role strains within role theory (see Secord and Backman, 1964). Clinical psychologists and sociologists have both studied in depth changes in the self concept (Rogers, 1951; Brim and Wheeler, 1966). Finally, a burgeoning area in clinical psychology is behaviour modification (Bandura, 1969).

Unfortunately, each of these sub-theories is compartmentalized. Paraphrasing Cassirer (1944, p. 21), each sub-theory is autonomous and becomes a Procrustean bed on which the empirical facts are stretched to fit a preconceived pattern. The result is a complete 'anarchy of thought'.

A confluence of the four aforementioned frameworks is proposed here leading to a general theory of personal change. A brief outline of the basic components of the framework are described along with the fundamental assumptions of the system of thought. A more elaborate description of each sub-system is developed later along with the connections between the sub-systems within the general

* This report was funded by the Office of Naval Research, Group Psychology Programs, under contract No. 00014-67-A-0446-0003.

theory of personal change. Although each sub-theory points towards a general theory of change, each has a limited purview and the framework of each does not provide an adequate basis for integrating the extensive research findings. Moreover, taken as a collective, the sub-theories fail to provide a working basis for a thorough understanding of personal change because they are unwieldy, are not generalizable in their entirety, and do not consider the joint effects of the differed frameworks. A synthesis is required which points out some of the shortcomings of the separate frameworks and leads to a restructuring of the frameworks at a higher level of abstraction for greater generalization.

The core of the personal change theory is a Guttmantype hierarchy of potentially changeable personal characteristics including attitudes, values, behaviours, roles, and self concepts. It is assumed here that the characteristics are ordered on an underlying dimension of ease of change. Attitudes are the least difficult to change, and the self concept is the most difficult to change. Values, behaviour, and role are ordered on a continuum somewhere between these two extremes.

| Self Concepts |
| Roles |
| Behaviours |
| Values |
| Attitudes |

In defining the components of this hierarchical system of personal change, a close association will be sought between the definition of the component and the method of measurement of the component usually used in the experimental literature. This approach is particularly important with regard to the definition of attitudes. Much of theory and research in the area of attitude change are closely related only if the reader is willing to overlook the fact that attitudes are usually measured through self reports with their inherent shortcomings. Under these conditions, the resulting theory can be deluding. Most importantly, however, directions for a new framework may be obscured. With regard to attitude change theory, it is proposed here that diffuse definitions of attitudes along with aggrandizing theories have served to truncate the development of a vital theory of attitude change within a system of personal change.

Nevertheless, the contribution of the research may be reclaimed by limiting the range of meaning of the studies and by organizing the findings within a more complete system of thought.

Attitudes

A frequent definition of attitude is a person's predisposition to behave in a certain way (Jones and Gerard, 1967). Newcomb (1950, pp. 118–19) defines attitude as a state of readiness for motive arousal. 'An individual's attitude toward something is his predisposition to perform, perceive, think and feel in relation to it.' In discussing the function of attitudes, Katz, Sarnoff, and McClintock (1956) have included an ego defensive function. In one way or another, these definitions indicate a link between attitudes and the remaining four components in the system of personal change. The nature of the association is not indicated, however.

In the present context, attitude is defined as a self report and a public statement of the person's disposition at that point in time to behave in a certain way. The self report nature of attitudes is stressed because most measures of attitudes used in experiments ask for a verbal self report or an opinion (Bem, 1967). The inherent shortcomings of the self report must be underscored here (Kelly, 1955, p. 268; Polanyi, 1966, p. 4).

In addition, however, the definition of attitude emphasizes its social component. The opinion is usually made public. The report is presented to someone. Thus, expectations between the self and the other become involved.

Values

Values are most often defined as a cluster of attitudes. In this sense, a higher level of abstraction is indicated. Values, too, usually are measured by public self reports. Nevertheless, it is often assumed that attitudes are more susceptible to change than values (Hollander, 1967, p. 117), again suggesting the proposed hierarchical ordering assumed here.

Behaviour

A behaviour is a response in relation to a situation as a stimulus. Behaviour occurs in the context of a situation as opposed to an attitude or value which occurs in response to a question. When a verbal statement is made in response to a question raised in a non-voluntary situation, the verbal response is distinctly not a behaviour in the present sense. If, on the other hand, the statement is volunteered by the individual, the verbal response approaches a behaviour as described here. In the latter case, the individual assumes a greater responsibility for the act. Watson (1930) included verbal responses within the behaviour category, but this assumption led to an unnecessary diffusion of the behaviour definition.

Role

A person occupying a place in a social relation, such as a mother, expects herself and is expected by others to relate and behave towards other persons in the social system according to certain norms. Certain behaviours are relevant to the role. If these behaviours are not forthcoming, the social system is less predictable leading to some interference in the group interaction, social processes, and perhaps reduced performance. In some roles the latitude of expectations is more narrow than other roles.

In some sense, a role assumes a degree of commitment to a social relationship. The person occupying a position expects and is expected to behave in certain ways because the members of the social system have made an implicit agreement to do so. It is also probably assumed by the members of the social system that they will signal the other members of the group before they change their behaviour in any appreciable degree. An element of trust is involved making for stability and predictability within the social unit.

Self Concepts

In the personal change system described here, the self concept is restored to a significant position. The self concept is more difficult than attitudes to measure, but we can scarcely afford to have theory construction dictated by the relative convenience of constructing measures.

It may be assumed that prediction is facilitated by the organization of relevant elements into a conceptual system. In the search for relevant elements, perhaps the most ubiquitous elements in the field should receive highest priority. The self concept, then, emerges as a high priority and crucial construct in the search for elements in social psychological theories of behaviour and behaviour change.

The self concept may be described as evolving within a context of associations and configurations with objects, persons, and other concepts. A multifaceted analysis of the self concept is proposed here. In keeping with Adler (1927), Sullivan (1953), Cooley (1899), and Mead (1934), however, the social nature of the self is emphasized, and it will be assumed that the individual's adaptation demands are primarily social in nature and involve the inherent conflicts between the self and significant others. These conflicts stem from competing needs for independence and dependence, autonomy and mutuality, self orientation and other orientation.

With regard to the cognitive level of the personal change hierarchy, it is proposed that social stimuli are screened and translated into personal meaning through crude topological descriptions of the self in relation to significant others (see Ziller, 1970; Ziller, 1969; Ziller, Hagey, Smith and Long, 1969).

SOCIAL STIMULI→SELF—OTHER CONSTRUCTS SOCIAL RESPONSE

For example, representation of the self as within as opposed to without the field of a set of significant others is associated with a tendency to be oriented towards positive rather than negative reinforcement (see Ziller, 1970). The evolving components of self–other orientation include self esteem, social interest, self centrality, complexity, majority identification, identification, power, marginality, inclusion, and openness. A description of self esteem will illustrate the approach.

Self-esteem is the individual's perception of his worth. In evaluating the self, the individual has recourse to comparisons of the self and significant others. Again the social context of self-esteem is underscored.

In this framework, it is proposed that self-esteem is the component of the self system through which the self system is maintained under conditions of strain such as during the processing of new information concerning the self. Thus, for example, either positive or negative evaluations do not evoke immediate, corresponding action by the individual with high self-esteem. New information relative to the self is examined in terms of its relevance and meaning for the self system. The organism is somewhat insulated from the environment or is not completely subject to environmental contingencies. It has been found, for example, that persons with high as opposed to low self-esteem are more consistent in their frequency of participation across group discussion sessions (Ziller, Hagey, Smith and Long, 1969).

Persons with low self-esteem, on the other hand, do not possess a well-developed conceptual buffer for evaluative stimuli. In Witkins's terms (Witkins, Dyk, Faterson, Goodenough and Karp, 1967), the person with low esteem is field dependent; the individual's behaviour is directly linked to environmental circumstances, and thereby is inclined towards oscillation or inconsistency.

Most significantly, in terms of the theory of personal change, the self concept is relatively stable. It is subject to change and is responsive to long term situational changes, but a lag in the change process is inherent. This lag assures a degree of stability within the personal system which serves as a point of reference in an otherwise kaleidoscopic social environment. Self–other orientations serve as control mechanisms for social adaptation by serving as screening and guiding representations.

Assumptions of the Personal Change System

THE HIERARCHICAL SYSTEM

It has already been indicated that the five components of the change system are assumed to constitute a hierarchy of difficulty of change. Attitudes are the least difficult and self–other orientations are the most difficult. The other components fall somewhere between. No simple scale is suggested, however.

COMMITMENT

The relative difficulty of change of the components is attributable, in part, to the relative commitment associated with each of the components. Commitment refers to a reduction in further alternatives associated with a particular choice (Roby, 1960). Having committed oneself at a particular level in the change hierarchy is associated with greater predictability for the individual. For example, having reported certain attitudes is less restricting than having accepted a certain role such as group leader. Violation of the expectations associated with the expression of an attitude is more acceptable to the self and others than violation of role expectancies. The greatest commitment is associated with the self–other orientations. The latter constructs are designed particularly to function rapidly under conditions of limited time demands and stress. The self–other orientations are associated with the stability, regularity, and consistency of personal behaviour. The individual ceases to monitor rigorously the thinking processes associated with these constructs. They serve as a subsystem of reference which facilitates adaptation. To change these on a daily basis would require a prohibitive amount of effort, or there would be much less opportunity to attend to matters external to the self.

Expression of an attitude on a questionnaire is associated with considerably less commitment. The self concept is associated with a reduction in alternatives and is subject to more controls. It is implied throughout that a more rapid change is possible as one moves down the hierarchy. Attitudes are subject to the most rapid change. Changes in self–other orientations are slow, but it is proposed here that this relative stability is functional. The instability of attitudes may also be functional in that a degree of flexibility is possible within a relatively stable personal system. Before exploring this possibility, however, it will be necessary to examine the assumption of the press towards consonance among the components in the personal system.

EQUILIBRIUM OF THE PERSONAL SYSTEM

The personal system is such that if one of the components is changed, a state of disequilibrium is effected within the system. It is assumed that in this imbalanced state there is a tendency for the components lower in the hierarchy to change in a way which will render the components congruent. For example, if an individual changes roles the next most probable change would involve attitudes, then values, followed by behaviours.

Even though there is a tendency for the press to move downwards in the hierarchy, it is assumed that a change in one component will also establish a press towards change in components higher in the system. A change in attitudes, for example, is assumed to exert some press towards changes on behaviour, role, and self concept but with diminishing force with regard to the higher level components.

A differential time factor for change is assumed to operate as one moves up the hierarchy as opposed to down the hierarchy. Thus, the press on behaviour change under conditions of attitude change is less than the press on attitude change under conditions of behaviour change. Nevertheless, if the press functions over time, it will increase. Still, it will take longer to change behaviour through a change in attitudes than it will to change attitudes through a behaviour change. For example, a change in attitudes toward pre-marital sex will not influence sexual practices to the same extent that a change in sexual practices will influence attitudes.

If more than one of the components are changed, the state of disequilibrium will vary in relation to the pattern of changed components. Under conditions where all components have been changed with the exception of the role, there will be a strong press towards changing roles. For example, if an individual's attitudes, values, behaviours, and self concept have changed regarding marriage, there will be a tendency to marry or obtain a divorce depending upon the original state. On the other hand, if only one's attitudes have changed towards marriage, the press towards change in the other components of the personal system with regard to marriage will be relatively weak, and the probability is higher that the attitudes will change in order to re-establish congruence in the system rather than a change in the entire system.

It is proposed that the individual is required to monitor the self–social system constantly in order to maintain the congruence of the self concept and social field. In the event of incongruence, the individual is most likely to alter his attitudes. It is assumed here that a change in attitudes requires the least effort and also is the least threatening to the self system as a control and predictive system. The change will have left intact the major components of the self system.

An attitude change also serves to reduce social pressure for change. In a sense, attitude change is a social defence mechanism. For example, overt agreement with the majority opinion is a low cost exchange which still permits covert disagreement. Indeed, in a sense each of the components below the self concept may be interpreted as a defence mechanism in that the individual may maintain the self system intact yet adapt to social presses through changes in attitudes, values, behaviours, or even roles.

As already stated, it is assumed that in the event of a change at one level in the hierarchy, the entire system is in jeopardy to some extent. A press is generated to change other aspects of the system towards congruence, especially those components lower in the hierarchy. Under conditions where more than one component has changed, the system is subject to greater strain. For example, if behaviour is changed in addition to an attitude change, the probability of changing values increases toward 1.00. The probability of changing roles also probably increases. It is quite likely, for example, that behaviour modification techniques are effected, in part, by a change in attitudes *prior* to behaviour change attempts. Indeed, when examined, most approaches to personal change will reveal a multiple entry strategy.

Since the greatest disequilibrium is created by changing components higher in the system, the optimal strategy of personal change would seem to be dictated: change the self concept. Self theorists base their approach on this premise. Yet, the foregoing sections have stressed some formidable obstacles to this approach. A more complete consideration of this problem is postponed for a later section.

The preceding discussion of the press towards balance in the personal system suggests that balance is the optimal state of the system. This would be true if the social and physiological fields of the person were constants. Given the continuous change of the environment, however, it is now proposed that a state of disequilibrium may suggest movement towards adaptation of the organism and the environment. In this sense, a tentative change in attitudes permits experimentation with the personal system with a minimum of cost; a pilot study of the personal system, if you will. Little commitment is involved, and the system may return to a state of equilibrium very rapidly and with relatively little difficulty if the self monitoring processess so indicate.

Increasing commitment is made as changes in the other components proceed. The hierarchy suggests an orderly progression up the scale. Attitude changes are tried first, then values, behaviours, roles, and finally the self concept changes, in turn, under favourable circumstances. But more dramatic changes in the personal system are possible. The probability of a high rate of change may itself be a characteristic of the personal system associated with risk. Indeed, Mossman and Ziller (1970), have recently found that persons with high acceptable rates of change for themselves tend to use coercion more frequently in a persuasion situation.

SELF—OTHER ORIENTATION HIERARCHY

The self concept is, therefore, the most crucial component of the system. It is the most resistant to change and more time is required for change. Moreover, if the self concept is changed, there is a higher probability that other components in the system will change.

As indicated in the definition of the hierarchical components, however, there are assumed to be multiple components of self—other orientations. It is now proposed that these components themselves may be arranged in a hierarchy associated with personal change. Three components of the self—other orientation framework are relevant: complexity of the self concept, social interest, and self esteem. It is assumed that complexity of the self concept is most amenable to change, social interest next, and self-esteem least.

Self-esteem has already been described in terms of consistency of the self system. The person with high self-esteem is presumed to have developed an integrated self system through which the individual readily assimilates new information or screens out irrelevant social stimuli. High self-esteem is assumed to underly personal stability.

Social interest (see Ziller, 1970; Ziller, 1969) is an Adlerian concept referring to the range of a person's affectionate interest and concern. In terms of self—other orientation, social interest is assumed to involve inclusion of the perception of the self with others as opposed to the perception of separation from others. Inclusion involves a willingness to be subject to the field of forces generated among others and the self. Social trust is suggested. Indeed, it has been demonstrated (Ziller, 1970) that persons with high as opposed to low social interest are more inclined to monitor a positive as opposed to a negative source of reinforcement. It is assumed here that the stability of persons with high social interest is maintained through group norms.

Complexity of the self (Ziller, 1970) concerns the degree of differentiation of the self concept, or in Lewin's (1935) terms, the number of parts composing the whole. A person with high complexity of the self concept requires more words to describe himself.

It is now proposed that the individual with the more complex theory concerning self–other relations is less likely to be seriously disturbed by new experiences which momentarily appear to be incongruent with the system. This proposition derives by extrapolation from a series of unpublished studies by Alex Bavelas of Stanford University concerning the etiology of superstition. It was observed that persons with more complex hypotheses or theoretical systems concerning a given phenomenon were able to assimilate new information into the system with greater facility.

Complexity of the self concept may be similar to 'self-actualization' as described by Maslow (1954). Maslow suggests that in self-actualized persons 'many dichotomies, polarities, and conflicts are fused and resolved'. Emerging from this, self-actualized persons are simultaneously selfish and unselfish, individual and social, rational and irrational, and so on. Essentially, Maslow seems to be proposing that self-actualized persons are not simply described or categorized; that is, they are complex. In the present context complexity of the self concept is also associated with stability of the self system through cognitive processes such as tolerance for dissonance.

The assumed hierarchy among these three components of self–other orientation again suggests that strategies of personal change directed towards the self concept may be accomplished with greater facility if they begin with a concern for complexity of the self concept, in order to render the self system more adaptive. Changes in social interest are also a concern for personal change in that the individual with high social interest is more responsive to positive reinforcements from others (Ziller, 1970). Finally, a change in self-esteem may follow in relation to a series of positive experiences associated with responsiveness to others. Indeed, an effective programme to change self-esteem directly may not be possible to achieve directly but rather must emanate from social interest and the attendant positive social reinforcements. Again, a multiple intervention strategy is suggested directed simultaneously at complexity of the self concept and social interest, but ultimately self-esteem.

Cognitive, Conative and Affective Components

The five components of the personal system derive in part from the classic classification of human process: knowing, acting, feeling. The cognitive component of the personal system concerns the organization of the information field into units which facilitate communication. These units are what has been referred to as attitudes and values. The latter is the more abstract unit.

The behavioural component has already been so named within the original system. To the behavioural component must be added the role component which incorporates the expectations of the others as well as certain behaviours.

Finally, the affective facet includes self–other orientations as they are described here. Here feelings are assumed to be expressed not by verbal reports such as attitudes, but rather in terms of the perceptions of the self in relation to significant others. The feelings have been incorporated within the self system. Indeed the feelings referred to here may be ineffable. Thus, self–other orientations cannot be measured using standard methods of communication. A meta-language is required. One such approach is the use of spatial para-logic (see DeSoto, London and Handel, 1965; Ziller, Hagey, Smith and Long, 1969). The system of personal change described here includes some of the most central characteristics of the human state, and it is in this sense that the proposed theory is general.

A Synthesis of Four Micro-Theories of Personal Change

The theory of Personal Change is essentially an integration of the theories of attitude change, behaviour modification, role theory, and the theory of self–other orientation. The Theory of Personal Change has almost appeared piecemeal in the literature. Usually, however, one or another of the components is emphasized to the exclusion of some and the de-emphasis of others. Often many of the components are described but are not incorporated within the framework. More general frameworks seem to be avoided in preference for more readily testable micro-theories, but in so doing the modesty of empiricism may lead to theoretical myopia.

I. ATTITUDE CHANGE THEORIES

As stated earlier, the topic of attitude change has been the component of personal change most studied by social psychologists. Indeed, McGuire (1969, p. 136) states unequivocally that attitude research in the last decade has returned to the dominant status within social psychology that it had thirty years ago. This emphasis is somewhat difficult to defend, however, on the basis of the relationship between attitude change and behaviour change (Fishbein, 1967). Fishbein concludes that traditional measures of attitude are not likely to be related to behaviour in any consistent manner. He contends that earlier investigators have usually questioned the measures of attitudes. They have argued that traditional measures are oversimplified. Most measures only consider an individual's 'affective feelings', and fail to take his cognitions and conations into consideration. Fishbein then suggests that most investigators attempt to resolve the attitude behaviour problem by expanding the definition of attitude to include affective, cognitive, and conative components. I would add that the social psychologists may also have been seduced by the relative ease of conducting attitude research, and reduced the dissonance by exaggerating the importance of the research topic.

Support for Fishbein's claim that investigators of attitudes expand its definition of attitude to include affective, cognitive, and conative components to offset the inadequacy of the measures of attitudes may be found in the definition of attitude by Newcomb (1950), and Secord and Backman (1964). Newcomb writes that an individual's attitude towards something 'is his predisposition to perform, perceive, think and feel in relation to it' (p. 118–19). Similarly, Secord and Backman (p. 99) note that 'In a broader sense, an individual's entire personality structure and hence his behavior may be thought of as organized around a central value system comprised of many related attitudes.' Both statements at least indicate that attitudes are merely part of a personal system. Unfortunately, the emphasis is misplaced on the attitude component of the system. More significantly for the development of a general Theory of Personal Change are the proposed relationships between attitudes and other components of the five-component helical personal system.

ATTITUDES AND VALUES. In reviewing studies which have examined the relationship between attitudes and the other components in the change hierarchy, there is convincing evidence that a person's attitude towards an object is a function of his value orientation (Fishbein, 1963; Rosenberg, 1960). Rosenberg's study may be used as a model to investigate the relative position of the components in the change hierarchy. In this study, eleven deeply hypnotized subjects were given post hypnotic suggestions part of which follows:

> When you awake you will be very much in favor of Negroes moving into white neighborhoods. The mere idea of Negroes moving into white neighborhoods will give you a happy, exhilarated feeling. . . . Also, when you awake you will be very opposed to the city-manager plan. The mere idea of the city-manager plan will give you a feeling of loathing and disgust (p. 43).

The subjects, of course, were told that they would have no memory of the suggestion when they emerged from the hypnotic state. Value questionnaires were administered to the hypnotized subjects and to a control group of non-hypnotized subjects both before and after the trance session. The hypnotized subjects showed a greater change than the non-hypnotized control subjects in the structure underlying their attitude towards the issues. It was concluded that the experimental subjects had adjusted their beliefs concerning the perceived instrumentality of furthering or hindering their values to bring them into greater agreement with the hypnotically induced change in attitude.

Unfortunately, the reverse procedure was not conducted to examine the effect of a change in values on attitudes. It is only through this approach that the hierarchy can be established. Unfortunately, too, the definitions of attitudes and values are not clear. In terms of the hypnotic induction, the study may easily be interpreted as involving self–other orientations (as induced) and attitude or value changes, thereby supporting the proposed change hierarchy.

Nevertheless, Rosenberg's approach may well serve as a model experiment for testing the relationship among the various components. For example, a change in self–other orientation may be induced hypnotically followed by an examination of changes in behaviour and attitudes. In a second phase of the study, behaviour change may be induced hypnotically followed by an examination of changes in self–other orientation and attitudes. A final phase of the study would involve hypnotically induced attitude change followed by an examination of behaviour change and change in self–other orientations.

ATTITUDES AND BEHAVIOUR. The first major breakthrough in attitude research leading to the Theory of Personal Change was made by Festinger (1957). Essentially, Festinger's theory concerning dissonance reduction indicates that a behavioural act is associated with an attitude change.

Festinger's ideas stem from a balance theory orientation (Heider, 1958). For example, when inconsistencies exist between two attitudes, the organism will strive for consistency by reducing or increasing the positive stance towards one of them. In point of fact, however, most of the experiments which examine the theory of dissonance–consonance are concerned with imbalances between behaviour and attitudes. In most instances, the subject finds that he has committed himself to a certain course of action which is inconsistent with his attitudes. Since behaviour involves more of a commitment, a change in attitude consistent with the behaviour is usually found. Equilibrium is re-established with a minimum of cost since it is easier to change one's attitude rather than try to redress a situation.

In one experiment (Smith, 1961), subjects ate chocolate fried grasshoppers as part of a survival training programme in a military setting. The subjects were instructed to eat the grasshoppers under the supervision of either a controlling (very military) or permissive leader. Under the more severe leader, the subjects reported that the taste of the grasshoppers was less objectionable.

The experiment clearly indicates the prepotent effect of act in relation to attitude. In an effort to highlight the dissonance–consonance framework, however, other facets of the experiment are overlooked which may place the experiment within the broader context of a Theory of Personal Change. Most significantly, the experiment was conducted under military classroom conditions. Under these conditions, the subjects may readily perceive themselves as models of military behaviour under the conditions where the leader was himself an exaggeration of the model military leader, or even more so when the leader did *not* assume the expected leadership role. The role of the subject must be underscored. The effects then stem not only from the act of eating the grasshopper, but most significantly from expectations associated with the role of an exemplar. It is quite likely that most experiments concerning personal change involve several of the components of the proposed hierarchy.

In support of the latter proposition, an experiment by Zimbardo (1960) is instructive. Pairs of friends were led to believe that they disagreed either a little or a great deal in their judgements of a case study of juvenile delinquency. The importance of the rating of the case was varied by telling some pairs that their judgements represented basic values, personality traits, and outlooks on important life problems. Other pairs were told that their judgements did not mean much. It was found that change towards the friend's position is directly proportional to the significance of the judgement in relation to the self. Thus, the self concept is an important consideration in attitude research. The question that is never asked, however, is the relative strength of influence on attitudes among self–other orientations (self-esteem, social interest, complexity of the self), roles, behaviours, and values. The focus is solely on attitudes rather than the personal system. More importantly for theory construction, it is necessary to separate the potential effects from the various components of the personal change system as they relate to attitudes. Focusing on behaviour as it relates to attitudes is likely to lead to a narrow analysis of the process, to diffuse definition of concepts, and even to misplaced emphasis.

Confusion is also introduced into the theoretical framework concerning attitude change in that the direction of the effect is not indicated, although it is sometimes implied that attitude change leads to changes in values, behaviour, and self concept.

Bem (1967) proposes a somewhat different interpretation of these studies and supports it with a series of pinpointing experiments. In his studies the individual is described as standing back and observing his own overt behaviour in relation to a situation and making inferences (attitudes) from the association of behaviour and the situation. For example, just as a communicator is more persuasive to others if he is known to be receiving no payment for his communication, so too, it is found that he is more likely to believe himself under such circumstances (Bem, 1965). Although self-observation is central to Bem's framework, the concept of the self is eschewed.

Bem's explanation is supported in a study (Davidson and Valins, 1969) using drug inductions. It was found that if an individual believes that he is responsible (the subject is told that what he was told was a drug injection was, in fact, a placebo) for engaging in a behaviour which is inconsistent with his own attitude, his attitude will more readily change and become consistent with this behaviour than if he believes that external forces (a drug injection) are responsible for his behaviour.

In these studies by Festinger, Bem and Davidson and Valins, the relationship is analysed between behaviour change and attitude change. Behaviour change is found to be the more dominant variable.

ATTITUDES AND ROLES· The next level of the hierarchy after behaviours pertains to role changes. Evidence has already been cited to support the relationship between role change and attitude change, but the more directly applicable studies involve role playing and attitude change.

The relation between the second level in the personal change hierarchy (roles) and the fifth level (attitudes) has also been explored extensively. The usual experiments examine role-playing as it relates to attitude change (Janis and King, 1954; King and Janis, 1956; Scott, 1957; Brehm and Cohen, 1962). Subjects who verbalized the other person's point of view changed their attitudes more than subjects who were merely exposed to the other's point of view. These experiments have been seriously questioned, however, in terms of design (Zimbardo, 1965). Nevertheless, if the subject perceives himself as playing the role of *teacher or student*, through the act of presenting an argument to two other persons, there is an increased likelihood that the subject will incorporate the attitudes in question in accordance with the expectations of others and himself relative to the role of teacher or student. Proper adoption of the role may become the issue of central concern, and attitudes consistent with this role are readily adopted. Commitment to a role takes precedence over commitment to an attitude.

Of course, commitment to a role is far greater in a natural situation than under conditions of role playing, and attitude change would be expected to accompany role changes. A unique opportunity to examine the relationship between role change and attitude change occurred in an industrial setting where some rank and file workers were promoted to foremen and others to shop stewards. Later, some of these same recently promoted foremen were returned to their former positions (Liebeman, 1956).

Individuals whose attitudes were the same before they changed positions showed consistent changes in attitude in the direction of their new reference groups, shop stewards or foremen. Moreover, the foremen who returned to their rank and file status reverted to their attitudes of three years earlier.

To this point, the possible effects of attitude change on role change has not been considered. Executive training programmes often assume that a change in attitudes relevant to the role leadership will create sufficient imbalance in the personal system to effect a change in role behaviour. It is hoped that by changing crucial attitudes, role behaviour may be effected. Since the role is defined by the expectations of others as well as the self, however, the probability of such a change is extremely small. In addition, there is always the question as to whether or not attitudes crucial to the role have been selected for change. It is entirely possible that only the actor's perceptions can determine this. Thus, the self–other schemas of the actor become a consideration.

ATTITUDES AND SELF CONCEPTS. The association between self–other orientations and attitudes is being stressed increasingly by investigations (Smith, 1968; Sherif and Sherif, 1967; Jones and Gerard, 1967). Smith, for example, refers to attitudes as mediators of self–other relations. Somewhat earlier Lifton (1961) referred to a 'death and rebirth' process associated with attitude change. He suggests that a revulsion within the individual is required before attitude change is effective. A similar process was described by Schein (1951) with regard to the Chinese attempts to 'unfreeze' the attitudes of American prisoners of war prior to re-indoctrination (brainwashing). The process is not unlike that used by military recruiters in re-socializing new members of the military services in the United States (Smith, 1949; Erikson, 1958).

The integration of personality, behaviour, values, and attitudes is perhaps best illustrated in the following statement by Secord and Backman (1964, p. 99): 'In a broader sense, an individual's entire personality structure and hence his behavior may be thought of as organized around a central value system composed of many attitudes.'

Sherif and Sherif (1968), however, have made the link between the self concept and attitudes central to their theory of attitude change. They state (p. 2) that a 'person's attitudes defines for him what *he is* and what he is *not*, that is, what is included within and what is excluded from his *self*–image'. More than this, however, Sherif and Sherif suggest that the self concept is the most cogent determinant of the personal system. It is assumed, first, that regardless of the nature of the environment, the individual is the centre of his social space. It is the individual's apprehension of the environment that is incorporated and translated into beliefs, values, and actions. Of course, extrapersonal stimuli are important causal antecedents, but these stimuli are first subjected to selective and modifying processes within the individual. 'The self serves as the final screen channeling the course of development of social attitudes' (p. 19). In terms of the Self–Other Orientation framework described earlier (Ziller, 1970), the screening processes referred to by Sherif are assumed to utilize self–other schemas or images. Furthermore, these images are relatively enduring making for a degree of personal stability.

As the components of the personal system become more distal to each other, the probability diminishes that a change in the lower component in the hierarchy will influence the higher level component, particularly with increasing age. It has been noted repeatedly that the consistency of children's attitudes increases with age (Horowitz, 1936; Stevenson and Stewart, 1958; Vaughan, 1964; Wilson, 1963). This suggests that as the personal system stabilizes, attitude change is less likely to create a press towards change in other components of the personal system.

Earlier, self-esteem was defined in terms of consistency or stabilization of behaviour. It may be expected, then, that persons with high self-esteem are more likely to move towards redressing disequilibrium. For example, it may be expected that persons with high self-esteem are less likely to change their attitudes to begin with. In response to a dissonant situation, the person with high self-esteem is also more likely to overcome the imbalance by cognitive work; that is, Festinger's dissonance–consonance hypothesis is more likely to be upheld by persons with high self-esteem. The latter proposition was upheld in studies by Gerard, Blevans and Malcolm (1964) and Malewski (1962). A large number of studies have confirmed the positive relationship between self-esteem and susceptibility to persuasion (Janis and Field, 1959; Cohen, 1959; Leventhal and Perloe, 1962).

In examining the relationship between attitude change and the self concept, it becomes increasingly clear that the investigators of attitude change hope to extend their findings with regard to attitudes to the topic of the self or even more generally to personality by the simple expedient of expanding the definition of attitudes to embrace the concepts of the ego and behaviour. In so doing, social psychologists may have paralleled the perils of psychotherapists who accepted the changed self reports of clients in a clinical setting as equivalents of behaviour changes and personality changes.

Kelman (1961) suggests that there are three distinct processes of social influence: compliance, identification, and internalization. *'Compliance* can be said to occur when an individual accepts influence from another person or from a group because he hopes to achieve a favorable reaction from the other' (p. 62). The expression of an opinion even though the person privately disagrees with the expression is instrumental. At the very least, it is a defence mechanism. In the personal change hierarchy, compliance is equivalent to attitude change.

'Identification can be said to occur when an individual adopts behavior derived from another person or a group because the behavior is associated with a satisfying self-defining relationship to this person or group' (p. 63). This definition approximates the social learning approach to behaviour modification which is the third level of the personal change hierarchy.

'Internalization can be said to occur when an individual accepts influence because the induced behavior is congruent with his value system' (p. 65). Literally interpreted, internalization is similar to a change in the self concept.

To refer to all of these as attitude changes aggrandizes the concept of attitudes and results in a misplaced emphasis on attitude research and the theories derived thereof. Indeed, it is proposed here that the emphasis of research should be distributed over the five levels, but that the major concern should be with the self concept rather than attitudes.

2. BEHAVIOUR CHANGE

Approaches to behaviour change which derive from a learning framework are grouped under the rubric of behaviour modification (Bandura, 1969; Frank, 1969). The approaches include modelling, positive reinforcement, negative reinforcement, and desensitization.

Usually, the approach pertains to the clinical goal of treatment (Watson, 1962). The behaviour modification approach usually is directed towards a narrowly defined behavioural objective. For example, the objective of the personal change training may be the elimination of smoking behaviour. The approach avoids focusing upon inner agents and forces associated with smoking or even attitudes towards smoking. The objective is no more than the elimination of smoking behaviour itself. Moreover, role considerations and the self concept are usually outside the field of concern. Change is effected through positive reinforcement of the desired behaviours or behaviours in the direction of the desired outcome or punishment of undesirable behaviours in the Skinnerian tradition (Skinner, 1953). Under some problem conditions, modelling of the desired behaviours is reinforced.

One of the other characteristics of the behaviour modification approach to personal change is the flexibility, or indeed creativity, encouraged on the part of the trainer. The nature of the reinforcement is often selected for the particular subject and circumstance.

For example, Ayllon and his associates conducted an extensive programme of research in the development of reinforcement procedures for the change of gross behaviour disorders in adult psychotics. In the early studies (Ayllon and Michael, 1959), nurses and hospital attendants were trained to record 'base line' data of the frequency with which patients exhibited certain behaviour. Reinforcement contingencies—usually in the form of social attention and food reward—were arranged in the hospital setting to bring about the desired changes. Bizarre forms of behaviour were ignored or were not reinforced with social attention. More rational response patterns were supported by the nurses. In so doing, psychotic verbalizations were markedly reduced or completely eliminated (Ayllon and Haughton, 1964).

BEHAVIOURS AND ATTITUDES. The relation between attitudes and behaviour from the point of view of behaviour modification is quickly dismissed by Bandura (1969) as relatively inconsequential. He avers that persons who profess to be interested in attitude change are not interested in attitudes *per se*; their principal aim is behaviour change. It is proposed that the attitude-change approach is selected as a means of behaviour change under conditions where the behaviour in question cannot be directly elicited and reinforced for practical or other reasons. However, the available data provide little or no support for the effectiveness of persuasive communications with regard to overt actions (Fleishmann, Harris and Burtt, 1955; Levitt, 1965; Maccoby, Romney, Adams and Maccoby, 1962).

BEHAVIOURS AND ROLES. The relationship between role change and behaviour change is rarely discussed directly in reference to behaviour modification. It is now proposed, however, that the topic of social learning and imitation (Bandura and Walters, 1963) may meaningfully be discussed in relation to role changes and behaviour changes.

Perhaps the most common definition of role (Biddle and Thomas, 1966) is the set of prescriptions defining what the behaviour of a member in a given position should be. In terms of social learning, this definition suggests that only certain behaviours consistent with the expectations of the group members are reinforced by the group members. For example, it has been found that lower-class patients expect a therapist to assume an active, medical role in the interview, and if he does not, they don't return (Overall and Aronson, 1963). Given the social forces directed towards the individual occupying a given social position to behave in prescribed ways, a change in roles congruent with a desired change in behaviour would appear to be a most simple and direct method of personal change. The same forces that prescribe role behaviours, however, also tend to prevent or restrict role change. The actor becomes dependent upon given reinforcements associated with role behaviours. Role changes occur infrequently, however. But role playing is a suitable and readily available substitute.

In the usual role-playing situation (Cameron, 1947; Moreno, 1934; Newcomb, 1950) there are no explicit instructions of how the actor should behave, although they may be aided by descriptions of positive models. In contrast, role playing in the experimental or therapeutic situation usually involves instructions to the subject or patient to imitate the behaviour of a real-life or symbolic model (Bandura and Walters, 1963). As Bandura and Walters point out (p. 91), role playing is particularly effective (in experimental situations, at least) since the role player dependently accepts the assigned role and then is reinforced for reproducing the model's behaviour.

Exposure to modelling stimuli may be viewed as a variation of role playing or vicarious role playing. A model, often on film, is positively reinforced or punished for a particular behaviour or behaviour sequence. The viewer's subsequent behaviour in similar situations is observed to be related to the model's behaviour. Bandura (1969, p. 120) attributes the effects of modelling to three factors: (1) the observer may acquire new response patterns; (2) observation of modelled behaviour and their consequences to the performer may strengthen or weaken inhibitory responses in observers; (3) the behaviour of others serves only as discriminative stimuli for the observer. An example cited is the situation where a person gazes intently into a display window and others respond in a similar manner.

The relation between behaviour change and role change is not thoroughly analysed as a synthesis of role theory and behaviour. In the description of social learning and imitation, behaviour modification approaches attempt to subsume role theory. A more balanced view suggests that imitation and social learning processes depend to a large extent upon a change in the role of the subject. The subject assumes the role of student. The therapist often assumes the role of teacher along with the attendant expectations involving the subject as a student. Or, for example, when a behaviour modifier intervenes in a family or group situation, the therapist disturbs the existing status pattern and generally makes possible a restructuring of the status hierarchy. In addition, the decision to participate in the experience with the change agent may itself represent an attitude change which may be propaedeutic to behaviour change. All those who base their personal change processes on one of the components in the personal change hierarchy attempt to incorporate a wide number of psychological processes within the framework by broadening the definition of the process or by failing to recognize the contribution of other frameworks.

BEHAVIOURS AND SELF CONCEPTS. By way of amelioration, behaviour modification theorists have recently attempted to incorporate mediating constructs such as self-esteem within their framework (Bandura, 1969, p. 91; Wahler and Pollio, 1968). Wahler and Pollio demonstrated that behavioural changes produced in a boy through social reinforcement altered favourably his self evaluation as well as his evaluation of others. In another instance, Bandura (1969, p. 37) invokes the concept of self-esteem to explain personal stability under conditions of minimal external social support or conflicting contingencies of reinforcement which are frequently encountered in the social environment. Eysenck (1959) anticipated a facet of the proposed Theory of Personal Change when he suggested that the way to change the self concept is to change behaviour.

More generally, behaviour therapists are compelled to consider cognitive factors which influence human behaviour and even autonomic functioning (Rackman and Teasdale, 1969). In aversion therapy as applied to alcoholism, for example, it may be necessary to invoke cognitive factors to explain why a patient avoids drinking outside the treament room even though he knows that drinking will not be followed by an electric shock.

Cognitive factors have been shown to have a profound influence on conditioning and extinction (Spence, 1965; Grings, 1965). As early as 1937 Cook and Harris reported that the magnitude of a GSR was increased when the subject was told that he would receive an electric shock, and decreased when he was told he would not receive shock. It is proposed here, that cognitive factors associated with the social self influence social behaviour in a way similar to that in which experimental sets influence learning behaviour.

Furthermore, it is proposed here that role frameworks and the imaginal processes associated with self–other orientations may be necessary to explain the long-term effects of behaviour modification. One of the questions which haunts the behaviour modifiers is the long-term effect of a change in a given behaviour. Few follow-up studies have been conducted. It is recognized, however, that return of the patient to his original environment frequently leads to the attenuation or extinction of the trained response. Similar observations have been made by T-group trainers (Dunnette and Campbell, 1969).

In an effort to make the individual less susceptible to the development of future maladaptive behaviour without the assistance of a therapist, behaviour therapists have begun to teach their patients self-control procedures. In these procedures, the subject is at once the patient and therapist (Fester, Nurnberger and Levitt, 1962; Goldeamond, 1965; Homme, 1965). For example, in an effort to control eating behaviour, an individual can arrange to buy food on a daily basis, and he can buy food which requires a great deal of preparation (Ferster, Nurnberger and Levitt, 1962). Self–other orientations are assumed to be cognitive control mechanisms or, in a sense, self-control mechanisms in that the self–other orientations

E

presumably developed under conditions of behaviour therapy are extended to similar situations thereby extending the treatment.

The above observations are consistent with the personal change framework proposed here, which assumes that an imbalance in the system at any one level creates a state of disequilibrium in the system. This imbalanced state is rectified most easily by altering the elements lower in the hierarchy, in this case, the specific behaviour rather than the role or self concept.

For example, it is frequently noted that individual therapy with married adults not infrequently is associated with a subsequent divorce. The divorce, it is now assumed, may be a change in the personal system congruent with a behaviour change or change in the self concept leading to stabilization of the personal system. It is also suggested that unless a change in role and self concept is observed, the behaviour change will be relatively short-lived. A synthesis of the levels of the personal system must be effected before change is assured at any one level.

Behaviour change processes are seen to involve attitude changes, role changes, and changes in the self concept; that is, behavioural change must be viewed within the context of the personal change system. A compelling question is whether or not there is an optimal level to begin the process of personal change. Consideration of the behaviour modification approach to fear responses is suggestive (Bandura, 1969, p. 74–5).

Bandura proposes that the establishment of complex social behaviour and the modification of existing response patterns can be achieved most effectively through a gradual process in which the subject participates in an orderly learning sequence that guides him stepwise towards more demanding performances. A sequence of intermediate goals should be outlined that lead gradually to more complex modes of behaviour.

With regard to fear responses such as snake phobias, the therapist first devises a ranked set of situations to which the client responds with increasing degrees of anxiety. Initially, the subject is exposed to the least threatening event under favourable conditions (the therapist is present) until his emotional responses are extinguished. Subsequent steps in the treatment process involve a gradual increase in the fear arousing properties of the aversive situation until emotional responsiveness to the most threatening stimuli is extinguished.

The personal change hierarchy may be assumed to be a similar stepwise guide towards more demanding performance. Attitude change is the least demanding, followed by value change, behaviour change, role change, and changes in the self concept.

3. ROLE CHANGE

Definitions of role usually indicate the relationship of the concept with other components of the personal change system but particularly behaviours and the self. Newcomb, Turner and Converse (1965, p. 323) write that role 'refers to the behavioral consistencies on the part of a person as he contributes to a more or less stable relationship with one or more others'. More generally, role is usually defined in terms of the behavioural expectations of the self and others for a person in a particular place in a social unit (Sarbin, 1954). In terms of behaviour modification, a role is a set of social behaviours which tend to be supported consistently by other members of the social unit, by the self, and by other individuals in the social field. In cognitive terms, role is an abstract pattern of ideas that is learned by the members of a social system (Jackson, 1966).

The ease with which an individual can conform to the expectations of others relative to a given role is assumed to vary from individual to individual as well as across roles. The difficulty in conforming to role expectations is usually referred to as 'role strain' or 'role conflict'. Role conflict may arise from a variety of sources (Secord and Backman, 1964, p. 488). Conflict may arise when: (a) one expectation requires behaviour that in some way is incompatible with another; (b) when an individual occupies two or more positions simultaneously; (c) when the individual's attitudes are incongruent with the role: and (d) when the individual's self concept is incongruent with the role expectations.

Thus, in describing role conflict, role theorists have had recourse to all levels of the Personal Change Theory. Again, however, no integrated approach to the levels was attempted, although the hierarchy is sometimes implicit. For examples, Reckless, Dinitz and Murray (1956) suggest that the self concepts of 'good' boys in a high-delinquency area serve as insulation against engaging in delinquent behaviour. The boys defined themselves in such a way that engaging in delinquent behaviour was incompatible with their self definitions.

A variety of processes have been described (see Secord and

Backman, 1964, pp. 519–20) which contribute to the resolution of role conflict. These include the development of a hierarchy of priorities in role obligations and restrictions on multiple position occupancy. Also actors who are particularly subject to sanctions are protected in a variety of ways. Finally, two roles may be amalgamated.

ROLES AND SELF CONCEPTS. Rarely do role theorists indicate a relationship between role change and changes in the self concept. Jackson (1966) pinpointed the difficulty of exploring the relation between self and role as the need for a more precise and operational definition of self as a system. Vincent (1964), however, found an increase in self-acceptance (using the California Personality Inventory) after marriage. An increase in self-esteem following election to the state legislature has also been noted by Ziller and Golding (1969).

Perhaps the most obdurate problem in role theory concerns the confluence of the concepts of self and role. The synthesis of these two concepts is critical in that a solution may lead to a more fruitful integration of individual psychology and sociology.

Newcomb (1950) confronted the problem and discussed it in terms of the relationship between self and others. He observed that since role behaviours involve a relationship between self and others, they are bound to be influenced by the ways in which oneself and others are perceived. The role behaviour of a politician who perceives himself as superior to others is quite certain to be different than a politician with a lower self-estimate.

Studies of occupational socialization also support the hypothesized selective interaction of self concept and role. Secord and Backman (1964) note that individuals reduce role strain by tending to interact only with those who confirm their self concept. Hoe (1962) also interpreted data relating discrepancies between the self concept and perception of the teacher role as indicating that large discrepancies led to dissatisfaction and drop-out from the profession. Finally, Stern and Scanlon (1958) found that selection of medical specialization was related to personality patterns, thereby minimizing the necessity of a change in the self concept. These studies again appear to support the assumption of the Personal Change Theory that the self concept is more resistant to change than role.

Newcomb (1950) also suggests that the adoption of social norms associated with certain roles become 'interiorized' in that they become part of the psychological make-up. The child, for example, not only *absorbs* but comes to use the frames of reference which he finds the people around him using. Thus, Newcomb assumes an inter-action between self–other concepts and roles. Role behaviours may influence the self concept, and the self concept may influence role behaviours.

In a more recent statement of role theory, Sarbin (1968) elaborates on the concept of interiorization. He refers to the intensity of role enactment as 'organismic involvement'. At the low end of the assumed continuum, the actor participates with minimal effort and visceral activity. The example is cited of a ticket seller at a neigh-bourhood theatre during a slow period of business. At the other end of the continuum such as may occur during religious conversions, the self and role are as one. An extreme example of the role's usurpation of the self is under voodoo conditions.

Sarbin (1968) also hypothesizes that the congruence of self and role leads to more convincing role enactment. Self-role congruence is assumed when the person seems to like the role, is involved in it, and is committed to it. This fit between the self and role is ordinarily described by saying that a person is not well suited to a particular role or that the job does not fit his personality. This statement in itself assumes the dominance of the self concept over the role. Indeed, Sarbin assumes implicitly the self–other orientation and role be-haviour hierarchy described here in the personal change system (see Sarbin, p. 524). Sarbin also assumes implicitly the remaining ele-ments of the personal change hierarchy, although he suggests that attitudes and behaviour levels are equivalent and are expected to change simultaneously following a role change (p. 555–6).

ROLE AND BEHAVIOURS   The most explicit statement of the relation-ship between role and behaviour as well as role and attitudes was found in an earlier report by Sarbin (1964). Sarbin cites evidence that gastric hunger contractions are influenced by role enactment (Lewis and Sarbin, 1943).

Role enactment also influences performance. Moreno's pioneer work in psychodrama (1934) is based partially on this assump-tion.

Sarbin also indicates the bridge between role enactment and be-haviour modification (1964, p. 197). In the usual role-playing situation the actor is in the presence of an audience which provides cues for expected behaviour and also reinforces behaviour which meets those expectations. For example, Zimmerman and Bauer (1956) showed that an imagined audience characterized as holding certain attitudes that were in opposition with the material to be learned and remembered influenced the retention of the material. Again, although the other components of the personal change system are sometimes related to role theory, the framework is constricted. The identity of the theory is preserved at the cost of narrowness.

The bridging concept between role theory and behaviour modification is socialization. Socialization is usually defined (Secord and Backman, 1964) as an 'interactional process whereby a person's behavior is modified to conform with expectations held by members of the groups to which he belongs' (pp. 525–6). Both attitudinal and behavioural changes occurring through learning are relevant. It has remained for behaviour modifiers, however, to make the major contribution to the socialization framework (Bandura and Walters, 1963; Parke, 1969). The latter works, in turn, have not benefited from a consideration of the role theory. Each group of investigators appear to be content within the more defensible but more limited micro-theories (Merton, 1957). A move towards the amalgamation of the two frameworks is suggested in Sarbin's (1968) updating of the role theory chapter in *Handbook of Social Psychology*. He devotes one page to behaviour modification and social learning (p. 548). More concretely, Jackson (1966) has developed a measurement model for norms and roles which provides a tool for investigating whether more emphasis is placed upon reward or punishment in the social control process.

4. SELF THEORIES

The Personal Change Theory proposes that the self concept is the anchoring characteristic of the system. Assuming the hierarchical arrangement of the elements in the system, it is readily understandable why the history of the study of personal change is dominated by a concern with the self in relation to significant others. If a change in the self can be effected, a higher probability is created for changes in the remaining elements. Yet, those who have subscribed to self theories have not demonstrated convincingly the efficiency of their frameworks.

Self theories are phenomenological. The individual's subjective view of himself in relation to significant others is presumed to mediate social stimuli and social responses. The serial order effects involved among these variables are not ignored with impunity.

As has already been indicated, the self concept emerges as an overarching cognitive category out of the individual's interaction with his environment. The self concept, in turn, increasingly acts as a regulator of behaviour particularly in critical or novel situations (Jones and Gerard, 1967, p. 184). The self concept is a personal theory of behaviour to which the individual has recourse under novel conditions or when inconsistency threatens. The phenomenal self assumes monitoring and steering functions under conditions of stress, but is itself shaped by outcomes of behaviour.

It is assumed here, that through the self concept as a mediating construct the individual maintains stability yet permits adaptability of the personal system through social monitoring procedures. The monitoring processes focus upon personal records of changes in the social environment as well as changes in personal attitudes, values, behaviours, and roles. The monitoring processes vary in degree of systematization, but at the very least, gross deviations from some informal base line is assumed to be within the range of awareness of most persons.

For the most part, the monitoring processes function in the service of the stability of the self concept: the maintenance of a congruence between the phenomenal field of experience and the conceptual structure of the self. Such a condition of congruence Rogers notes (1951, p. 532) would represent freedom from internal strain and anxiety.

In support of the proposed hierarchy of personal change, Rogers (1951) observes that the individual will maintain a self picture completely at variance with reality. The individual hopes that events will change so that it won't be necessary to change the self concept.

Adaptability of the personal system derives from the characteristics of the system which permits incongruence among one or more elements of the hierarchy. As noted at the outset, it is assumed that attitudes may be changed without too much threat to the personal system. The disequilibrium created by a change in attitudes is not so great as to force a restructuring of the entire system. The conflict among levels of the personal system may remain 'encapsulated' at that level.

Similarly, values, behaviours, and even roles may each be returned to the initial state of equilibrium. Thus, for example, it is proposed that unless a positive change in self-esteem accompanies changes in behaviour of the child following behaviour modification procedures, the therapy should be continued until such time as the desired change in the self concept is observed.

Indeed, clients are assumed to function with different ranges of acceptable rates of change, and these rates, in turn, have been found to be related to social behaviour (Mossman and Ziller, 1970). Acceptable rates of change of the self system is itself, then, another aspect of the self concept.

Several other facets of the self concept (here, self–other orientations) have been described earlier in this paper. They include self-esteem, social interest, and complexity of the self. Of these, self-esteem is assumed to be associated with the stability of the self system. Persons with high self-esteem are more consistent in their behaviour across situations (Mossman and Ziller, 1968). This consistency is assumed to derive, in part, from the subject's willingness to impose personal structure on the system, thereby exerting some control over the situation. The person with high self-esteem in contrast to those with low self-esteem is less a victim of his environment and more a controller or even creator of his environment.

The second component of self–other orientations is social interest or the perception of the self as included within the force field of significant others. It has previously been found that persons with high social interest tend to monitor positive as opposed to negative social reinforcements. It is readily seen that unless the social interest of the individual is changed, very little may be accomplished by changing his attitudes towards other persons.

Although Rogers' Self Theory is consistent with many of the propositions of the present framework, approaches to personal change which stem from his Self Theory also suffer from the failure to consider other elements of the personal change hierarchy. Also, Rogers was compelled to depend upon self reports for his measures of the self concept.

One of Rogers' major assumptions was that the self concept can be changed directly. It was assumed that (a) the self develops out of the organism's interaction with the environment, (b) the self may intraject the values of other people, (c) the self strives for consistency, (d) the organism's behaviour is consistent with the self, and (e) the self may change as a result of maturation and learning.

In order to change a dysfunctional self concept, a non-threatening therapeutic micro-social environment is arranged through a client-therapist dyad. Under these warm and accepting conditions the person is encouraged to explore slowly the feelings which threaten his security. Slowly, too, these hitherto threatening feelings are assimilated into the self-structure. Rogers also posits the need for a continuous monitoring process to see whether a change in the client's value structure is required.

For an evaluation of the self concept, Rogers relied on Stephenson's (1953) Q-technique. In this approach a number of items describing the self ('I am a submissive person') are sorted along a scale in terms of how the client sees himself. Next, the same cards are again sorted along the same scale in terms of how the person would most like to be.

Although in terms of the personal change hierarchy the Rogerian method may be subsumed under the self–other orientation level, it is apparent again that a multi-level strategy is probably in operation. By the act of volunteering for counselling, the person becomes a client with the therapist. The client is subtly encouraged to play the role of therapist with regard to himself under the supervision of a master therapist. Certain behaviours under these role conditions are supported by the therapist. Finally, and unfortunately, the outcome of the therapy is not a change in the self concept but rather a self report of change. In terms of the personal change framework, the focus of the therapy is not the self but simply a series of attitudes about the self. An index of the extent to which these attitudes are interiorized is outside the scope of the measuring devices.

As suggested earlier, perhaps a direct approach to changing the self-esteem component of the self concept is impossible. A change in the self concept is the desired outcome of personal change procedures but the change processes must involve changes in attitudes, values, behaviours, and roles. Only when these changes are reflected in the self–social schemas of the person is there much assurance that the personal system has reorganized and has achieved a new state of equilibrium required for personal stability. If the desired changes in the self–other orientations have not been achieved, the client is likely to revert to earlier attitudes, behaviours, and roles.

The pivotal point of the Theory of Personal Change concerns the proposed cognitive outcomes and the communication of the proposed social schemas (Ziller, Megas and De Cencio, 1964; Ziller, Long,

Ramana and Reddy, 1968; Ziller, 1969; Ziller, 1970). It is assumed here that the human organism finds it expedient to order and categorize or to structure generally the multitude of self-surrounding stimuli. The processes used by the respondents to structure the environment and especially the social environment are expected to be somewhat idiosyncratic, but owing to commonality among human experience, sensory processes, and classification systems, the evolving abstraction systems possess a sufficient common basis for a communication system. Some of these processes include extent of separation between objects (Kuethe, 1962), number of objects in a category, and the ordering of objects (De Soto, London and Handel, 1965).

For example, with regard to the social schema of self-esteem the most relevant ordering process is what De Soto, London and Handel refer to as 'spatial paralogic' and 'linear ordering'. It is observed that people are prone to place elements in a linear ordering to the exclusion of other structures, and that they handle linear ordering more easily than most other structures (Coombs, Raeffa and Thrall, 1954; De Soto, London and Handel, 1960). Indeed De Soto, London and Handel note that serial ordering proceeds more directly in a rightward direction than in a leftward direction. The tendency to attribute greater importance to the object placed at the extreme left position in a horizontal display has been noted by Morgan (1944).

The measure of self-esteem developed here utilized the serial ordering predilection of the subjects within a social context. The measure involves presenting a horizontal array of circles and a list of significant others (including the self) such as those used by Kelly (1955). The task requires the subject to assign each person to a circle. The score is the weighted position of the self. In accordance with the cultural norm, positions to the left are assumed to be associated with higher self-esteem. It has been found, for example, that depressed neuropsychiatric patients have lower self-esteem than other patients (Ziller, Megas and De Cencio, 1964), that persons with high self-esteem participate more frequently and more consistently across group discussion sessions (Mossman and Ziller, 1968), and that political candidates who are elected to office tend to rise in self-esteem, whereas those who lose tend to drop in self-esteem (Ziller and Golding, 1969). Studies repeatedly show that low-status social elements such as 'someone you know who is unhappy' are located more frequently on the right side of the assumed left–right hierarchy (Ziller, Hagey, Smith and Long, 1969).

A number of social schemas have been identified including social interest, complexity of the self-concept, self-centrality, openness, identification, inclusion, power, and marginality (Ziller, 1970). These cognitive maps of self and others are assumed to screen and order social stimuli and in general mediate the social response. They are assumed to operate a cognitive control mechanism to which the organism has recourse particularly under conditions of stress. It is also assumed that these schemas are enduring relative to roles, behaviours, values, and attitudes, but like the other components of the personal change hierarchy, they too are subject to change albeit much more slowly.

Heretofore self theorists have been concerned almost exclusively with the social schema of self-esteem (Wylie, 1961; Coopersmith, 1967). The emphasis on self-esteem may have been determined, in part, by difficulties of measurement which may have discouraged the proliferation of self constructs. With the advent of a component approach to social schemas, self theories need no longer be restricted to the narrow confines associated with the concept of self-esteem. Programmes of personal change may be designed to fit the patterns of self–other orientations which are most significantly involved for the individual. It is not necessary to assume that every personal problem stems from concerns with self-esteem, although it does appear to be a key concern. Moreover, more complex patterns of personal change may now be explored and the outcomes evaluated. Recently, for example, the alienation syndrome has been identified and operationally defined in terms of low self-esteem, low social interest, and high self-centrality (Ziller, 1969).

The major criticism of self theories comes from those concerned with behaviour theories, but particularly those who adhere to the behaviour modification framework (Bandura, 1969; Mischel, 1968). Usually the utility of internal constructs is denied. The criticisms are well founded and stem from the history of psychoanalysis with the proliferation of constructs which elude measurement and experimental verification.

The conflict between these two theoretical positions is one of the oldest in psychology. The initial conflict between S–R theories versus gestalt psychology has given way to the conflict between behaviour modification and self theories. Increasingly, however, one finds that each school of thought moves in the direction of the opposing school. S-R theories have introduced intervening constructs leading to more extended connections between the stimulus and the response (see Berger and Lambert, 1968). Cognitive theorists have remained somewhat less compromising (see Zajonc, 1969). Bandura (1969) uses the concept of self-esteem repeatedly, and in another classic account of behaviour modification frameworks (Frank, 1969), a critique of behaviour modification suggests that this area too may have recourse to intervening constructs such as the subject's perception of the situation.

In the present paper, self theorists are combined with cognitive frameworks to develop a Theory of Self–other Orientation and accompanying measures of the central constructs employing cognitive maps of self and others. Concepts of the self are discussed by most theorists in the area of personal change. These concepts are dismissed with alacrity by many but with reluctance by some. Progress in science is tripartite and includes theory, measurement, and research. Perhaps the Theory of Personal Change has been truncated by the failure to develop adequate measures of the self concept.

Overview

An omnibus framework for personal change has been described here which incorporates theories of attitude and value change, behaviour modification, role theory, and self theories. The pivotal construct concerns self–other schemas, cognitive maps of the self in relation to significant other persons. It is assumed that these social schemas include self-esteem, social interest, self-centrality, self-complexity, power, identification, majority identification, openness, inclusion, and marginality. These constructs are assumed to mediate social stimuli and social responses. Changes in social schemas are assumed to be the ultimate objective of all approaches to personal change.

Five approaches to personal change were discussed beginning with attitude change, value change, behaviour change, role change, and changes in the self concept. The five change approaches are assumed to describe a hierarchy of personal change. The hierarchy derives from the relative resistance to change associated with the five components. For example, attitudes are less difficult to change than behaviours. Social schemas are the most resistant to change and make for the stability of the system. The individual is less committed to attitudes than self concepts. The ease of change at some levels in the hierarchy makes for flexibility within stability of the personal system. Given the flexibility within the system, the organism is required to constantly monitor changes in attitudes, values, behaviour, roles, and the self in order to maintain congruence among these components of the personal system.

Under conditions where one of the elements of the hierarchical system is changed, a state of disequilibrium is effected and a press towards equilibrium is generated. The press is greater towards components lower in the hierarchy, however. A change at the higher levels is assumed to be associated with greater imbalance and a greater likelihood of a change in the self system. Thus, changes at several levels of the hierarchy simultaneously may be expected to lead to a change in the self system.

The Theory of Personal Change contrasts with most micro-theories of personal change reviewed here which emanate from a few basic constructs such as attitudes or roles. Within a limited field, these uni-factor theories seem to summarize most elegantly the existing research, and undoubtedly form the basis for useful processes of personal change within a limited area of application. The shortcomings of these micro-theories appear when they are aggrandized and used in lieu of a more general theory of personal change. It is then that micro-theories serve as the Procrustean beds for many applied situations which do not fit neatly within the limited purview. More importantly, however, micro-theories tend to truncate the development of more universal frameworks by fostering chauvinism.

A more helical approach to theory development is required. Micro-theories may serve as points of reference within a more open theoretical system.

One of the crucial tests of the proposed helical Theory of Personal Change should involve two groups of subjects under conditions of behaviour modification in relation to a given behaviour disorder. It is maintained that the duration of the treatment effects will be longer for those subjects whose behaviour changes are accompanied by appropriate changes in self–other orientations.

Perhaps the topic of alienation may serve to illustrate the efficacy of the helical approach. Alienation is a protean term. Feurer (1963) proposed that the term 'is used to convey the emotional tone which accompanies any behavior in which the person is compelled to act self-destructively'.

Early measures of the concept involved the subjects' attitudes. For example, one of the items used by Dean (1961) was 'Sometimes, I feel all alone in the world.'

Seeman (1959) attempted to clarify the concept in terms of five major components: powerlessness, meaninglessness, normlessness, isolation, and self-estrangement. Several of these components were described in terms of reinforcements or expectation of reinforcement. For example, powerlessness is conceived as 'the expectancy or probability held by the individual that his own behavior cannot determine the occurrence of the outcomes, or reinforcements that he seeks' (p. 784). Estrangement is defined by Seeman as a condition in which the individual is engaged in activities which are not self rewarding.

Recently, Lewinson, Weinstein and Shaw (1968) have proposed a behaviour modification approach to alienationed individuals. A treatment of depressed women is described involving increasing the number of positive reinforcements received by the subject. The treatment also involves training the subjects in the requisite social skills for eliciting social reinforcements.

In terms of role theory, alienation may be seen as role strain. Certain roles associated with minority group members and the aged are frequently cited as examples of alienation (Josephson and Josephson, 1962).

In terms of the self concept, it is proposed (Ziller, 1969) that three self–other orientations are definitive with regard to social adaptation: self-esteem, social interest, and self-centrality. Self-esteem as used here is concerned with the individual's stability of behaviour stemming from his recourse to self-reinforcement under conditions of stress. The person with high self-esteem is somewhat insulated from moment to moment changes in the environment or lack of reinforcement from the environment, whereas the person with low self-esteem is particularly subject to environmental contingencies, either positive or negative, and is inclined towards inconsistency. Faunce (1968) has suggested that alienation is an incongruence in self evaluation and the evaluation by others.

Social interest is used here to represent the perception of inclusion of self and other, and the expectation of positive reinforcement from the other. Social interest is associated with knowledge and acceptance of the norms of a primary group.

In terms of alienation, Seeman's (1959) component of isolation may be similar to the concept of social interest. Isolation refers to the detachment of the individual from common cultural standards.

Self-centrality as used here concerns the use of the self as opposed to others as the key point of reference. The concept is associated with withdrawal from social situations. The high centrality individual disengages himself from others or from social norms and develops a private frame of reference.

Inherently, the socialization process involves conflict between satisfaction of individual and group needs. The inability to maintain a workable degree of stability under conditions of self–other conflict is assumed to stem from inadequate guides for behaviour (low self-esteem and low social interest) which are assumed to lead to withdrawal (high self-centrality).

Since self-esteem is socially derived and reinforced, reduced social interest also is associated, in turn, with reduced self-estimate, which, in turn, is associated with increased self-centrality and reduced social interest. The process is cyclical and degenerative. Increased self-centrality tends to lead to further reduction in social interest and so on, as a function of the situation. The cycling and interaction effects of low self-esteem, low social interest, and high self-centrality is assumed to be the essence of the concept of alienation.

In a series of studies (Ziller, 1969) the alienation syndrome was found among behaviour problem children, neuropsychiatric patients, and a minority group (French Canadian children in Montreal, see Henderson, Long and Gantcheff, 1970), and to some extent among the ageing and Negro children in 1965.

Consistent with the helical theory of personal change, it is now maintained that attitude, behaviour, roles, and self–other orientations must all be considered in the study of alienation. Attitudes may indicate an inclination towards alienation, as do behaviours and certain positions in the social system, but a clear set towards alienation cannot be assumed until the three self–other schemas associated with the alienation syndrome are in evidence: low self-esteem, low social interest, and high self-centrality.

Essentially a chain of middle range theories of personal change has been proposed here. Links have been proposed between theories of attitude change, value change, behaviour modification, role theory, and the self system. Perhaps, however, this chain of theories or helical approach is but an intermediate step towards the development of a more unified theory of personal change. Nevertheless, the helical approach to theory construction is an alternative to middle range theories (Merton, 1957) and general theories.

REFERENCES

ADLER, A. *The practice and theory of individual psychology.* New York: Harcourt, 1927.

AYLLON, T. & HAUGHTON, E. Modification of symptomatic verbal behavior of mental patients. *Behavior Research and Therapy*, 1964, 2, 87–97.

AYLLON, T. & MICHAEL, J. The psychiatric nurse as a behavioral engineer. *Journal of the Experimental Analysis of Behavior*, 1959, 2, 323–34.

BANDURA, A. *Principles of behavior modification.* New York: Holt, Rinehart, Winston, 1969.

BANDURA, A. & WALTERS, R. H. *Social learning and personality development.* New York: Holt, Rinehart, Winston, 1963.

BEM, D. J. An experimental analysis of self-persuasion. *Journal of Experimental Social Psychology*, 1965, 1, 199–218.

BEM, D. J. Self-perception: An alternative interpretation of cognitive dissonance phenomena. *Psychological Review*, 1967, 74, 183–200.

BERGER, S. M. & LAMBERT, W. W. Stimulus-response theory in contemporary social psychology. In G. Lindzey & E. Aronson (eds.), *Handbook of Social Psychology*, I, 2nd edition. Reading, Massachusetts: Addison-Wesley, 1968, pp. 81–178.

BIDDLE, B. J. & THOMAS, E. J. *Role Theory.* New York: Wiley, 1966.

BREHM, J. W. & COHEN, A. R. *Explorations in cognitive dissonance.* New York: Wiley, 1962.

BRIM, O. G. JR. & WHEELER, S. *Socialization after childhood: two essays.* New York: John Wiley & Sons, 1966.

CAMERON, N. *The psychology of behavior disorders, a bio-social interpretation.* Boston: Houghton-Mifflin, 1947.

CAMPBELL, J. P. & DUNNETTE, M. D. Effectiveness of T-group experiences in managerial training and development. *Psychological Bulletin*, 1968, 70, 73–104.

CASSIRER, E. *The essay on man.* New Haven: Yale University Press, 1944.

COHEN, A. R. Some implications of self-esteem for social influence. In C. I. Hovland & I. L. Janis (eds.), *Personality and Persuasibility.* New Haven: Yale University Press, 1959, pp. 102–20.

COOLEY, C. H. Personal competition. *Economic Studies,* 1899, 4, 73–183.

COOMBS, C. H., RAEFFA, H, & THRALL, R. M. Some views on mathematical models and measurement theory. *Psychological Review,* 1954, 61, 132–44.

COOPERSMITH, S. *The antecedents of self esteem.* San Francisco: Freeman, 1967.

DAVISON, G. C. & VALENS, S. Maintenance of self-attributed and drug-attributed behavior change. *Journal of Personality and Social Psychology,* 1969, 11, 25–33.

DEAN, D. G. Alienation: its meaning and measurement. *American Sociological Review,* 1961, 26, 753–9.

DESOTO, C. B., LONDON, M. & HANDEL, S. Social reasoning and spatial paralogic. *Journal of Personality and Social Psychology,* 1965, 2, 513–21.

ERIKSON, E. H. *Young man Luther: A study in psychoanalysis and history.* New York: Norton, 1958.

EYSENCK, H. J. Learning theory and behavior therapy. *Journal of mental science,* 1959, 105, 61–75.

FAUNCE, A. *Problems of industrial society.* New York: McGraw-Hill, 1968.

FERSTER, C. B., NURNBERGER, J. I. & LEVITT, E. B. The control of eating. *Journal of Mathetics,* 1962, 1, 87–110.

FEUER, S. What is alienation? the career of a concept. In M. Stein & A. Vidlich (eds.), *Sociology on trial.* Englewood Cliffs, New Jersey: Prentice-Hall, 1963.

FESTINGER, L. *A theory of cognitive dissonance.* Evanston: Row, Peterson, 1957.

FISHBEIN, M. An investigation of the relationship between beliefs about an object and attitude toward that object. *Human Relations,* 1963, 16, 233–9.

FISHBEIN, M. Attitude and the prediction of behavior. In M. Fishbein (ed.), *Readings in attitude theory and measurement.* New York: Wiley, 1967.

FLEISHMANN, E., HARRIS, E. & BURTT, H. *Leadership and super-*

vision in industry: An evaluation of a supervisory training program. Columbia-Ohio State University, Bureau of Educational Research, 1955.

FRANK, C. M. *Behavior Therapy.* New York: McGraw-Hill, 1969.

GERARD, H. B., BLEVANS, S. A. & MALCOLM, T. Self evaluation and the evaluation of choice alternatives. *Journal of Personality,* 1964, 32, 395–410.

GOLDIAMOND, I. Self control procedures in personal behavior problems. *Psychological Reports.* 1965, 17, 851–68.

GRINGS, W. Verbal-perceptual factors in the conditioning of autonomic responses. In W. Prokasy (ed.), *Classical conditioning.* New York: Appleton-Century Crofts, 1965, pp. 71–89.

HEIDER, F. *The psychology of interpersonal relations.* New York: Wiley, 1958.

HENDERSON, E. H., LONG, BARBARA H. & GANTCHEFF, HELENE. Self-other orientations of French and English Canadian adolescents. *Canadian Journal of Psychology* (in press).

HOE, BETTY H. Occupational satisfaction as a function of self-role congruency. Unpublished master's thesis, University of Nevada, 1962.

HOLLANDER, E. P. *Principles and methods of social psychology.* London: Oxford University Press, 1967.

HOMME, L. E. Perspectives in psychology—XXIV: Control of coverants, the operants of the mind. *Psychological Record,* 1965, 15, 501–11.

HOROWITZ, E. L. The development of attitudes toward the Negro. *Archives of Psychology,* 1936, 28. No. 194.

JACKSON, J. A. conceptual and measurement model for norms and roles. *Pacific Sociological Review,* 1966, 9, 35–47.

JANIS, I. L. & FIELD, P. B. Sex differences and personality factors related to persuasibility. In C. I. Hovland & I. L. Janis (eds.), *Personality and persuasibility.* New Haven: Yale University Press, 1959, pp. 55–68.

JANIS, I. L. & KING, B. T. The influence of role-playing on opinion change. *Journal of Abnormal and Social Psychology,* 1954, 49, 211–18.

JONES, E. E. & GERARD, H. B. *Foundations of social psychology.* New York: Wiley, 1967.

JOSEPHSON, E. & JOSEPHSON, MARY. *Man alone: alienation in modern society.* New York: Dell publishing Company, 1962.

KATZ, D. I., SARNOFF, I., & McCLINTOCK, C. G. Ego defense and attitude change. *Human Relations*, 1956, 9, 27–46.

KELLY, G. A. *The psychology of personal constructs*. New York: Norton, 1955.

KELMAN, H. C. Processes of opinion change. *Public Opinion Quarterly*, 1961, 25, 57–78.

KING, B. T. & JANIS, I. L. Comparison of the effectiveness of improvised versus non-improvised role-playing in producing opinion changes. *Human Relations*, 1956, 9, 177–86.

KUETHE, J. L. Social schemas. *Journal of Abnormal and Social Psychology*, 1962, 64, 31–6.

LECKY, P. *Self-consistency: A theory of personality*. New York: Island Press, 1945.

LEVENTHAL, H. & PERLOE, S. I. A relationship between self-esteem and persuasibility. *Journal of Abnormal and Social Psychology*, 1962, 64, 385–8.

LEVITT, T. *Industrial purchasing behavior: A study of communication effects*. Boston: Harvard University Press, 1965.

LEWIN, K. *A dynamic theory of personality*. New York: McGraw, 1935.

LEWINSON, P. M., WEENSTEIN, M. S. & SHAW, D. A. Depression: A clinical-research approach. *Proceedings of the American Association of Behavior Therapy*, San Francisco, 1968 (in press).

LEWIS, J. H. & SARBIN, T. K. Studies in psychosomatics: The influence of hypnotic stimulation on gastric hunger contractions. *Psychosomatic Medicine*, 1943, 5, 125–31.

LIEBERMAN, S. The effects of changes in roles on the attitudes of role occupants. *Human Relations*, 1956, 9, 385–402.

LIFTON, R. J. *Thought reform and the psychology of totalism: A study of brainwashing in China*. New York: Morton, 1961.

MACCOBY, M., ROMNEY, A. K., ADAMS, J. S. & MACCOBY, E. E *'Critical periods' in seeking and accepting information*. Stanford: Stanford University Institute for Communication Research, 1962.

MALEWSKI, A. The influence of positive and negative self-evaluation on post-decisional dissonance. *Polish Sociological Bulletin*, 1962, 3–4, 39–49.

MASLOW, A. H. *Motivation and personality*. New York: Harper & Brothers, 1954.

McGUIRE, W. The nature of attitudes and attitude change. In L. G. Lindzey & E. Aronson (eds.), *Handbook of Social Psychology*,

2nd edition, vol. III. *The individual in a social context*. Reading, Massachusetts: Addison-Wesley, 1968.

MEAD, G. H. *Mind, self, and society*. Chicago: University of Chicago Press, 1934.

MERTON, R. K. *Social theory and social structure*. Glencoe, Ill.: Free Press, 1957.

MISCHEL, W. *Personality and assessment*. New York: Wiley, 1968.

MORENO, J. L. *Who shall survive?* Washington, D. C.: Nervous and Mental Disease Publication Co., 1934. New York: Beacon, 1953.

MORGAN, J. J. B. Effects of non-rational factors in inductive reasoning. *Journal of Experimental Psychology*, 1944, 34, 159–68.

MOSSMAN, B. M. & ZILLER, R. C. Acceptable rates of change and the use of coercion in a persuasion situation. Paper read at the West Coast Small Group Meetings, Los Angeles, California, 1970.

MOSSMAN, B. M. & ZILLER, R. C. Self esteem and consistency of social behavior. *Journal of Abnormal Psychology*, 1968, 73, 363–7.

NEWCOMB, T. M. *Social Psychology*. New York: Dryden Press, 1950.

NEWCOMB, T. M., TURNER, R. H. & CONVERSE, P. E. *Social Psychology*, New York: Holt, Rinehart, and Winston, 1965.

OVERALL, BETTY & ARONSON, HARRIET. Expectations of psychotherapy in patients of lower socioeconomic class. *American Journal of Orthopsychiatry*, 1963, 33, 421–30.

PARKE, R. D. *Readings in social development*. New York: Holt, Rinehart, and Winston, 1969.

POLANYI, M. *The tacit dimension*. New York: Doubleday, 1966.

RACHMAN, S. J. & TEASDALE, J. Aversion therapy: An appraisal. In C. M. Franks (ed.), *Behavior Therapy*. New York: McGraw-Hill, 1969, pp. 279–320.

ROBY, T. B. Commitment. *Behavioral Science*, 1960, 5, 253–64.

RECKLESS, W. C., DINITZ, S. & MURRAY, ELLEN. Self-concept as an insulator against delinquency. *American Sociological Review*, 1956, 21, 744–6.

ROGERS, C. R. *Client-centred therapy: its current practice, implications and theory*. Boston: Houghton, 1951.

ROSENBERG, M. J. Cognitive reorganization in response to the hypnotic reversal of attitudinal affect. *Journal of Personality*, 1960, 28, 39–63.

SARBIN, T. R. Role theoretical interpretation of psychological change.

In P. Worchel & D. Byrne (eds.), *Personality Change*. New York: John Wiley & Sons, 1964, pp. 176–219.

SARBIN, T. R. Role theory. In G. Lindzey & E. Aronson (eds.), *Handbook of Social Psychology*, I, 2nd edition. Reading, Massachusetts: Addison-Wesley, 1968.

SCHEIN, E. H. *Coercive persuasion*. New York: Norton, 1951.

SCOTT, W. A. Attitude change through reward of verbal behavior. *Journal of Abnormal and Social Psychology*, 1957, 55, 72–5.

SECORD, P. F. & BACKMAN, C. W. *Social psychology*. New York: McGraw-Hill, 1964.

SEEMAN, M. On the meaning of alienation. *American Sociological Review*, 1959, 24, 783–91.

SHERIF, CAROLYN W. & SHERIF, M. (eds.), *Attitude, ego-involvement and change*. New York: Wiley, 1967, pp. 458–67.

SKINNER, B. G. Operant behavior. *American Psychologist*, 1963, 18, 503–15.

SKINNER, B. F. *Science and human behavior*. New York: Macmillan, 1953.

SMITH, E. E. The power of dissonance techniques to change attitudes. *Public Opinion Quarterly*, 1961, 25, 626–39.

SMITH, M. B. Attitude change. In D. L. Sells (ed.), *Encylopedia of the social sciences*. New York: Crowell-Collier & Macmillan, 1968.

SMITH, M. B. Untitled memorandum. In S. S. Stauffer *et al*. The American Soldier. Vol. I: *Adjustment During Army Life*. Princeton University Press, 1949.

SPENCE, K. W. Cognitive factors in the extinction of the conditioned eyelid response in humans. *Science*, 1965, 140, 1224–5.

STEPHENSON, W. *The study of behavior*. Chicago: University of Chicago Press, 1953.

STERN, G. C. & SCANLON, J. C. Pediatric lions and gynecological lambs. *Journal of Medical Education*, 1958, 33, 12–18.

STEVENSON, H. W. & STEWART, E. C. A developmental study of racial awareness in young children. *Child Development*, 1958, 29, 399–409.

SULLIVAN, H. S. *The inter-personal theory of psychiatry*. New York: Norton, 1953.

VAUGHAN, G. M. The development of ethnic attitudes in New Zealand school children. *Genetic Psychology Monographs*, 1964, 70, 135–75.

Vincent, C. E. Socialization data in research on young marrieds. *Acta Sociologica*, 1964, 8.

Wahler, R. G. & Pollio, H. R. Behavior and insight: A case study in behavior therapy. *Journal off Experimental Research in Personality*, 1968, 3, 45–56.

Watson, J. B. *Behaviorism*. New York: Norton, 1930.

Watson, R. I. The experimental tradition and clinical psychology. In A. J. Bachrach (ed.), *Experimental Foundations of Clinical Psychology*. New York: Basic Books, 1962.

Wilson, W. C. Development of ethnic attitudes in adolescence. *Child Development*, 1963, 34, 247–56.

Witkins, H. A., Dyk, R. B., Faterson, H. F., Goodenough, D. R. & Karp, S. A. *Psychological differentiation*. New York: Wiley, 1962.

Wylie, Ruth C. *The self concept*. Lincoln: University of Nebraska Press, 1961.

Zajonc, R. B. Cognitive theories of social psychology. In G. Lindzey & E. Aronson (eds.), *Handbook of Social Psychology*, I, 2nd edition. Reading, Massachusetts: Addison-Wesley, 1968, pp. 320–411.

Ziller, R. C. The alienation syndrome: A triadic pattern of self–other orientation. *Sociometry*, 1969, 287–300.

Ziller, R. C. *The social self schemas of the self and significant others*. New York: Holt, Rinehart, Winston (in press).

PART III The Assessment of Personality

6 Personality and Social Behaviour

MICHAEL ARGYLE

Historical Introduction

Social psychologists have been aware for a long time that there are wide individual differences in the behaviour of experimental subjects which cannot be accounted for in terms of the experimental conditions. These variations are assumed to be due to the 'personalities' of the subjects. However we have also been aware for some time that there is little consistency in persuasibility, conformity, etc. across different situations, and that existing personality tests give very poor predictions of such behaviour (Mann, 1959). We were therefore very interested in recent developments in personality research, which showed that there is little consistency in other areas of behaviour, and seemed to cast doubt on the usefulness of traits (Mischel, 1968).

What I shall call the 'traditional trait model' was taken over from the study of intelligence, and led typically to the factor analysis of tests and measures of various kinds. It was hoped that, as in the case of intelligence, the factors would prove to have some degree of generality across different kinds of responses, and that the latter could in turn be predicted from tests of some kind. This model also involved S–R thinking, where a trait can be seen as a disposition to respond to a range of S's by a similar kind of R (Alston, Chap. 4). However it was always supposed that a wide range of situations would lead to a similar response. It was also recognized that the situation was also a source of variance; indeed experiments were concerned with the effects of varying the situation. It was however believed by many that persons would be more powerful predictors than situations—while sociologists usually believed the opposite. This controversy led to the person v. situation variance studies, which will be discussed below. The view which was widely accepted for a time was a dispositional model, which allowed for an additive effect of situation.

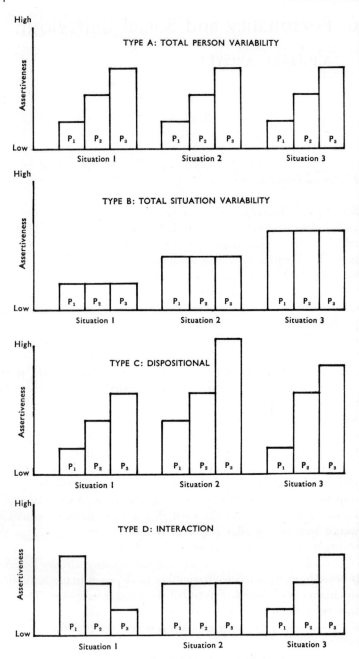

Fig. 1. Four types of variability in social behaviour
(from Argyle & Little 1972)

Most traits theorists also believed that there should be consistency between persons, in that if A is found to be more extraverted than B in one situation, the same rank order should be found in other situations. In fact such consistency is found to be very low; another way of describing this is to say that there is a lot of $P \times S$ variance. Consider the typical lateness of Tom, Dick and Harry in three situations. Traditional trait theory would expect something like Table 1.

TABLE 1
(from Argyle, 1975)

Minutes late for	Lecture	Tutorial	Coffee	Person means
Tom	0	3	6	3
Dick	3	6	9	6
Harry	6	9	12	9
situation means	3	6	9	6

Very often, however, the pattern is more like that shown in Table 2. Here there are low or negative correlations between situations, there is $P \times S$ variance, and 'inconsistency' across the situations, though the person and situational means are the same as before.

TABLE 2
(from Argyle, 1975)

Minutes late for	Lecture	Tutorial	Coffee	Person means
Tom	−6	3	12	3
Dick	3	6	9	6
Harry	12	9	6	9
situation means	3	6	9	6

For this and other reasons the traditional trait model has been abandoned by most psychologists, in favour of the 'interactionist' model. The Lewin formula $B = f(P, S)$ was revived, and traits were thought of as unseen properties of persons which interacted with properties of situations to generate behaviour. This formulation was by no means new in psychology, and had been proposed by Murray,

Lewin and others (Ekehammer, 1974). It was now associated with two kinds of research, one of them new. A long series of studies was carried out to apportion variance between persons, situations and P × S interaction. And special interest was taken in studies in which both personality and situational variables were manipulated. This in turn led to attempts to categorize, dimensionalize and generally measure situations. In addition new ways were sought to conceptualize persons in ways which would avoid the difficulties of traits (e.g. Mischel, 1974; Alston, op. cit.).

The interactionist model is still being actively debated (Endler and Hunt, 1976), but a number of difficulties have become clear—for example the impossibility of partitioning variance in a meaningful way, and the fact that persons both choose and alter situations. Research on situations casts some doubt on the usefulness of a dimensional analysis. I shall put forward an alternative approach, in which situations are seen as discrete structures, with distinctive generative rules.

The Traditional Trait Model

I. VARIANCE DUE TO PERSONS AND SITUATIONS

A great deal of interest has been focused on the extent to which persons are consistent, and in particular their degree of consistency across different situations. It is the outcome of these studies that, rightly or wrongly, has led many psychologists to abandon the traditional trait model in favour of the interactionist model.

The early studies of consistency across situations, like the Harteshorne and May (1928) research on honesty, used correlations between behaviour in pairs of situations, usually followed by factor analysis. Recent work has used analysis of variance to divide variance between that due to persons, to situations, and to P × S interaction. This was first done by Endler and Hunt (1966) and others have used a similar statistical procedure. It was hoped that this would decide between the trait model (P the main source of variance), the situational model (S the main source), and an interactionist model (P × S the main source). Olweus (1976) has argued that no clear test of these models can be made in this way, since it has never been specified, for example, how much situational or P × S variance would be inconsistent with the trait model. On the other hand, it would probably be agreed that the trait model requires a substantial amount of P variance (or fairly high correlations across situations).

An objection to analysis of variance here is that even if there is perfect rank-order consistency of persons, there may still be relatively little P variance—if the situations are sufficiently diverse. There could be high consistency, with low person variance, if P × S variance is very small—which usually it is not.

TABLE 3

Minutes late for	Lecture	Tutorial	Coffee	Person means
Tom	−1	5	11	5
Dick	0	6	12	6
Harry	1	7	13	7
situation means	0	6	12	6

Thus with the same degree of consistency of persons, as measured by correlations, P variance may be large or small, depending on how vigorously situations are manipulated. Golding (1975) concludes that the analysis of variance design is inappropriate here, and that a correlational approach is better. He suggests the use of Cronbach's coefficient of generalizability (1973) which assesses how far a number of persons have the same relative scores across a range of situations.

However it is of some interest to know whether some aspect of behaviour is primarily a function of persons (like emotions, see below), or of situations. The trouble is that it is impossible to design a study in which persons and situations are both sampled over equivalent ranges; the variances obtained depend on how varied are the persons and situations. In the Argyle and Little study (1972) for example, a rather homogeneous group of persons and a rather varied set of situations led to low P variance—16.1 per cent, and high S variance—43.6 per cent, which is atypical. Although no exact solution to this problem has so far been devised, we can now inspect the variance results for a sample of *investigations* (Bowers, 1973). Or we could work towards studies of samples of whole populations, using a wide range of the most commonly experienced situations.

So far we have discussed studies using two-way analysis of

variance, persons and situations being the two sources. A number of investigations, however, have used three-way analysis, 'mode of response' being the third variable. By this is meant, for example, the answers to different questions about anxiety (Endler and Hunt, op. cit.). In three-way analysis this third source of variance and its interactions with the others accounts for a lot of the variance and accordingly suppresses percentages of variance from the other sources. Olweus (op. cit.) has reanalysed some of Endler and Hunt's data to show what the two-way percentages would be.

TABLE 4

Reanalysis of Endler and Hunt's (1966) 3-way analysis as a 2-way analysis
(Olweus, 1976)

| | *Anxiety inventory, 169 students percentage of variance* | |
	Original 3-way	*Reanalysed 2-way*
Persons	5.8	26.5
Situations	5.3	22.9
P × S	10.0	50.7

I too think that three-way analysis gives a misleading picture of the true situation, and that two-way analysis is preferable.

We turn now to the results of the analysis of variance studies. Endler and Hunt (1968) report a study of 51 *samples* of subjects, nearly 5,000 in all, who filled in a questionnaire about feeling anxious and hostile in 11–18 situations (in different versions) and reported 10–14 forms of anxiety or hostility. Their results are similar to those shown and reanalysed in Table 2. Other studies have used observations of overt behaviour rather than self-reports. Moos (1969) observed 16 psychiatric patients in 6 situations, on two occasions, and recorded 8 categories of social behaviour. The results for the second observation (when the patients were somewhat recovered) based on a series of two-way analyses of variance, were as shown in Table 5.

If questionnaires and self-report studies (like Endler and Hunt's) are compared with observational studies (like Moos's), there is a tendency for person variance to be greater in the former, and situational variance greater in the observational studies (Bowers, op. cit.)

The proportions of person and situation variance also differ between forms of response, as can be seen from Table 3. There is no room here to review the findings in this area, but the results of a number of studies show that the behaviour which is most due to persons appears to include (a) emotional states; (b) smiling, gaze, scratching, and other aspects of non-verbal communication; (c) addictive behaviour, i.e. smoking; (d) self-presentation. The behaviour which is most due to the situation appears to include (a) amount of talk, or other aspects of social activity; (b) formality and friendliness of social behaviour; (c) amount of intimate information revealed (e.g. Moos, 1968, 1969; Argyle and Little, 1972).

TABLE 5

Percentage of variance accounted for by different sources of variance in behaviour categories—second observations (Moos, 1969).

Category	Source			
	Persons	Settings	P × S	Within
Hand and arm movement	17.2	13.8	29.6	39.3
Foot and leg movement	27.3	13.0	31.2	28.6
Scratch, pick, rub	26.3	18.2	27.6	27.9
General movement and shifting	23.1	4.4	48.2	24.3
Nod yes	4.6	56.5	21.3	18.5
Smile	33.4	8.3	36.1	22.3
Talk	7.4	60.1	19.9	12.5
Smoke	36.5	12.2	10.2	41.1

The proportions of person and situation variance also differ for different types of person, and for different kinds of situation, and the evidence on this will be discussed below.

I conclude that P × S variance studies can usefully be carried out if (1) attempts are made to sample persons and situations equally widely, (2) overt behaviour is used, and (3) two-way analyses are performed. Samples of studies which approximate these conditions show that person variance falls in the range of 15–30 per cent, situation variance 20–45 per cent, and P × S variance 30–50 per cent. These results give powerful support to an interactionist position. However there are some further limitations of P × S studies which will be discussed later—people normally choose their situations, and they can alter these when they get there. Further, the modes of response which can be used in situations differ, so that this method is restricted to aspects of behaviour, like anxiety, and amount of gaze or talk, which can occur in any situation.

2. THE ATTRIBUTION OF VARIANCE TO PERSONS AND SITUATIONS

In the early stages of this controversy it was believed that laymen act as trait theorists when they observe the behaviour of others (Mischel, 1968). Traditional person perception research methods compelled then to do so by asking for impressions of personality based on samples of behaviour. Attribution theory research took this a step further by finding that dispositions (or traits) were inferred from behaviour under special conditions—when a person behaves in a distinctive way (i.e. different from other people), and does so consistently across time and situations (Kelley, 1967). In another kind of person perception study, subjects are asked to predict the behaviour of target persons in a number of distinct situations (Cline, 1965), which they are quite well able to do. Research in the attribution theory tradition asks a different question of subjects—the extent to which they think some behaviour is primarily due to the person or the situation. The main conditions for person attribution are (1) he is seen to be free of pressure, e.g. of high social status, not closely supervised, not rewarded for his behaviour; (2) the causes of his behavour, e.g. aggressive behaviour, are not seen; (3) he is thought to have a number of choices open; (4) his behaviour is out of role, is unsuccessful, or not socially desirable (Jones *et al.*, 1972).

Recent research has found a number of points at which these attributions are incorrect.

(a) SELF V. OTHERS. Jones and Nisbett (1971) proposed, and found evidence, that people account for their own behaviour primarily in terms of the situation ('I tripped because it was dark'), but account for the behaviour of others in terms of traits ('she tripped because she's clumsy'). This result has been widely confirmed. Two alternative explanations were offered by Jones and Nisbett: environmental stimuli are more salient to actors than to observers, and actors are more aware of their own variability between situations.

(b) FOCUS OF ATTENTION. Arkin and Duval (1975) found that the effect described above is reversed if a TV camera is pointed at actors. Presumably this focuses their attention on themselves, as opposed to environmental stimuli, thus supporting the first of the two explanations given above.

(c) P × S VARIANCE. Clearly Mischel was wrong in supposing that laymen act as trait theorists—they are well aware of the effects of situations. But are they aware of P × S interaction? There are probably some instances where people are aware of P × S variance—the specificity of phobic responses, and the differential behaviour of authoritarians to high and low status others, for example.

(d) SUCCESS OR FAILURE. There is consistent evidence that if a person is successful he will be more likely to attribute the success to his own efforts (compared with the attributions of observers for example). This has been found where the task is teaching someone else, and with competition between teams at games or laboratory tasks. On the other hand there is little evidence of 'self-protective' bias, i.e. people do not increase their attributions to external factors when they fail. External attributions are however increased when the outcome is unexpected, and internal attributions when the desired outcome is obtained (Miller and Ross, 1975).

3. OTHER KINDS OF CONSISTENCY

(a) DIFFERENT MEASURES OF THE SAME TRAIT. Research workers often study the correlations between different measures of the same trait. These correlations are sometimes very low; for example there is almost no correlation between physiological and questionnaire measures of anxiety. On the other hand, Eysenck used a wide variety of different measures in his studies of neuroticism (1952) and extraversion (1957); he did find generally positive correlations, though they were usually very low. Campbell and Fiske (1959) observed that correlations between different measures of the same trait are often no greater than correlations between different traits using the same methods. Their multi-trait–multi-method matrix provides a method of establishing the existence of traits over and above the use of particular measures, and their method has been used by a number of investigators. This has led to the idea of construct validity (Campbell, 1960). However, as Alston (op. cit.) points out, this aspect of consistency is irrelevant to the trait problem—it merely shows that 'not all the measures studied are (good) measures of the same thing' (p. 83).

(b) DIFFERENT SUB-CLASSES OF THE SAME KIND OF RESPONSE. A good example of this is the Sears (1963) study of the correlations between

F

the frequencies of five kinds of dependency behaviour in preschool children. He found that only one of the 20 correlations was significant (boys and girls being taken separately). Factorial studies of various aspects of social behaviour have often shown that there are often a number of independent forms of aggressiveness, suggestibility, rigidity, and so on (Mischel, 1968). However as Alston (op. cit.) points out, all this shows is that individuals have their own individual styles of aggressiveness. We can accommodate such results within trait theory either by conceptualizing traits as rather narrow, or by conceptualizing traits differently, as Alston suggests (p. 84 below). Fishbein and Ajzeh (1975) have found that attitude scales can predict much better to multiple-act criteria, i.e. adding up a range of alternative behaviours, than to a single-act criterion.

(c) CONSISTENCY BETWEEN DIFFERENT QUESTIONNAIRE ITEMS. Many traits have been arrived at by the factor analysis of self-report questionnare items; a number of items of apparently related behaviour (e.g. dominance) are found to correlate together, and the factor is labelled accordingly. Over 950 factors have been identified in this way (Borgatta, 1968). The questions asked refer to forms of social behaviour, but they do not specify the situation—the subject is invited to describe 'typical' behaviour on his part. This is quite unlike a mental test item, where the subject does as well as he can; self-report items can be answered in any way the subject chooses, and are affected by a number of extraneous factors. If two items, or scales, correlate, this is not necessarily because they are different aspects of the same trait. It may be because (a) they contain the same or similar items, (b) they are unaffected by the same response sets of acquiescence or social desirability, (c) both are affected by intelligence or educational level. It is now familiar that self-report measures usually have very low correlations with overt behaviour, a point that has now been extensively documented (Argyle and Little, 1972; Mann, 1959; Mischel, 1968). The reason for this is now clear—self-report is behaviour in a particular situation, with its own motivations, rules and social pressures, which may or may not be similar to those affecting overt behaviour in other situations.

(d) CONSISTENCY BETWEEN RATINGS OF BEHAVIOUR. There are two ways in which ratings or impressions of others appear to generate consistent traits. In the first place factor analyses of ratings lead to factors

like *agreeable, extraverted, dominant/assertive,* etc., and rather
similar factors have appeared in different studies (e.g. Norman,
1963). However there is evidence to support Mischel's conclusion
that these dimensions do not reflect the personalities of those rated,
but rather the social stereotypes and conceptual dimensions of the
judges, since the same dimensions were found when complete
strangers were rated, so that the dimensions obtained couldn't
possibly reflect the organization of attributes in those rated (Passini
and Norman, 1966). And the three dimensions listed above, obtained
for example by Hallworth (1965), clearly correspond to the three
dimensions of the semantic differential.

Impressions of others appear to be consistent in a second way—
those we know give an impression of consistency, stability and
predictability—they seem to be the same people in different situations. However we tend to see those we know in a limited set of
similar situations, in which there is an important constant element—
the presence of ourselves, and where the person observed may be
motivated to present a consistent image. As we have seen, if behaviour is recorded objectively, the level of consistency is actually
rather low.

(e) CONSISTENCY OVER TIME. A number of longitudinal studies have
investigated the extent to which persons show stability over time.
Block (1971) studied his subjects when they were adolescents and
20–25 years later; ratings on aspects of dominance and other dimensions of behaviour across this time-span, correlated at 0.35 or above.
Similar results have been obtained in other studies, though as Mischel
(op. cit.) points out this is partly due to the existence of a stable
environment. And, as everyone knows, we all change in the course
of time, partly by simply getting older, so that there is a limit to this
kind of consistency. In any case these findings are irrelevant to the
trait problem.

4. WHICH PERSONS ARE MOST CONSISTENT?

One outcome of research in this area has been a set of findings about
which kinds of person are most consistent across different situations.

(a) NEUROTICISM, PSYCHIATRIC DISTURBANCE. In a number of studies it
has been found that mental patients, i.e. people who are emotionally

disturbed, show more consistency than normals. For example, Moos (1968) studied 22 patients and 10 staff in a mental hospital, with a questionnaire asking about 9 situations and 5 factors of responses.

TABLE 6

Source	Patient	Staff
Persons	30.0	6.8
Situations	1.7	12.6
Persons × Situations	17.0	25.4

This finding could be explained in terms of the differences in role or status between staff and patients. However, other quite different studies have obtained similar results. Endler (1973) gave samples of normals, neurotics and psychotics his anxiety questionnaire. Some of the results were as follows:

TABLE 7

Source	Normals	Neurotics	Psychotics
Persons	2.9	12.1	18.8
Situations	23.7	5.8	5.3
Persons × Situations	21.5	22.1	8.3

Note: this was a three-way analysis, but the third source has been omitted here.

It has been found in other studies that as patients recover, the proportion of situation variance increases (Moos, 1969; Rausch et al., 1960). It is possible that this change is due to their becoming more familiar with the hospital and the demands of the different situations within it.

The difference between patients and others has been offered by Wachtel (1973) as an explanation of the different views about personality, put forward by clinicians and social psychologists—patients being relatively consistent across situations give more support to a trait approach. Social psychologists study normal students who are less consistent. This difference certainly makes the point that there is nothing abnormal about varying behaviour considerably between situations—it is abnormal people who are consistent—though there may perhaps be individuals who vary their behaviour to a degree which is not only statistically unusual, but is associated with failure of adjustment.

(b) INTERNAL-EXTERNAL CONTROL. A number of studies from a different tradition of research have found that people scoring high on
internal control are more resistant to social influence of various kinds,
including conformity pressures, influence of authority figures and
verbal reinforcement (Phares, 1976); it follows that they will appear
to be more consistent across situations where social pressures make
different demands in each. Bem and Bem (1974) used a similar way
of discovering consistent persons. Firstly they asked subjects to rate
themselves for their consistency in friendliness and conscientiousness;
secondly they gave subjects a questionnaire about their friendliness
etc. in different situations, and measured the variability of response.
The subjects who came out as consistent on these two measures were
found to be consistent when a number of measures of friendliness
in different situations were used. The average intercorrelation of
measures of friendliness for the consistent subjects was 0.57, while
for the other subjects it was 0.27. This does not lead to the isolation
of subjects who are consistent in general, but only in relation to
particular trait domains.

Snyder and Monson (1975) devised a 25-item questionnaire to
measure 'self-monitoring' tendencies, self-monitoring meaning sensitivity to situational cues. 'High' items include 'When I am uncertain how to act in a social situation, I look to the behaviour of others
for cues', and 'I'm not always the person I appear to be.' 'Low' items
include 'I have trouble changing my behaviour to suit different
people and different situations', and 'I can only argue for ideas which
I already believe.' It was found that high self-monitoring subjects conformed more in a public (v. private) experimental condition, as S's low
in neuroticism, and that high self-monitoring S's reported a greater
variation in generosity, honesty and hostility across situations.

(c) EXTREMES OF PERSONALITY DIMENSIONS. May and Harteshorne (1927)
discuss the degrees of consistency shown by subjects with different
dispositions to cheat, over a series of cheating test, with different
thresholds. Those at each extreme behave most consistently. The
same is true of answers to items on attitude scales and questionnaires.
Those in the middle of a dimension like extraversion check half the
items and appear to be inconsistent (Campbell, 1968). There is some
advantage in the use of 'ipsative' measures of individuals, i.e. describing them primarily in terms of the dimensions for which they are
most extreme—and most consistent.

(d) SEX DIFFERENCES. Are women really more inconsistent, as is often believed? The Endler and Hunt data (Table 4) suggests that they are more affected by situations in the spheres of anxiety and hostility. There is widespread evidence that women conform more to social norms. Several studies have found that females score higher on external control and similar measures. There does seem to be a certain amount of evidence for a general sex difference here.

(e) CULTURAL DIFFERENCES. It has been suggested that there is more situational variability in some cultures than others. Argyle, Shimoda and Little studied the implicit personality theories of English and Japanese subjects. As predicted, the Japanese S's attributed more variance to situations than did the English S's, though there were reversals of this effect on certain scales.

5. THREE STATISTICAL SOLUTIONS

The trait approach has been defended by putting forward elaborations on the original simple model, which depend on additional statistical procedures.

(a) MODERATOR VARIABLES. Sometimes variables A and B have little statistical relationship, but a moderator variable C can be found, so that for subjects within certain limits of C there is an A–B relationship. Sometimes there is a different A–B relation for the remainder, sometimes no relationship. Thus, for some S's at least, there may be more consistency than at first appeared. Grooms and Endler (1960) found that an Academic Aptitude Exam and High School grades predicted College grade average at 0.63 for high-anxiety subjects, but only 0.19 for low anxiety subjects. This principle has sometimes been used for personal selection: Furneau (1962) found that success at engineering could be predicted from mental tests for stable extraverts, but not for neurotic introverts. The moderator variables which have been most widely used are sex, intelligence, and anxiety or neuroticism.

The method can be applied to consistency of behaviour across different situations. Kogan and Wallach (1964) found that risk-taking in different situations was more consistent for females, and for subjects scoring high on test anxiety and defensiveness—though the findings are not at all clear-cut, as Wallach and Leggett (1972) observe.

Although the right moderator variables are often discovered by luck or good judgement, there are systematic methods for doing this. Argyle and Delin (1965) proposed the method of 'artificial correlations': variables A and B are plotted against each other; a line is drawn through the means at a slope proportional to the standard deviations; parallel lines are drawn to cut off a diagonal slice comprising 10–15 per cent of the subjects; the A–B correlation for these subjects is high and positive; the means of the artificial sample and the remainder are compared on as many variables as possible to see if any could act as moderator variables. In one such study it was found that guilt feelings and church attendance correlated, for Protestant females over the age of 15.

If moderator variables are used simply to define the minority of subjects who are consistent in relation to the experimenter's group of situations, this does not help much with the general prediction and explanation of behaviour. However, moderator variables have been used with success in a number of studies—for example, where males and females are found to obey different empirical laws (p. 158). We shall also consider cases where the situation acts as a moderator variable (p. 173).

(b) ACTUARIAL PREDICTION. In several fields of psychology it is common to work out actuarial methods of predicting behaviour. The predictors may be test scores, e.g. on the MMPI, or items of past behaviour; the behaviour predicted may be job success, recidivism, clinical prognosis, etc. The mathematical function can take a variety of forms, the most common being to weight the predictor variables and then add the weighted scores (Sines, 1966). This method has been used successfully in the fields mentioned above, where it usually predicts better than 'clinical' combinations of the same data (Meehl, 1956). It has often been used in personal selection, where combinations of objective biographical material, test scores, and interview material may be combined (Dunnette, 1966). The predictions obtained in this way are often very good—well in excess of correlations of 0.30. Indeed correlations of 0.60–0.70, or successful estimates of parole performance etc. of over 85 per cent are quite common.

This method enables the prediction of a specific piece of behaviour, though this is often a fairly global aspect of behaviour like job success. To predict a second aspect of behaviour a completely new equation is needed in which there may well be different predictor variables. This method has not been used systematically in the field of social behaviour, and it is not known what the predictor variables should be. However, the weighting for any one situation would have to be different for different situations. Take the prediction of conformity from individual differences in achievement motivation: McClelland *et al.* (1953) found that 13 per cent of those above the n.Ach median conformed compared with 87 per cent of those below it. In other studies the reverse has been found, and it appears that the effect of n.Ach on conformity depends on whether conformity or deviation appears to lead to achievement.

It seems very likely that the actuarial approach, whether using questionnaire or other data, could provide a means of predicting behaviour in specific social situations. But to predict behaviour in a range of related situations, e.g. conformity, entails working out a series of *different equations*, each with different empirical weights. And while the method may predict, it doesn't explain: it provides blind predictions from a set of fairly meaningless equations.

(c) INDIVIDUAL TRAITS AND P—TECHNIQUE. Allport (1937) regarded a trait as 'a generalized and focalized neuropsychic system (peculiar to the individual) with the capacity to render many stimuli functionally equivalent, and to initiate and guide consistent (equivalent) forms of adaptive and expressive behaviour' (p. 295). In other words the grouping of consistent responses can be different for each person. Most research into traits has used correlations across numbers of subjects, so that only common traits are found. What methods can be used in the discovery of traits which are unique to individuals?

Bem and Bem (1974), in the study described above, used a method of finding the subjects whose unique traits match those conceptualized by the investigators. In part of this study the investigators initially included 'neatness' (of appearance) in their trait of conscientiousness, but it turned out that neatness was not part of this trait, in most of the subjects. In another study they found that masculinity and femininity were traits only for some subjects, and that others are better regarded as 'androgynous'.

There is an older approach to the discovery of individual traits—Cattell's P technique (1943). The technique consists of making a number of measures of an individual's behaviour on a considerable number of successive occasions, working out correlations between pairs of measures across time (n is the number of occasions), and extracting factors unique to that individual (consisting of responses that co-vary over time). A number of such studies have now been carried out, and some of the individual factors found have appeared in a number of cases and have been regarded as general or replicated factors (Luborsky and Mintz, 1972). These replicated factors appear to be mainly emotional states, such as 'activation v. torpor' and 'general diurnal fatigue'.

A related method, called 'chain P technique' by Cattell (1966), involves correlation across time for individuals, where the situation is varied. This method was in effect used in a study by Argyle and Little (1972), which will be described later. In this study the self-reported behaviour of individuals in a number of situations for a number of modes of response was factor analysed for each subject.

The individual trait approach leads to the discovery of that minority of subjects whose traits match those of the investigators. In this way it is similar to the moderator variable approach. The analysis of unique traits by P-technique leads to common emotional states. But the analysis of individual responses to situations appears to be a way of plotting the unique pattern of individual social behaviour across a wide range of situations. It does not provide an economical means of assessing or conceptualizing individuals, or of predicting behaviour from traits. It may have to be accepted that human social behaviour varies with the situation in a very complex way. We know that anxiety comes to be associated with specific situations as the result of particular learning experiences. Similarly a person's degree of social skill or his style of social behaviour in different situations depends on the opportunities he has had for acquiring certain social skills.

6. CONCLUSIONS

(a) The most important kind of consistency is between situations; the results are clear—for many aspects of behaviour this kind of consistency is low, and a lot of variance is due to situations and P × S interaction.

(b) There are several other kinds of consistency but these are either low, or irrelevant to the trait issue.

(c) Inter-situational consistency is highest for the mentally disturbed, internal controllers, those at extremes of dimensions, and women.

(d) It is possible to isolate consistent persons by means of moderator variables, to predict from tests by actuarial methods and to discover traits unique to individuals. However none of these methods provide predictions for ranges of situations, or understanding of the processes involved.

The Interactionist Approach, $B = f(P,S)$

The simple trait model has been replaced, for most psychologists, by some kind of interactionist model. Such models emphasize the contributions of persons and of situations, and of interaction between them. Lewin (1935) suggested the formula $B = f(P, S)$. Other psychologists have suggested similar models, such as Murray (1938) with his needs which operate in conjunction with corresponding environmental 'presses'. Cattell (e.g. 1950) suggested the use of 'specification equations', where

$$R = S_1 T_1 + S_2 T_2 + \ldots S_n T_n$$

where $T_1 T_2$, etc. are traits, and $S_1 S_2$, etc. the weights which specify the relevance of each trait to a particular situation, as in actuarial prediction.

The interactionist approach has a fairly long history, which Ekehammer (1974) has traced. The interactionist approach leads both to $B = f(P,S)$ equations, and to the partition of variance between P, S, and P × S sources (as described above). Both kinds of research assume that P can be measured in a way independent of S, that S can be measured, and they are both confined to forms of B that are manifested in a range of different situations.

We shall now consider how the four elements of Lewin's equation can be filled in.

'*B.*' As Lewin intended it, 'B' referred to the choice of one action from a range of possibilities (Lewin, 1935). However in most research B is conceived as measurable along dimensions of some kind, e.g. amount of anxiety, talk or gaze. These are all aspects of behaviour which can be used over a variety of situations. And we shall take it to mean behaviour as measured by the investigator.

(a) THE MEASUREMENT OF P. Lewin himself though of P in structural terms—individual goals, barriers, etc., but his concepts have fallen into disuse. We now know that surface traits, defined in terms of behaviour, do not lead to good predictions. In order to be able to apply the interactionist equation we need to be able to measure P in a way that is independent of behaviour in any particular situation. A number of personality measures exist which are intended to do this. For example Spielberger (1966) devised questionnaire measures of state and trait anxiety, where the latter is a measure of anxiety proneness. Although a person's behaviour changes between situations, his physiological properties and presumably his psychological ones do not. There are several kinds of measures of personality properties which remain the same, but which generate different behaviour in different situations. These include physiological, cognitive and other kinds of measurement.

TABLE 8

Personality variables affecting gaze

Demographic factors
    Age Gaze falls from childhood to adolescence then increases.
    Sex. Gaze and mutual gaze greater for females.
    Culture. Arabs and SE Europeans high: some American Indians low.
Physiological
    Extraversion. Extraverts gaze more.
Motivation
    Affiliative. Interaction with situation only; no main effect (see below).
Cognitive structures
    Internal-external control. Interaction with situation only.
    Field dependence. Field dependent gaze more.
Mental Health, classification
    Autism. Very low gaze.
    Schizophrenics. Reduced gaze; short glances.
    Depressives. Reduced gaze; look down.

To demonstrate the empirical success of such measurements we must turn to studies in which they have been used to predict individual behaviour in different situations. We shall give examples of the working out of $B = f(P,S)$ equations later. Here, however, we give a rather longer list of examples of the operation of P variables, in a special sphere, research on gaze. B here is the percentage of S's gaze or the percentage of mutual gaze between two persons. A considerable number of studies have been carried out, showing the effects of P, S, and $P \times S$ interaction on gaze and the details of $B = f(P,S)$ equations. Detailed references to this research are not given, since this research is reviewed by Argyle and Cook (1976).

Table 8 takes no account of the independent effects of situations, which will be discussed below. It simply mentions those stable P variables which have been shown to affect gaze, or to contribute to P × S interaction. It is only intended to make the point that there are a number of diverse measures of P, as a stable entity, which are able to predict some form of B.

(b) THE MEASUREMENT OF S. Very little research has been carried out on situations, compared with the volume of work on personality. It is only during recent years that environmental psychology has produced systematic research in this area (e.g. Proshansky et al., 1970), and research workers have tried to identify the dimensions of situations. In order to apply our formula it is not enough to show that behaviour is different in different situations: behaviour must be shown to be a function of some measurable or scalable property of situations, when other aspects are held constant. These may be aspects of situations which can be measured by the investigator, e.g. physical properties, or properties derived from a consensus of subjective ratings.

In a sense all psychological experiments involve the manipulation of situations, and therefore take account of ways in which situations vary. And such experiments may show which aspects of situations affect behaviour. However they have not led to a systematic analysis of the dimensions or categories that are appropriate for situational analysis. Sociologists like Barker and Wright (1955) list large numbers of social situations which are found in community life, in which behaviour is different, but again this has not led to general dimensions or categories, or understanding of how situations affect behaviour.

One approach to situational measurement is in terms of physical description, or other objective terms. Research on gaze, for example, has found the following results:

> *Distance.* More gaze at greater distance.
> *Density.* Less gaze with more density.
> *Conditions of visibility.* More gaze through one-way screen or dark glasses.

Studies of others aspects of behaviour have shown, for example, the effects of temperature on behaviour (Moos and Insel, 1974). Environmental psychologists have factor analysed the contents of sitting-rooms. Laumann and House (1970) studied the contents of 800 living-rooms, and produced two main factors which were interpreted as (i) social class, (ii) traditional-modern style. The first at least would be expected to affect the social behaviour of those present.

An objective classification can be made of the task activity in different situations. Krause (1970) suggested the following categories: joint working, trading (negotiating), fighting, teaching, serving, self-disclosure, and play. To this would need to be added purely social activity, family life, and rituals.

However there are limitations to a purely physical assessment of situations. Most physical aspects of situations affect behaviour because of their meaning to those present. Here are some examples:

Colour – suggests emotional mood, e.g. red for warm and cheerful.
Relative height – dominance is created by the positions which people are placed, e.g. height.
Social activity symbolized – rooms can be decorated to suggest love, work, interrogation, etc.

Since the meanings above cannot be assumed to be universal, it is necessary to find their meaning for the participants.

One method of studying situations subjectively is to ask participants to fill in rating scales. For example Moos and Houts (1970) compared the atmosphere of 8 psychiatric wards, by analysing the ratings of 20–30 patients in each ward. The Ward Atmosphere Scale has 12 sub-scales, of which 8 significantly differentiated between wards, and also had clear relationships with satisfaction and liking other patients. Magnusson (1971) used multi-dimensional scaling as a means of finding which situations were judged as most similar, Forgas, at Oxford (in press), used this method with the 25 situations found to be most common by samples of Oxford students and housewives and included regressive analysis with marker scales to identify the dimensions. The dimensions which discriminated best between situations for these S's were as follows:

	Housewives	*Students*
I.	Intimacy, degree of involvement	Friendly-unfriendly
II.	Know-how to behave, self-confidence	Know-how to behave
III.	Pleasant-unpleasant	Organized-disorganized

The three dimensions for the students are shown in Figure 2.

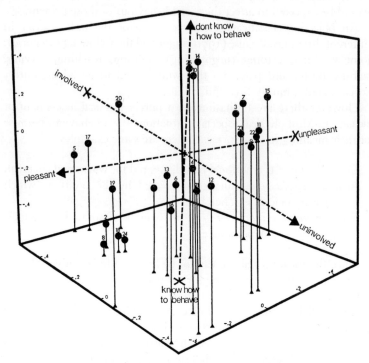

Fig. 2. Multi-dimensional scaling of 25 situations
(from Forgas in press)

Experimental research on gaze has found that the following subjective aspects of situations affects the amount of gaze.

Cooperation–competitive. Interaction with situation only, no main effect (see below).
Difficulty of task. Less gaze for difficult topics.
Intimacy of topic. Less gaze for intimate topics.
Friendly–hostile relations. More gaze for friendly.
Same–equal status. More gaze at higher status person.

Although these have been listed as subjective dimensions, some of them at least could be defined objectively, though not exactly in physical terms. Perhaps situational variables should be classified into four types: (1) purely physical, e.g. distance, (2) task variables, (3) social structure, e.g. status relations, (4) subjective, e.g. pleasant–unpleasant.

(c) DETERMINING THE CHARACTERISTICS OF 'f'. In order to discover the functional relationship involved, it is necessary to carry out investigations in which both P and S are varied systematically. In experimental psychology there are many studies showing, for example, how learning curves differ for subjects of different intelligence or extraversion, how anxiety is a function of trait anxiety and the stressfulness of situations, and so on. Preferably there should be at least three levels of both P and S, so that curvilinear relations can be shown, but this has rarely been done. When f has been specified then we should be able to understand the personality mechanisms involved; and they will be mechanisms involving interplay between person and situation.

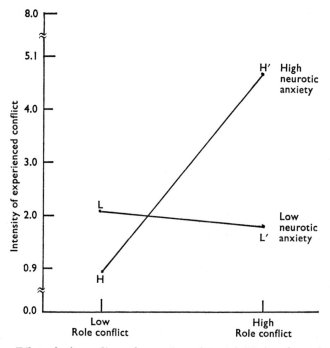

Fig. 3. Effect of role conflict and neurotic anxiety on intensity of experienced conflict. (Kahn *et al* 1964)

In the first place f will specify whether B is primarily a function of P, S, or P × S interaction. We shall consider later some examples, which differ in this respect. More important, f specifies the nature of the functional relationships between B and aspects of P and S.

In our first example, B is affected by all three of these sources of variance, and involves one P variable, and one S variable. Kahn *et al.* (1964) found that experienced role conflict was affected by neurotic anxiety and objectively ascertained role conflict. Here there are significant effects due to personality, situation and P × S interaction.

Our second example involves two P variables, one of which produces interactive but no mean effects, and one S variable. Exline (1963) studied the effect of sex, affiliative motivation and cooperative–competitive situations on gaze. He found the pattern of effects shown in Figure 4 opposite.

It can be seen that (1) sex acts as a moderator variable, and there is also a sex difference in level of gaze, (2) neither the P nor the S variables have any direct effects, but (3) there is a strong interaction between them for females. Affiliative females look more in cooperative situations, and vice versa.

The two examples above depend on the results of empirical research. Our third example is rather different, and is a theoretical model put forward to account for a wide range of person–situation interactions.

McGuire (1963) proposed that being persuaded depends on two mediating processes: reception of the message and yielding. He proposed that personality variables affect these two processes in opposite ways. So an intelligent person is more likely to receive a message, but less likely to yield. If the two mediating processes are to be multiplied together, it follows that being persuaded will be a curvilinear function of intelligence (and also self-esteem).

There is a certain amount of evidence that this relationship is correct. In McGuire's model it is also proposed that (a) there are interactions of intelligence, anxiety, and other P variables with a variety of S factors, and (b) sex operates as a moderator variable.

We have seen that the determination of f has been accomplished in a number of studies, which demonstrate the utility of the $B = f(P,S)$ model to account for variance and to predict behaviour.

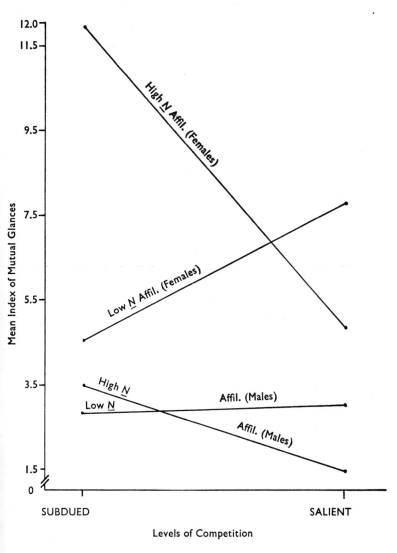

Fig. 4. Mean percentage of time each sex spends in mutual visual interaction for each of two levels of *n* affiliation at two levels of competition (Exline, 1963)

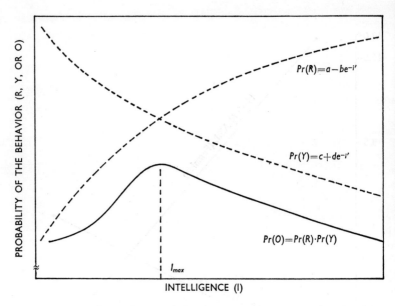

Fig. 5. Proposed curvilinear relationship between influenceability and intelligence, due to intelligence having opposite effects on the two mediators, reception and yielding. (McGuire, 1968)

(d) INTERACTIONIST CONCEPTUALIZATIONS OF PERSONALITY. As we saw above, a number of earlier approaches to personality adopted an interactionist point of view—Lewin, Murray and others. Recent work on consistency has led to further developments in this direction.

Mischel (1974) has combined the social learning and cognitive traditions to suggest what is inside the person that enables people to respond differently to different situations. He postulates a number of primarily cognitive constructs in persons:

First, people differ in their *construction competencies*. Even if people have similar expectancies about the most appropriate response pattern in a particular situation, and are uniformly motivated to make it, they may differ in whether or not (and how well) they *can* do it, i.e. in their ability to construct the preferred response. For example, due to differences in skill and prior learning, individual differences may arise in interpersonal problem-solving, empathy and role-taking, or cognitive-intellective achievements. Response differences also may reflect differences in how individuals *categorize* a particular situation (i.e. in how they encode, group and label the events that comprise it) and in how they construe themselves and others. Differences between persons in their performances in any situation depend on their behaviour-outcome and stimulus-outcome *expectancies*, i.e. differences in the expected outcomes associated with particular responses or stimuli in particular situations. Performance differences also may be due to differences in the subjective *values* of the outcomes expected in the situation. Finally, individual differences may be due to differences in the *self-regulatory systems* and plans that each person brings to the situation. (p. 275.)

It is evident that each of these cognitive constructs interacts with situations to produce behaviour. These components have been used in a number of previous formulations, for example Atkinson's account (1957) of achievement motivation. This scheme does not include any purely physiological or temperamental aspects of persons, except in so far as they are reflected in cognition. My own suggestions about the way persons should be conceived are set out later.

Alston (Chap. 4, this book) argues that the traditional trait model does not apply very well to needs, abilities and attitudes, and offers his 'purposive–cognitive' model as an alternative. In my opinion the traditional model does fit abilities rather well, if what is being predicted is level of performance, as in the case of intelligence tests. Nor do I find his distinction between traits as dispositions and as theoretical terms a very useful one. I am however in sympathy with Alston's general approach, and his suggestion that a wide range of aspects of P become operative in particular situations, and interact with the properties of those situations.

(e) LIMITATIONS OF THE $B = f(P,S)$ MODEL. However there are a number of important limitations on this model, especially where social behaviour is concerned.

(1) As we showed above the exact proportions of variance due to P, S and $P \times S$ cannot be determined, since there is no way of sampling P and S in a comparable way. Therefore the weights to be given to P and S variables cannot be found, though they can be given for a defined, subject population and range of situations.

(2) In a dyadic situation, P_1 constitutes part of the situation for P_2,

and vice versa. It is found that the outcome does not depend on their absolute but rather on their relative attributes. Thus Carment, Cervin and Miles (1965) found that the *more* extraverted member of an otherwise homogeneous dyad spoke first in 26 out of 33 pairs, spoke more in 24 out of 33 pairs, and persauded the others to change their minds in 39 out of 43 pairs. The effects of differential intelligence were slightly greater. Meltzer *et al.* (1967) found little consistency between individuals in measures of their amount and loudness of talking, between different groups. However, measures of relative amplitude, talking time, and interruptions in one group correlated with similar measures for other groups at over 0.50. Similar considerations apply to the prediction of leadership in informal groups; it is the person with the *highest* level of the abilities needed by the group in their main task who is likely to lead.

Another approach is to assess the compatibility of two people. Schutz (1958) was able to create incompatible groups by having more than one person keen to dominate, or by having some group members with strong affiliative needs, others with weak ones. In fact nearly all combinations of two or more people will be incompatible to some degree, in the sense that their preferred styles of behaviour do not easily fit together. Some mutual accommodation is necessary, and this is done by a kind of non-verbal group problem solving. A doesn't say 'I want to talk most of the time'; instead he makes use of non-verbal synchronizing cues that enable him to do so (Argyle, 1969).

The prediction of interpersonal attraction depends very much on the similarity of two people, and in some respects their complementarity. Whether or not A likes B is more a $P \times P$ interaction than a function of P alone.

(3) A problem of a different kind for students of $P \times S$ interaction in the case of social behaviour is that people normally choose their situations, these choices reflecting their personalities (Bowers, 1973). Experimental designs in which people are allocated to situations miss this important aspect of P functioning, as well as perhaps placing them in unfamiliar settings. One example of persons choosing situations is the way in which people choose jobs which fit their pattern of interests, as measured, for example, by the SVIB. Another is the way people choose social atmospheres which suit them: in the U.S.A. it has been found that authoritarians often join military academies rather than universities (Stern *et al.*, 1956). There is con-

siderable evidence for the general hypothesis that people seek out and are most satisfied by environments which 'fit' their personalities (Pervin, 1968).

(4) Wachtel (1973) points out that people often produce certain responses in others—bad temper, intimidation, or shyness, for example. It is possible to 'define situations' in different ways, and special signals are sent suggesting possible definitions. Symbolic interactionists have emphasized the importance of such moves in social interaction; ethnomethodologists have argued that the way to analyse what happened is to elicit verbal accounts from the participants (Harré and Secord, 1972). We should not exaggerate the power individuals have to change situations; some people have very little effect and some situations can't be changed much. This should perhaps be rephrased to say that one way in which P contributes to behaviour is by changing the behaviour of others, and the way the situation is defined. In the changed state of affairs P may feel that he is confronted by an objective situation.

(5) In the analysis of 25 situations by Forgas, using multi-dimensional scaling (Fig. 2), it can be seen that there are a number of tight clusters of situations. However close inspection reveals that the cluster 3–7–23 consists of the situations 'Discussing an essay during a tutorial', 'Acting as a subject in a psychology experiment', and 'Attending a wedding ceremony'—three situations which are totally different in objective respects and in the behaviour required. While people can classify situations, or place them on seven-point scales, this taps only a very small part of their knowledge about these situations. Dinner parties may be felt to be more friendly than seminars, but participants have to know a great deal more than this in order to take part in such social situations. What we need are new research methods capable of exploring subjective knowledge and conceptualization of situations. I shall argue below that situations cannot wholly be classified in terms of dimensions: they can also be discrete and discontinuous.

(6) I shall also argue that the aspects of behaviour which are most relevant in, for example, a game of hockey, a Scottish ball and a psychology seminar are quite different, so that there is no common aspect of B to be predicted. This can be partly met by the use of wider, more abstract categories of behaviour. Thus 'gives information', one of the Bales categories, could include bidding at an auction, and giving a sermon in church. Or both could be assessed

for the lengths of the utterances involved. Either analysis however would miss the most important aspects of the behaviour in question.

CONCLUSIONS

(1) The interactionist model is superior to the traditional trait model, since it can deal with different proportions of P, S, and P × S variance, it has led to the dimensional analysis of situations, and to functional equations showing the joint effects of P and S.

(2) However, no satisfactory way of apportioning P and S variance has been discovered, people choose and change situations, and different kinds of behaviour occur in different situations, so that the approach is limited to universally occurring elements of behaviour like amount of talk or gaze. There are also serious doubts about whether situations can usefully be measured along continuous dimensions.

A Generative-Rules Approach to P × S Interaction

We have just seen that there are a number of limitations to the usual interactionist approach. In particular the forms of behaviour which are relevant in different situations differ, and it seems doubtful whether situations can be arranged along continuous dimensions. The generative-rules approach has been very successful in linguistics, and has been applied to the study of social behaviour (Clarke, 1976). I propose to develop here the idea that situations can be regarded as a source of such generative rules.

(a) THE BASIC RULES-GAMES MODEL. There is an almost infinite variety in the contents of what people may say. Partly for this reason in linguistics there is no attempt to predict what anyone will actually say. The goal is to arrive at a finite set of rules which will demarcate the (infinite) set of acceptable utterances in a language from the set of unacceptable ones (Chomsky, 1957). This is a less ambitious goal as far as prediction is concerned, but it does lead to understanding the structure of language, and enables others to be taught these principles. There is a second reason for abandoning the goal of complete prediction—the possibility that human behaviour is in part unpredictable.

The model has an obvious application to the study of games; the approach would be to discover the rules of, say, cricket, rather than to predict who will win, etc. The discovery of such rules requires new research methods, such as deliberate rule-breaking, interviewing the socially mobile, and consulting rule books. Garfinkel (1963) was the first person to use rule-breaking as a research procedure. In one of his experiments subjects played noughts and crosses; at one point E placed his mark on one of the lines, instead of between them, and the reactions of subjects were studied.

If two or more people want to play a game they must decide what game it is to be, and then agree to keep the rules. Otherwise there is chaos. Social episodes appear to be introduced by a series of negotiating signals by means of which the definition of the situation is agreed. In games there appear to be two kinds of rules, those which are fundamental to the game (putting O's in the squares at noughts and crosses), and social conventions, such as wearing white clothes to play cricket.

Similar considerations apply to social situations. I have found, for example, that interviewers report that they would be unable to cope with interviewees who speak the wrong language, tell lies or ask all the questions, but are not worried about interviewees' appearance or posture. However there are also intermediate cases of rule-breaking, which fall short of total disruption, and there is rarely a total collapse of social interaction, but rather attempts to restore it (Goffman, 1971). It is sometimes possible for two people to play slightly different social games, e.g. A is receiving a tutorial, B is having an affair. However the point remains that there has to be a sufficient degree of cooperation in keeping to the same set of intrinsic rules for social interaction to take place.

(b) THE ANALYSIS OF SITUATIONS. I suggest that social situations are akin to the chemical compounds, in being discrete, not continuous entities. Each situation, e.g. a dinner party or auction sale, like cricket and hide-and-seek, is a structured system of interdependent parts. The situation 'cricket' cannot be dimensionalized by removing e.g. the ball, or adding some more or larger balls. If situations are discontinuous, like chemical compounds (or elements) but unlike length and temperature, it follows that intermediate cases cannot be found. Clearly there is no continuous set of games intermediate between chess and cricket, but are there situations continuously intermediate between church services and psychology conferences? Almost certainly there are not, though there are mixed cases, and there are dimensional variations, like size of conference, for example.

In order to take part in a game of cricket, a tutorial, to visit a riding stables or attend College guest night, the interactors must master the basic components of these situations. These include:

Behaviour. Each situation defines certain social acts as relevant and meaningful. The signals used at auction sales would be ignored in church, the moves at Scottish dancing would be regarded as insane at a dinner party. While amounts of speech and gaze etc. are universal to all situations—their meaning and relevance is not; and social acts are often specific to situations.

So we have a new interactionist equation:

$$\text{Behavioural categories} = f(S).$$

This has been confirmed in a series of our studies in which the main categories have been established for interviews, tutorials, conversation over coffee, buying and selling, etc.

Structural/motivational themes. In any situation a number of different motivational themes may be present, and constitute the underlying structure of that situation. For example a dinner party involves:

social/cooperative
male–female relations
joint work (for hosts only)
self-presentation
eating

It does not involve buying and selling, therapy, teaching, etc.

Rules. It would be possible to define situations entirely in terms of rules of different kinds, but I have chosen to use other ideas as well. Rules specify what should and should not happen, including who may be present, what should be worn, and appropriate sequences of behaviour. In the case of rituals the rules specify what is to happen in some detail. Competitive games can be subdivided on the basis of their rules, as can different kinds of rituals and interviews. A dinner party has rules about time, order of courses, dress, topics of conversation, seating, etc.

Roles. Most situations generate social roles. Dinner parties have hosts, guests and sometimes servants, as well as male/female roles and senior/less senior guests.

Pieces. Most situations involve special environmental settings or props. Cricket needs bat, ball, stumps, etc., a seminar requires blackboard, slides, projector, and lecture notes. There are rules governing the use of such pieces, each of which has a special social meaning, and implications for interaction.

Concepts. To take part in Scottish dancing one must know the significance of 'second corner', 'the ladies' side' etc.; to play cricket one must know what an 'innings' and an 'over' is. We suggest later that more expert and experienced performers use more elaborate concepts, e.g. in Scottish dancing 'poussette' and 'rondel', in chess 'fork', 'discovered check', 'open game', and 'Sicilian defence', or the terms used in different schools of psychotherapy to describe the state of the patient or the therapy—'resistance' and 'negative transference'.

Traits. Finally, the dimensions in terms of which other people are classified, and in which one thinks of oneself, are also a function of the situation. A recent study by Argyle, J. Forgas and G. Ginsburg has found that the dimensions used are to a considerable degree a function of the situation, and also of the group of persons involved.

(c) THE ANALYSIS OF PERSONS. Establishing the generative rules tells us the range of possible behaviour, but does not predict any actual behaviour. In order to do this we must take account of individual motivation, style, skill, or other kind of variation *within* the rules.

To begin with there are person variables governing the choice and grouping of situations.

Choice of situation. There are individual differences in the range of situations chosen. Some people spend a great deal of time making speeches, others chatting, others watching TV. The systematic analysis of range situations is potentially a most interesting aspect of individual differences.

Grouping of situations. As I shall show below, there are differences in the ways in which situations are subjectively grouped, and presumably in the behaviour produced in them, e.g. level of skill, the anxiety produced, etc. This is shown in some of the results of the Argyle and Little study (1972). Principal components analysis for individuals produced a mapping for each person of the way situations were grouped (see Fig. 5).

In order to predict individual behaviour in a particular situation, it is necessary to carry out a regression analysis, using those aspects of persons which are likely to be relevant. It is also possible to use a restricted $B = f(P,S)$ approach within a grouping of situations of similar structure, and using dimensions of situations, like size or density, which make sense for that grouping. There are several aspects of persons that are likely to be useful here.

Motivation. There is a certain degree of variation in the forms of motivation which are relevant to each situation. In informal social situations there can be variations in needs to affiliate, dominate or engage in self-presentation and sexual behaviour; in games there is variation in the desire to win, in Scottish dancing to do it perfectly, or flamboyantly.

Ability. Variations in ability at non-social activities can be relevant, e.g. in determining leadership of working groups. Variations in social skills are found in all situations; these affect the performance of the individuals in question and the whole course of interaction. These effects are probably least in rituals, where variation is only in the manner of performance.

Knowledge of rules and concepts. If a person doesn't know the rules, he will not be likely to obey them. If he has learnt a somewhat different set of rules for a situation, he will be an unwitting rule-breaker. This is one of the main sources of trouble in inter-cultural encounters, including inter-class and inter-age interaction. If a person has not mastered the concepts he will also be in difficulty. Bannister and Salmon (1966) obtained evidence to show that one trouble with schizophrenics is that they do not have adequate concepts for persons. Just as gardeners need a concept of 'weed', and Scottish dancers a concept of 'second corner', so do participants in all social situations need concepts of persons and social performance.

(d) FUNCTIONAL RELATIONS, AND THE PREDICTION OF INDIVIDUAL BEHAVIOUR. Some degree of prediction can be made from the rules alone, without considering the individual at all. In order to predict the next move a player will make at chess we have to understand the game, and know the present state of play. There are degrees of prediction: (1) only moves within the rules are possible—a pawn cannot move like a knight; (2) a whole range of moves are very unlikely since they would be to the player's obvious disadvantage; (3) the prediction within the remaining moves is more difficult, and depends on the player's skill, and the strategies he has learnt. It may be suggested that the more formal a situation is, the smaller the P variance, and the more predictable behaviour is from the situation.

There appear to be rules for the sequence of utterances in a conversation which operate in a similar way. A simple and universal example is the question–answer sequence. A more elaborate one, including non-verbal components, is often used by school-teachers: teacher gives information—teacher asks question—children hold up hands—teacher points at one child—he answers—teacher comments or asks further questions. Systematic work in discourse analysis will probably lead to general rules for the sequence of utterances. Clarke's research at Oxford (1976) has shown already that subjects have sufficient implicit knowledge of such rules to reconstruct the original order of a set of utterances, which have been shuffled into random order, with a very much above chance degree of accuracy.

We can add information about individual differences, in order to predict individual behaviour. This can be done by applying the $B = f(P,S)$ equation within a limited range of similar situations. The relevant aspects of P and S are included in the analysis, as outlined above. The aspects of P and S which are used will be relatively specific aspects of each, rather than any general dimensions.

Application

(a) SELECTION, AND OTHER KINDS OF PREDICTION. The simple, general trait model has been widely used for predictive purposes, and as we have seen has proved remarkably unsuccessful. The same person behaves differently in different situations, and tests for these traits rarely correlate more than 0.2 with any actual behaviour.

We have seen that people are consistent *over time*, and Mischel (1968) argues that this provides the most accurate method of prediction.* Indeed numerous parole-selection schemes have made successful use of this method (e.g. Mannheim and Wilkins, 1955). Interviewers often try to discover how applicants performed in past situations most similar to the job situation. Academic performance can be predicted quite well from past success, in similar subjects at

---

* For a detailed exposition of the biographical approach see Chapter 7, (Ed.).

least. This is, however, not possible if the individuals in question have not been observed in similar situations in the past.

The interactionist approach suggests that the relevant $B = f(P,S)$ equation be established for the behaviour to be predicted, and for both P and S to be assessed accordingly. This is usually a theoretical ideal rather than a practical possibility. A method of doing this for individuals, using self-reports, was developed by Argyle and Little (1972), in a study of the self-reported social behaviour of 23 apprentices in relation to 12 different persons, as rated on 18 scales. Principal components analyses were carried out for each individual subject. For most subjects two main dimensions appeared, and these were fairly similar over the rather restricted range of subjects. However the loading of the 12 situations (i.e. target persons) was quite variable. An example of the results for one subject is given in Figure 6.

This method shows the way in which an individual groups situations together ('renders them functionally equivalent'—Allport), and the pattern of behaviour which is used for each group of situations. In one case analysed, a professional woman was found to treat her mother in much the same way as she treated her subordinates at work.

The generative-rules model, as explained above (p. 174), enables predictions to be made simply from the situational rules. Further prediction of individual performance requires the assessment of relevant individual qualities of ability, style, motivation, etc., for a specific situation.

(b) THERAPY, THE UNDERSTANDING AND TREATMENT OF INDIVIDUALS. For some years we have been treating patients with neurosis and behaviour disorders who have social anxieties or are inadequate in social situations, by means of role-playing with video-tape playback, and related methods (Argyle, Trower and Bryant, 1974; Argyle, Bryant and Trower, 1974). Some of the research from this project can be interpreted in terms of the P × S models presented in this chapter.

Is there a general trait of social incompetence or anxiety? Bryant and Trower (1973) surveyed 223 Oxford students, asking them to report how much anxiety or difficulty they experienced in 30 everyday situations. A principal components analysis yielded a first component of general social difficulty; a second component distinguished between situations involving making initial contacts with strangers, and situations involving more intimate relationships.

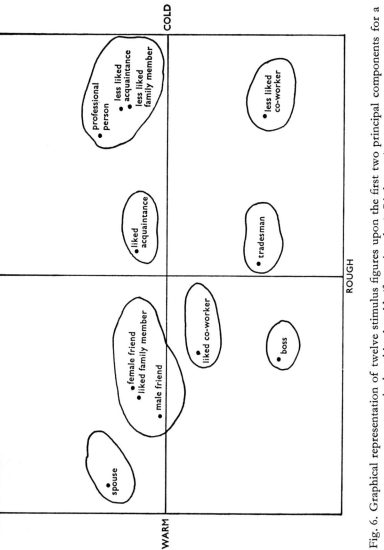

Fig. 6. Graphical representation of twelve stimulus figures upon the first two principal components for a single subject's grid. (from Argyle & Little 1972)

Clearly the situation is important but we have not as yet studied the dimensions of situations which are important here.

When a patient reports difficulty with a particular kind of situation, it is useful to be able to form some idea of how far this reflects general P tendencies, and how far P × S interaction, i.e. an abnormal reaction to this situation. In the second case one possibility is for him to avoid the situation where possible, and otherwise to concentrate social skills training on this situation alone.

There are some patients who report difficulty with quite specific social situations, such as parties or interviews. It doesn't look as if dimensions of situations are relevant and we can now adopt the generative-rules approach. The treatment includes explanation of the purposes, rules, etc. of the situation in question—of which the patient sometimes proves to be unaware. He may also need coaching in the skills involved.

2. RACIAL PREJUDICE, INTER-CULTURAL COMMUNICATION

Certain aspects of inter-cultural communication can be tackled by the interactionist model. Where it is found that there are differences of proximity, gaze, orientation, etc. between two cultures, culture can be regarded as a systematic source of P variance. Collett (1971) succeeded in training Englishmen to deal with Arabs on this basis. It may turn out that the dimensions of situations which affect behaviour, or other aspects of the $B = f(P,S)$ equation, are different in two cultures.

The variance due to P and S may also vary between cultures. Ruth Benedict (1946) observed that the Japanese were more affected by situations than Americans or Europeans. Argyle, Shimoda and Little (unpublished) carried out a study of variance attributed to P and S replicated in England and Japan, and found that for most of the dimensions of reported behaviour studied, variance attributed to S was significantly higher, and that attributed to P lower, for the Japanese.

The generative-rules model has more direct practical applications. Many difficulties in inter-cultural contact arise out of different rules for situations, e.g. eating, buying and selling, dealing with women, which in turn are related to different concepts and goals. The system of buying and selling in an Arab market is totally different from that in a European or American department store. In the Illinois Culture

Assimilator, instruction is given on understanding behaviour in 50–100 types of situations or encounters, found to be troublesome in critical incident surveys (Fiedler *et al.*, 1971).

ACKNOWLEDGEMENTS

I am indebted to David Clarke, Petei Collett, Rom Harré and Brian Little for some of the ideas in this paper, and to the SSRC and the Oxford Regional Hospital Board for supporting the research reported.
The last part of this chapter draws on material presented in another paper (Argyle, 1976), presented at the Stockholm Conference, organized by Norman Endler and David Magnusson.

REFERENCES

ALLPORT, G. W. *Personality: a Psychological Interpretation.* New York: Holt, 1937.

ALSTON, W. P. Traits, consistency and conceptual alternatives for personality theory. *J. Theory Soc. Beh.* 1975, 5, 17–48 (Chap. 4 this volume).

ARGYLE, M. *Social Interaction.* London: Methuen, New York: Aldine, 1960.

ARGYLE, M. Do personality traits exist? *New Behaviour*, 3 July 1975, 176–9.

ARGYLE, M. (in press) Predictive and generative rules models of P × S interaction. In D. Magnusson and N. Endler (eds.) *Personality at the Crossroads: Current Issues in Interactional Psychology.* Hillsdale, N. J.: L. Erlbaum Assoc. (J. Wiley).

ARGYLE, M., BRYANT, B. & TROWER, P. Social skills training and psychotherapy. *Psychol. Med.*, 1974, 4, 435–43.

ARGYLE, M. and COOK, M. *Gaze and Mutual Gaze.* Cambridge University Press, 1975.

ARGYLE, M. & DELIN, P. Non-Universal Laws of socialisation. *Human Relations*, 1965, 18, 77–86.

ARGYLE, M. and LITTLE, B. B. Do personality traits apply to social behaviour? *Journal for the Theory of Social Behaviour*, 1972, 2, 1–35.

ARGYLE, M., TROWER, P. & BRYANT, B. Explorations in the treatment of personality disorders and neuroses by social skills training. *Brit. J. Med. Psychology*, 1974, 47, 63–72.

ARKIN, R. M. and DUVAL, S. Focus of attention and causal attributions of actors and observers. *J. exp. soc. Psychol.*, 1975, 11, 427–38.

ATKINSON, J. W. Motivational determinants of risk-taking. *Psychological Review*, 1957, 64, 359–72.

BANNISTER, D. and SALMON, P. Schizophrenic thought disorder: specific or diffuse? *Brit. J. Med. Psychol.*, 1966, 39, 215–19.

BARKER, R. G. & WRIGHT, H. F. *Midwest and its Children: the Psychological Ecology of an American Town*. Evanston, Ill: Row, Peterson, 1954.

BEM, D. J. and ALLEN, A. On predicting some of the people some of the time: the search for cross-situational consistencies in behavior. *Psychol. Rev.*, 1974, 81, 506–20.

BENEDICT, R. *The Chrysanthemum and the Sword*. Boston: Houghton-Mifflin, 1946.

BIRDWHISTELL, R. *Kinesics and Context*. Univ. of Pennsylvania Press and London: Allen Lane the Penguin Press, 1971.

BLOCK, J. *Lives through Time*. Berkeley, Calif.: Bancroft, 1971.

BORGATTA, E. F. Traits and persons. In E. F. Borgatta and W. W. Lambert (eds.), *Handbook of Personality Theory and Research*. Chicago: Rand McNally, 1968.

BOWERS, K. S. Situationism in psychology: an analysis and a critique. *Psychological Review*, 1973, 30, 307–36.

BRYANT, B. & TROWER, P. Social difficulty in a student population. *Brit. J. Educ. Psychol.*, 1974, 44, 13–21.

CAMPBELL, D. T. Social attitudes and other acquired behavioural dispositions. In S. Koch (ed.), *Psychology: A Study of a Science*. *VI.* New York: McGraw-Hill, 1963, pp. 94–172.

CAMPBELL, D. and FISKE, D. Convergent and discriminant validation by the multitrait-multimethod metric. *Psychol. Bull.*, 1959, 56, 81–105.

CARMENT, D. W., MILES, C. S. & CERVIN, V. B. Persuasiveness and persuasibility as related to intelligence and extraversion. *Brit. J. soc. clin. Psychol.*, 1965, 4, 1–7.

CATTELL, R. B. The description of personality. I. Foundations of trait measurement. *Psychol. Rev.*, 1943, 50, 559–94.

CATTELL, R. B. *Description and Measurement of Personality*. Yonkers-on-Hudson: World Book Co., 1946.

CATTELL, R. B. Personality structure and measurement. I. The operational determination of trait unities. *Brit. J. Psychol.*, 1946, 36, 88–103.

CATTELL, R. B. *Personality: a Systematic, Theoretical and Factual Study*. New York: McGraw-Hill, 1950.

CHOMSKY, N. *Syntactic Structures*. S'Gravenhage, Netherlands: Mounton, 1957.

CLARKE, D. The use and recognition of sequential structure in dialogue. *Brit. J. soc. clin. Psychol.* (in press).

CLINE, V. B. Interpersonal perception. *Progress in Experimental Personality Research*, 1964, 1, 221–84.

COLLETT, P. On training Englishmen in the non-verbal behaviour of Arabs: an experiment in intercultural communication. *Int. J. Psychol.*, 1971, 6, 209–15.

CRONBACH, L. J. *et al.* *The dependability of behavioural measurements: theory of generalizability for scores and profiles*. New York: Wiley, 1973.

D'ANDRADE, R. G. Trait psychology and componential analysis. *Amer. Psychol.*, 1965, 67, 215–28.

DUNETTE, M. D. *Personnel Selection and Placement*. London: Tavistock, 1966.

EKEHAMMER, B. Interactionism in personality from a historical perspective. *Psychol. Bull.*, 1974, 81, 1026–48.

ENDLER, N. S. The person versus the situation—a pseudo issue? *J. Pers.*, 1973, 41, 287–343.

ENDLER, N. S. & HUNT, J. McV. Sources of behavioral variance as measured by the S–R Inventory of anxiousness. *Psychological Bulletin*, 1966, 65, 336–46.

ENDLER, N. S. & HUNT, J. McV. S–R variations of hostility and comparison of the properties of variance from persons, response, and situation for hostility and anxiousness. *J. pers. soc. Psychol.*, 1968, 9, 309–15.

ENDLER, N. S. & MAGNUSSON, D. *Interactional Psychology and Personality*. Washington: Hemisphere, 1976.

EXLINE, R. V. Explorations in the process of person perception: visual interaction in relation to competition, sex and need for affiliation. *J. Pers.*, 1963, 31, 1–20.

EYSENCK, H. J. *The Scientific Study of Personality*. London: Routledge & Kegan Paul.

EYSENCK, H. J. *The Dynamics of Anxiety and Hysteria*. London: Routledge & Kegan Paul, 1957.

FIEDLER, F. E., MITCHELL, T. & TRIANDIS, N. The Culture Assimilator: an approach to cross-cultural training. *J. appl. Psychol.* 1971, 55, 95–102.

FISHBEIN, M. & AJZEN, I. *Belief, Attitude, Intention and Behavior.* Reading, Mass.: Addison-Wesley, 1975.

FORGAS, J. P. The perception of social episodes: categorical and dimensional representations in two different social milieus. *J. pers. soc. Psychol.* (in press).

FURNEAU, W. D. The psychologist and the university. *Universities Quarterly,* 1962, 17, 33–47.

GARFINKEL, M. Trust and stable actions. In O. J. Harvey (ed.), *Motivation and Social Interaction.* New York: Ronald, 1963.

GOFFMAN, E. *Relations in Public.* London: Allen Lane the Penguin Press, 1971.

GOLDING, S. L. Flies in the ointment: methodological problems in the analysis of variance due to persons and situations. *Psychol. Bull.,* 1975, 82, 278–88.

GROOMS, R. R. & ENDLER, N. S. The effect of anxiety on academic achievement. *J. Educ. Psychol.,* 1960, 51, 299–309.

HALLWORTH, H. J. Perception of Children's personalities by experienced teachers. *Educ. Rev.* 1966, 19, 3–12.

HARRÉ, R. & SECORD, P. F. *The Explanation of Social Behaviour.* Oxford: Blackwell, 1972.

HARTESHORNE, H. & MAY, M. A. *Studies in the Nature of Character.* New York: Macmillan, 1928.

JONES, E. E. & NISBETT, R. E. The actor and the observer: divergent perceptions of the causes of behaviour. In E. E. Jones (ed.), *Attribution: Perceiving the Causes of Behavior.* Morristown, N.J.: General Learning Press, 1971.

JONES, E. E. *et al. Attribution: perceiving the causes of behavior.* New York: General Learning Press, 1972.

KAHN, R. L., WOLFE, D. M., QUINN, R. P. & SNOEK, H. D. *Organizational Stress.* New York: Wiley, 1964.

KELLEY, H. H. Attribution stress in social psychology. In D. Levine (ed.), *Nebraska Symposium on Motivation.* Lincoln: University of Nebraska Press, 1967.

KOGAN, N. & WALLACH, M. A. *Risk Taking. A Study in Cognition and Personality.* New York: Rinehart and Winston, 1964.

KRAUSE, M. S. Use of social situations for research purposes. *Amer. Psychol.,* 1974, 25, 748–53.

LAUMANN, E. V. & HOUSE, J. J. Living room styles and social attitudes: the patterning of material artefacts in a modern urban community. *Sociol. Soc. Res.*, 1970, 54, 321–42.

LEWIN, K. *A Dynamic Theory of Personality*. New York: McGraw-Hill, 1935.

LUBORSKY, L. & MINTZ, J. The contribution of P-technique to personality, psychotherapy, and psychosomatic research. In R. M. Dreger (ed.), *Multivariate Personality Research*. Baton Rouge: Claitor's, 1972.

McCLELLAND, D. C., ATKINSON, J. W., CLARK, R. A. & LOWELL, E. L. *The Achievement Motive*. New York: Appleton-Century, 1953.

McGUIRE, W. J. Personality and susceptibility to social influence. In E. F. Borgatta and W. W. Lambert (eds.), *Handbook of Personality Theory and Research*. Chicago. Rand McNally, 1968, Chap. 24, 1130–87.

MAGNUSSEN, D. An analysis of situational dimensions. *Perc. Motor Skills*, 1971, 32, 851–67.

MANN, R. D. A review of the relationships between personality and performance in small groups. *Psychol. Bull.*, 1959, 56, 241–70.

MANNHEIN, H. & WILKINS, L. T. *Prediction Methods in Relation to Borstal Training*. London: H.M.S.O., 1955.

MAY, M. A. & HARTESHORNE, H. First steps towards a scale for measuring attitudes. *J. Educ. Psychol.*, 1927, 17, 145–62.

MEEHL, P. E. *Clinical versus Statistical Prediction*. University of Minnesota Press, 1954.

MELTZER, L., HAYES, D. T. & SHILLENBERG, C. Consistency of vocal behavior in discussion. Paper to A.P.A., 1967.

MILLER, D. T. & ROSS, M. Self-serving biases in the attribution of causality: fact or fiction? *Psychol. Bull.*, 1975, 82, 213–25.

MISCHEL, W. *Personality and Assessment*. New York: Wiley, 1968.

MISCHEL, W. Toward a cognitive social learning reconceptualisation of personality. *Psychol. Rev.*, 1973, 80, 252–83.

MOOS, R. H. Situational analysis of a therapeutic community milieu. *Journal of Abnormal Psychology*, 1968, 73, 49–61.

MOOS, R. H. Sources of variance in responses to questionnaires and in behavior. *Journal of Abnormal Psychology*, 1969, 74, 405–12.

MURRAY, H. A. *Explorations in Personality*. New York: C.U.P., 1938.

NORMAN, W. T. Toward an adequate taxonomy of personality

attributes: replicated factor structures in peer nomination personality ratings. *J. abnorm. soc. Psychol.*, 1963, 66, 574–83.

OLWEUS, D. 'Modern' interactionism in personality psychology and the analysis of variance components approach, a critical examination. In N. S. Endler & D. Magnusson (eds.), (in press).

PASSINI, F. T. & NORMAN, W. T. A universal conception of personality structures. *J. pers. soc. Psychol.*, 1966, 4, 4–49.

PHARES, E. J. *Locus of Control in Personality*. Morristown, N.J.: General Learning Press, 1976.

PERVIN, L. A. Performance and satisfaction as a function of individual-environment fit. *Psychol. Bulletin*, 1968, 69, 56–68.

PROSHANSKY, H. M. *et al.* (eds.), *Environmental Psychology: Man and his Physical Setting*. New York: Holt, Rinehart and Winston, 1970.

RAUSCH, H. L., FARBMAN, I. & LLEWELLYN, L. G. Person, setting and change in social interaction. II. A normal-control study. *Human Relations*, 1960, 13, 305–32.

SCHUTZ, W. C. *FIRO: A Three-Dimensional Theory of Interpersonal Behavior*. New York: Holt, Rinehart and Winston, 1958.

SEARS, R. R. Dependency motivation. In M. R. Jones (ed.), *Nebraska Symposium on Motivation*. Lincoln, Nebraska: University of Nebraska Press, 1963, 25–64.

SINES, J. O. Actuarial methods in personality assessment. *Progress in Experimental Personality Research*, 1966, 3, 133–93.

SNYDER, M. & MONSON, T. C. Persons, situations, and control of social behavior. *Journal of personality and social Psychology*, 1975, 4, 637–44.

SPIELBERGER, C. D. (ed.) *Theory and Research on Anxiety*. New York: Academic Press, 1966.

STERN, G. G., STEIN, M. I. & BLOOM, B. S. *Methods in Personality Assessment: Human Behavior in Complex Social Situations*. New York: Free Press, 1956.

WACHTEL, P. Psychodynamics, behavior therapy, and the implacable experimenter: An inquiry into the consistency of personality. *Journal of Abnormal Psychology*, 1973, 82, 324–34.

WALLACH, M. A. & LEGGETT, M. I. Testing the hypothesis that a person will be consistent. Stylistic consistency versus situational specificity in size of children's drawings. *Journal of Personality*, 1972, 40, 309–30.

7 The Personality of Individuals

J-P. DE WAELE and ROM HARRÉ

Introduction

The immensely complex and difficult topic of the person and his personality cannot be adequately investigated by any simplistic application of the old-fashioned experimental method. The conceptual problems which must be solved before empirical work begins are too pressing. It is our aim in this paper to make a start on the prior theoretical formulation of the problem and on the basis of our theory to propose various empirical investigations which stand some chance of being both informative and useful.

An adequate conception of 'personality' must satisfy certain *desiderata*. It must be based upon an explicitly defined philosophical basis. The unsatisfactoriness of recent work in this field stems very largely from the quite unfounded assumption that empirical investigations will somehow generate conceptual clarity. Secondly, the conception of personality that we finally find acceptable must be associated with an adequate assessment methodology which will not, of course, be independent of the theory in terms of which it is formulated, and by means of which some understanding of the results of assessment can be made. Connected with this is the conception of personality that we finally find acceptable must be capable of application to fields other than the narrow problem of psychological testing.

Together with its conceptual system, it must have application in all those fields in which the personality of a human being is the subject of investigation and the basis of predictions or at least prognoses of the future course of life of that individual. Typical fields are the penal system and clinical and educational psychology. Finally both theory and methodology must be such that they do not, in the end, lead to the elimination of the person, as such.

There are two central problems in the study of people and their personalities. Why is it that human beings have distinct personalities? What features of the genetic and social situation of human beings call forth this peculiar way of structuring an individual and the style of his actions? The most superficial analysis reveals a highly complex situation. At the centre of all human action is the self—that which is the referent of personal pronouns, that which is the ever-invisible monitor from the standpoint of which we observe, comment upon and control our actions. The enormously difficult conceptual problems which the use of this concept generates are too formidable for us to tackle in this paper. For our purposes we shall take a quite uncritical common sense attitude to the self and turn our attention to aspects of the person which, though complex, are far less difficult to handle.

It can hardly be disputed that the field of personality study and assessment is now very largely in disarray. This is illustrated no less by the mounting criticism of the trait theory (Argyle and Little, 1972) as by a decline in confidence in the definitions of personality whose inadequacy is only too manifest (McKinnon, 1944). In this field, as in many other areas of psychological study, the culprit seems to have been an uncritical positivism which has led psychologists to be satisfied with attempts to conceptualize personality from a wholly external point of view. We hold no brief for such naïvety and will take for granted that the ultimate intention of any scientific theory worthy of the name is the investigation of hypotheses about the inner natures of the entities with whose behaviour it is concerned, in the search for an explanation of the forms of that behaviour, and such stabilities in self-presentation as we recognize as personality.

An Outline of the Theory

We begin with a common-sense contrast between the essential unity of a person as a biological individual and his multiplicity when conceived of socially and with respect to his psychological functioning. This multiplicity or complexity arises in two dimensions. A person is capable of the manifestation of a multiplicity of personas— that is, of identifiably different styles of behaviour, each unified by the idea of a type of social person. We shall suggest a number of intersecting typologies, some role-based, some situation-based, and some dramaturgical, by which some order can be brought into this matter. The other dimension of complexity that characterizes people is their capacity for observing or monitoring their own actions and then observing or monitoring that monitoring, and so on. The immensely difficult problem of the self appears if we try to press prematurely the general question as to the nature of the standpoint from which this kind of observation is made.

No doubt, these dimensions of complexity are found to some extent in other primates. It is perhaps instructive to observe that primate studies reflect to a very large extent our current conceptions of ourselves. A primate is always a little simpler than a human being, so it is assumed, and for every conception we have of ourselves we devise a concept for bringing order to our investigations of the life of the primates which is only a little less complex than our self concept. It is very clear that the new-style primate studies, exemplified by Jane Goodall's investigation of the lives of chimpanzees, are anthropomorphic in the best possible sense, drawing for analytical concepts upon a refined but commonsensical view of human nature and society (Goodall, 1971). But however much we may want to identify intelligent and even Machiavellian behaviour in the social life of chimpanzees, the capacities upon which these ways of living are founded have reached such a stage of elaboration in human beings that they must be regarded, with language, as the most central and important feature on which all forms of behaviour depend.

Central to our conception of the person is the idea that his resources for social performance are not genetically fixed but grow in the manner sketched by Shotter (Ch. 2). A human being has a biography and the existence of a personal history is a necessary condition for the growth and development of the kind of complexity which he is found to have. Only by paying attention to his biography can we understand his individuality, since his particular resources are, we believe, quite as much a product of what he has experienced as they are of what he is, though what he *can* experience is directly related to what he is, and what he comes to be. A human life must be conceived in terms of the acquisition and loss of possibilities, quite as much as a chronicle of 'What actually occurred'.

Our investigations will be carried out within the general framework of what has come to be called the ethogenic theory of human performance.

I. ANALYSIS OF ACTION (PERFORMANCE I)

According to that theory we should not look primarily for the stimuli to which some action is a response because there may be no such stimuli. Instead, we should look for the cognitive and perceived and interpreted environmental conditions which shape the spontaneous flow of a person's actions into a meaningful structure.

2. ANALYSIS OF PERSONS (COMPETENCE)

When a person shows himself to have a certain power or capacity for action of a certain kind we will seek for the source of that power in his nature. In many cases the conditions which shape action are to be found in the nature of the acting individual, a nature which has both personal and universal characteristics, and which we shall follow the linguists in identifying as a form of knowledge.

3. ACCOUNTING (PERFORMANCE 2)

A connection between action and person is developed through the analysis of the speech accompanying and justifying action, a second route to the revelation of competence as grounded in social knowledge.

The powers/nature conceptual system is used as a thoroughgoing substitute for both the trait conceptual system (with its essentially passive characterization of human performance) and quality/substance theory. For example, according to the powers/nature point of view the scientific meaning of ascribing a colour (quality) to an apple (substance) is to say that a certain structure of elementary force fields (the *nature* of the apple) has the *power* to reflect light of a certain wavelength. The powers of human beings are both actively exercised, often monitored, and always potentially under the control of a person through the organized structure of his cognitive and other resources, his nature, and so are both variable and modifiable by self-intervention. They cannot therefore be traits. A person's performances are exercises of his competences or powers, and his powers are grounded in his nature, the whole complex of elements, that is his inner structure, including his biological properties in so far as they are endowed by him with meaning.

How is personality to be conceived in terms of this general standpoint? It is to be identified with the resources upon which a person draws in giving form and meaning to his actions as social performances. These resources are the basis for what one could call his social competence. So in a general way this theory falls into the competence–performance category of theories of human behaviour. Thus it differs, on the one hand, from the kind of theory which sees personality as an ensemble of traits for which no coherent internal organization is postulated and no groundings hypothesized. On the other, it differs from theories such as the psychoanalytic which regards the crucial features of the inner organization of the person as somehow immune from his personal discovery, and needing both revealing and interpreting. So from our point of view it is not sufficient simply to attribute certain social competences to an individual. The basis of those competences both in specific features of his nature as an individual and generic features as a human being must be uncovered. Furthermore, we would regard the general standpoint of biological anthropology as relevant to certain of our questions, in particular to the general question of why it is that human beings have the power to present themselves in society in such distinct ways, that is what it is about them which has led to the development of this power, and the associated powers of self-reflection, self-intervention and accounting.

In conceiving of the personality as the social resources of a human being, we must look for another term to express the internally coherent but different 'faces' which he or she manifests from time to time. Both for etymological and scientific reasons we would like to fasten on the word 'persona' for this purpose. We would like to direct the consciousness of the reader rather towards the work of Anselm Strauss (1959) than towards the ideas of Jung by the choice of this technical term. How is the persona manifested? In our view, a persona appears in the style or qualification of actions. It is expressive rather than instrumental. A persona is built up in the perceptions other people have of the actor throughout all his actions that are related to them by the growing realization by the others that those actions are performed at least in their presence in a certain identifiable manner, and by the developing habit of the actor to perform in that particular way when with those particular people, though he will, no doubt, perform in other ways with others. It is then in the adverbs of action and their adjectival qualifications that the basic elements of persona presentation are expressed. As we say, 'He opened the door sulkily', 'He recited the poem cheerfully', 'He looked at his results despondently', and so on. It is of the greatest importance that the natural forms of language be preserved in the description of the ways in which personas are presented. If we pass from the common-sense qualification of action by adverbs and their dependent adjectives to the careless creation of substantives like cheerfulness and despondency, we create once again an opening for the discredited trait theory, if not something a good deal worse. If we create alleged attributes at the performance level, then we will be tempted to try and find quasi-entities such as traits which are logically identical with those attributes and so exist only at the level of performance. It is for this reason that we want to introduce a sharp terminological distinction between personas, which are identifiable unities in performance, from personalities, which are the set of properties, qualities, etc. upon which the power to give those performances and recognize the performances of others is based. Thus, the totality of those ways of qualifying action by a given human biological individual forms, we believe, differentiable sets of qualities, each of which forms a *recognizable* persona. There must, therefore, be an interplay between the persona that we create in interaction and the typology of personas with which our culture acquaints us. The interactions of the members of each society are constrained both by the possibilities of persona creation and the necessity for that creation to be recognized by other people. The demand that it be recognizable requires that it lies within the range of some type of persona already existing in the typology. The pervasiveness of common-sense typologies and their influence in creating clinical judgements have recently been noticed and we will return to elaborate this point.

We would wish to insist that personas are unities perceived in creations of the moment, called forth by the recognition of situations, i.e. by the endowment of contingent environments with meanings. However, we do not wish to be identified with what Kenneth Bower has recently called 'Situationism' (Bower, 1973). Though it will emerge that the notion of a defined situation is central to our conception of the resources required for social competence, that situation is not to be conceived of as an independent environment surrounding a wholly passive entity. The situations we find ourselves in are created by our own individual capacity to endow the world with

meaning and negotiate that meaning with others in search of a definition. They are not environments in the Skinnerian sense. The persona
presentation of human beings cannot then be examined in isolation
from an examination of the situations which a particular culture recognizes as distinct and the capacity for the creation and recognition
of which has been acquired by many of its members. For us, the persona actually presented depends in part upon the recognition by the
actor of the type of situation in which he is acting which may, of
course, be the end product of a negotiation with his interactor. For the
more Machiavellian amongst us, the creation of that situation may be
a deliberate and conscious act. This process is interactive, since the
persona that the other presents to him will be itself a product of
similar cognitive processes. We would also like to insist that the
manifestation of a persona may be 'locked into' the presence of a
specific other person who is himself 'locked in' with the actor. Thus,
in general, personas are produced dyadically, as interactor's images
of the actor, based upon a recognition of certain systematic or
invariant properties in a set of qualifications of actions done in the
presence of or with the other member of the dyad. Thus, in general,
we would accept the analytical schema of Secord and Backman
(1961) which sees the construction of a pair of social personas as an
interactive process, as a property of a dyad.

It follows from these preliminary hypotheses or principles that
human beings are not to be conceived of as having only one persona.
Indeed it is a confusion of thought, we hold, to identify personality
and persona as if a given human being was one simple, consistent,
social entity throughout all his dealings.

In speaking of the manifestation of personas as the exercise of a
competence we do not mean to imply that that competence or power
is always consciously exercised. The principles of persona production
are no more conscious on most occasions than are the principles of
grammar. However, just as one can speak by attention to rule so
one can control and organize the manner of one's actions in the
pursuit of the manifestation of a chosen persona. It is this possibility
that we refer to when we speak of a Machiavellian. It is a
possibility for humans because of their second dimension of complexity, the many orders of self-monitoring of which they are capable.
The psychologist's task, then, is to unravel the resources of human
beings that are the basis of their social competence and to look at
the semantic and syntactical structures of the adverbial qualifications

by which these personas are presented. Clues to part of these resources will be found in the language by which we explain, justify and comment upon the production and manifestation of a persona, that is in our 'accounts'.

While accepting much of Mischel's recent discontents with the state of personality studies and strongly endorsing his emphasis on cognitive factors in personality (Mischel 1973), we would regard his 'situation × person' scheme as not yet sufficiently sophisticated. Neither situation nor person can be generalized, and at the heart of this perception is the realization that a person, conceived as the bearer of certain social competences, has a unique structure, intelligible only because it contains many universal elements, coordinated in their social meaning by a common language. But 'situation' is not an independent 'variable' in this 'function'. Situations are constructed and endowed with meaning by people in terms of those very same cognitive resources upon which their social competence depends, and are only mildly constrained by their person-independent physical parameters. Thus, to take the mathematical rhetoric a stage further, the unit of social action is a non-linear function of cognitive social resources, not even of one person, unless that person is a very astute Machiavellian, but of two; the elementary dyad for whose interaction personas come forth.

Physical Anthropology and the Roots of Personality

On the ethogenic view of personality, which is based on the fundamental nature/powers paradigm, the basis of the social performances of an individual is to be found in his nature. As a realistic conception of personality cannot rest content with purely descriptive characterizations which would lead only to a definition in terms of nominal essences, the outward appearances of things, one must go further and try to reach 'real essences', the inner structures of things. It has to be shown that personality as conceived of by ethogenists is a reality, rooted in human nature as an essential basis. This means that it has to be demonstrated, (a) how personality and the exercise of social competences by which it manifests itself are possible, (b) why they are necessary. In anticipation it can be said that the conditions of possibility for personality are to be found in the specific biological make-up of human beings and their unique developmental characteristics, while the necessity of there being evolved a personality structure as we have outlined it has to be derived from the exigencies of socially defined, rule-governed conduct in highly differentiated organisms which are almost completely devoid of innate instinctive responses, at least as far as their social behaviour is concerned. Even the smile, biologically based though it is, acquires its range of human meanings culturally (Leach, 1972). In short, on the ethogenic view, personality is to be considered as the organized structure of competences which, in the process of self-domestication, man substitutes for the instinctive responses dominant in other species, in order to integrate the individual into various forms of social order.

This position should not be taken to mean that we are conceiving personality as an attribute exclusively possessed by man. On the contrary, ethogenic theory is not only quite consistent with recent findings concerning the behaviour of anthropoids, but moreover the inter-penetration of human biological nature and the culture on which it rests can only be understood if one takes into account modern data on the process of anthropogenesis in the course of which cultural developments and biological evolution have, so to speak, pushed each other forward to the present state reached by man.

Finally, it should be noted that in the ethogenic theory being proposed here, biological and cultural factors are not to be conceived as terms of a dichotomy between which some kind of interaction prevails, but as compresent processes of an open system in the functioning of which they represent two sets of determinable constraints.

During recent decades, anthropologists, biologists and philosophers have made several attempts to synthesize and interpret the data accumulated by physical anthropology, for instance, A. Gehlen (1955); O. Storch (1948); A. Portmann (1951); A. Keith (1948); G. Roheim (1950); K. Conrad (1963); A. Montagu (1965). It is our belief that the data they have gathered, as well as the theories they have elaborated, may, if properly fitted together, lead to a general conception of human nature in accord with the products of analysis of social life considered autonomously and analysed from a micro-sociological standpoint. This is particularly true of the work of Gehlen, Portmann and Conrad, whose very important contributions have not received, at least within the confines of the English-speaking world, all the attention they rightly deserve.

At this point we want to introduce a note of caution with respect to the assimilation of anthropological and biological data into psychological studies. In recent years there have been many attempts to apply concepts originally developed in ethology to the analysis of human social life. We do not believe that these attempts have yet risen much above the level of journalism. Indeed, we would be inclined to take the view that recent primate studies are more a product of sensitive anthropomorphism than a source of analytical concepts for understanding human life. Thus our concern is rather with the biological conditions of the cognitive conception of the genesis of social life than with a search for biological concepts by which social life could be analysed.

The fundamental concept from which one has to start is that the great majority of distinctively human morphological traits are markedly primitive or unspecialized in comparison with the development they have reached in other primates. This is in strong contrast to the elaborate and specialized social capacities of human beings, such as speech-competence. This lack of specialization means that they are not adapted to any specific environment. A long list of such organic primitivisms can be adduced. For example, the proportion of facial and cranial parts of the skull (small face and large brain case), the 'flatness' of the face, the retention of cranial flexure, the long neck, the forward position of the foramen magnum, roundheadedness, the relative hairlessness of the body, the persistence of cranial sutures, and so on. One difficulty of which we are aware is that the selection of primitivisms is relative to some theory of development. For example, of those that we have mentioned, some would be regarded as specializations by those who accept Sir Alistair Hardy's theory of anthropogenesis, the theory of aquatic man. (For a popular presentation, see Morgan, 1972). For example, he would regard roundheadedness and relative hairlessness as highly specialized characteristics related to life in the shallow waters of the ancient Rift Valley. It was the Dutch anatomist, L. Bolk (1926), who brought order into such primitivisms as can genuinely be identified by separating phylogenetic primitivisms from ontogenetic ones. As to the first of these, he hypothesized and confirmed by his comparative observations that the distinctively human unspecializations were the result of foetal characteristics or proportions that had become permanent, or as he put it, they were 'form characteristics or form proportions, which in the foetus of all other primates are transitory, ... stabilized in man'. This means that the very striking unspecialization of human morphological characteristics does not represent newly acquired characteristics which would be in contradiction with Dollo's law of the irreversibility of specialisms, but transitory stages common to all primates, which in anthropoids become more specialized although in man they are retained in the adult form of the individual. Ontogenetic primitivism, on the other hand, has to be understood as the kind of lack of specialization which results from a prolonged state of immaturity. As did many others, Bolk drew attention to another set of human characteristics —the slow growth, the long period of childhood, and the long post-reproductive phase. He then interpreted morphological primitiveness and slowness of development as the consequences of a typically human retardation of development (Bolk's so-called Retardation Law).

The theory of Bolk consists, then, in making phylogenetical foetalization a consequence of retardation processes. Slowing down of ontogenetical development would thus give rise to unspecified morphological characteristics by stabilizing them at some early stage of their development. Symbolizing his position about the origin of distinctive human traits, Bolk asserts, 'the essence of [human] morphology is the result of foetalization, the essence of life development the consequence of retardation'. Both these properties stand in close causal connection because foetalization of form is a necessary consequence of retardation.

This is not the place to discuss the detailed arguments in favour of Bolk's theory of neoteny or paedomorphosis, nor to point out its shortcomings as an overall theory of human morphology. It should, however, be noted that its acceptance, in a general way, implies a reformulation of Haeckel's famous biogenetic law: indeed, if there exists a causal relationship between retardation and foetalization then obviously ontogeny does not simply recapitulate philogeny, it creates it (Hardy, 1954).

Cephalization, the development of a relatively large brain, is another outstanding human characteristic. The degree of cephalization can be measured by the ratio of brain to body weight, which in human beings reaches sixty-four times the cephalization of the primitive mammal and is roughly proportional to the relative number of neurons in their respective nervous systems. Cephalization thus represents a typically human specialization that seems to run counter to the lack of specialization postulated by the neotenic theory. Erect posture, the structure of hands and feet etc., are other human specializations which are, perhaps, linked with cephalization. But it should be pointed out that the kind of specialization apparent in human anatomy does not result in a narrowly limited adaptation to specific environmental conditions, rather human specialization is in the direction of a capacity for survival in very various conditions. The same can be said of cephalization because it results in an organ that makes for plasticity, differentiation and variability in a generally unspecialized being.

As Hofstätter (1951) has shown, there exists a marked relationship between cephalization and psychomotor maturation. The higher the cephalization coefficient, the slower the psychomotor maturation. Not only does the maturation of an enlarged brain take more time, the learning processes which it makes possible also need time. And all the more so in that in order for learning in the usual sense to take place, not only do certain maturational conditions have to be met, but also some 'primary' learning has to take place. Whereas primary learning processes are essentially perceptual and lead to the establishment of new neuronal connections between incoming sensory stimulus patterns and corresponding cerebral networks, the secondary learning that takes place throughout life is based on the system of connections built up by primary learning.

A good deal of evidence has accumulated which shows that human encephalization implies retardation. Or to put it differently: a slow development is a necessary condition for a large brain to mature and to acquire by means of primary learning the kind of functional readiness it needs in order to be free for its numerous secondary learning tasks. The exact details of the process of primary learning and its relation to secondary are still obscure and in dispute. For example, it now seems likely that motor skills are built up of quite elaborate fixed routines which have a genetic origin (Bruner, 1974).

The helplessness of the newborn child has often been the subject of lyrical effusions, but its meaning and its connection with essential aspects of human nature have not always been properly understood. *Prima facie*, it would seem as if the prolonged state of immaturity at birth should place man among the nidicoles. Nidicoles are animals which are born after a relatively short gestation, as members of a litter composed of several individuals. Their immaturity at birth makes them completely dependent on their parents for survival. Nidifuges, on the other hand, are born after a long gestation period, a litter comprising only one or two individuals who, because of their sensory-motor maturity at birth, have a considerable degree of autonomy from their parents.

Though reptiles are, in general, nidifuges, birds and mammals show both patterns of relationship between birth-state and developmental maturity. Thus there appear to be two 'solutions' to the problem posed by increase in the duration of maturation and development as a consequence of increasing encephalization. Both solutions have their drawbacks. Too long a gestation time not only makes the female extremely vulnerable to various kinds of external changes, but also raises serious obstetrical problems. On the other hand, the nidicole solution makes the immature newborns very vulnerable. But if we consider the newborn human child to be a nidicole we immediately run into difficulties. Not only would he thereby deviate from all other primates which are nidifuges, but he exhibits a series of characteristics which he shares with nidifuges. For example, nidicoles are born with closed sensory organs but in man the eyes are open long before birth, and there are many other similar features. The contradictory aspects of the newborn human, who manifests both the helpless immaturity of the nidicole, while sharing a whole series of essential attributes with nidifuges, can be reconciled only by conceiving of man as a phylogenetic nidifuge who has become a secondary nidicole because of his premature birth. It is, indeed, only about one year after birth that the human child starts behaving as a real nidifuge, because it is only at that time that a sufficient degree of sensory-motor coordination is reached, walking becomes possible, and the first words are uttered. In other words, if a human child were to be born as a full-fledged nidifuge, gestation time would be at least twenty-one months. In itself, this is not biologically impossible, but a human infant must be born at a time when the development of its head is still compatible with its passage through the pelvic canal. Whatever their obvious importance, anatomical factors are not the only ones to be taken into account and the causes of the human infant's 'premature' birth still remain obscure.

The consequences of a long period of 'extero-gestation' are quite clear. The necessary intimacy of the child–mother relationship leads to the appearance of an interpersonal *Umwelt* as the first environment the infant encounters while still in course of development. Through the mother, or a partial mother substitute, the infant is exposed to continuous pressure towards socialization and domestication by means of various 'techniques' of management and schedules of care and feeding, manifestly directed towards it by one of its own kind. And, most importantly, from the first hours of its life the newborn infant is being communicated with both verbally and non-verbally. Most of his behaviour and accompanying expressions are being responded to and given verbal expression by the mother. The importance of speech which the mother directs to the child has been much emphasized in recent studies (Richards, 1974).

That the first year of life is to be considered an extra-uterine foetal year is also revealed by the relatively rapid growth that takes place during this period, though the human brain continues its growth throughout the first two decades of life. As Zeller (1957) has clearly shown, at the age of about six years the human form has an indubitable morphological unity. Before that age body proportions are characterized by the predominant volume of the head and the trunk over the volume of the limbs. At the time of what Zeller calls the first metamorphosis, childlike proportions substitute themselves for the former infantile proportions, for instance limbs show an increasing growth in proportional length. More important still, many new psycho-motor manipulations become possible, so that elementary tasks can be executed independently, and it becomes possible for the child to start learning to read and write. As we have argued elsewhere (Harré, 1974), it is just at this period that children begin to develop competence in and understanding of the ritual and dramaturgical devices by the development of which the management of the adult social world becomes possible.

The relatively late appearance of sexual maturity in the human life span, at about twelve to fifteen years after birth, is shared by some of the higher primates. The chimpanzee, for example, shares very much the same life proportions as the human being, but in man there exists a unique relationship between sexual maturity and growth. Whereas in higher mammals sexual maturity only appears after the major part of growth has taken place, in man puberty is accompanied by an intensification of growth processes.

Characteristics of this period of development is a general morphological disharmony which is frequently accompanied by a certain motor awkwardness. This phase concludes the second metamorphosis and leads to some further quantitative growth until in the early twenties the mature body form is attained.

At this stage, when no further changes in body proportions due to growth processes are to be expected, different body types become clearly discriminable. Starting with the work of Carus (1858) up to Rees and Eysenck (1945), several kinds of physical typologies have been elaborated. In spite of great differences in the methods used to establish them and of the great divergencies in their conceptualization, there exists a considerable degree of agreement between most of them. The best known of these constitutional typologies is undoubtedly the one presented by E. Kretschmer (1955). To judge by the enormous amount of research it has generated in psychology and in psychiatry, it has certainly been the most fertile. Its most outstanding achievement has been to demonstrate the existence of numerous correlations between body structure and psycho-pathological as well as other psychological characteristics.

However, the purely descriptive nature of Kretschmer's typology has been detrimental to its scientific development, for though clusters of correlations were discovered no explanatory theory was elaborated to account for their existence. So in the long run Kretschmer's theory came to exhibit a markedly static character. Futhermore, effective conceptualization based on the distinction of the polar types of the pycnic, the leptosome, and the athletic also hampered progress. It was K. Conrad (1963) who rescued Kretschmerian typology from this impasse by reformulating its basic concepts and by linking the formation of physical types and their psychological correlates to the distinctly human growth tendencies which have already been outlined. First of all, Conrad distinguishes two interdependent polar dimensions, the pycnomorph/leptomorph and the asthenic/athletic dimensions, which he calls respectively primary and secondary variations. To these he adds tertiary variations in order to take various forms of dysplastic and dismorphic growth tendencies into account. As Conrad clearly demonstrates, extreme pycnomorphs and extreme leptomorphs result from marked differences in body proportions. Making use of a great number of physical measurements, he then shows that the distinctively pycnomorph proportions are closely similar to those encountered in earlier stages of ontogenetic development, and more particularly those corresponding to the first metamorphosis. On the other hand, leptomorphic proportions bear a marked resemblance to those of the second metamorphosis. His developmental theory of constitutional types then consists in deriving the various body proportions that can be ordered on the pycnomorph/leptomorph

dimension from the relative prominence of conservative and propulsive growth tendencies in any given individual.

As far as the asthenic/athletic dimension is concerned, the athletic
body type is characterized by the intensification of the growth of
all extremities, of the shoulder-girdle and of the musculature. As the
fully developed athletic habitus appears after puberty, Conrad con-
siders it to be the result of some specific propulsive growth tendency.
As to the extreme asthenic type, its characteristics and its developmental origins are in all respects the symmetrical opposite of the
athletic type.

The importance of Conrad's theory lies not only in the fact that
it provides a developmental explanation of Kretschmerian types by
relating them to specifically human ontogenetic processes, its
explanatory power extends also to the physiological and psychological
characteristics related to the physical typology, as is evidenced by the
great wealth of data he uses in his demonstration. From our point
of view the social meaning attached to these body forms by oneself
and others, and the relative difficulty through diet and exercise,
clothing etc. to change them, show that they form a *relatively* stable
ground base to the primarily cognitive features upon which human
personality as social resources depends.

Considering the enormous amount of time and energy that has
already been spent on psychometric and factor-analytic research with
the aim of discovering fundamental typological dimensions, without
any comparable efforts at explaining the descriptive findings, we can
only wish that instead of looking exclusively for more refined
mathematical treatment, psychometricians would begin to formulate
their research in a developmental framework. The biological aspects
of human development which we have just sketched are the
conditions for and causes of the development of the specifically
human way of creating and maintaining a social order at the heart
of which is the process of persona production. However, to establish
this conclusion firmly we wish to show briefly how these anthro-
pogenetic conditions do in fact provide both the necessity for and
the possibility of a substitute for instinct.

In arguing for the elimination of any notion of instinctive action
in understanding the exercise of human social competences we are
not, of course, denying the obvious truth that there are certain
elements and patterns of action that are automatic. Instinctive action
must not be confused with reflexes or habits or actions on impulse,

or even unconscious actions. It is to instinct as identified positively by ethologists that we wish to deny a role in understanding human social behaviour. Instinctive behaviour is understood ethologically as a routine which is generated by an instinctive mechanism and that mechanism is present in the make-up of the animal through the usual selective processes of evolution. It is our contention that in human beings there are no such instinctive mechanisms. Their place is taken by structures which are no less responsible for routines of social action but are the product of processes which begin anew in each human individual and are not, in general, inherited, nor are their forms explicable in terms of evolutionary adaptation.

We do not, however, wish to deny that there exist what one might call instinct residues. These are plainly present in the motor field and are clearly exhibited during the first year of life. There are, for instance, such patterns as Darwin's grasping reflex, and we have already noticed the suggestion by Bruner that complex sensory-motor routines are structures not of elementary responses but of still complex sub-routines. It is plain, we believe, that in the first year of life such instinct residues disappear and are replaced pro-gressively by the possibility of self-control.

There remains another category of genetically based responses which are clearly involved in the social performances of human beings. We refer, for example, to the acts of grooming which people perform when slightly stressed, to the basic form of facial expression such as van Hooff (1972) has so carefully classified, and such apparently fundamental responses as those which are elicited by baby-sized and shaped objects. We are impressed by the fact that the domestic cat is roughly the same shape and size as a three-month human infant. However, it is our contention that none of these residual bases or forms of action are of sufficient generality to allow us to formulate a purely ethological theory of human social action. The residues which survive the first year of life are frag-mentary and unspecific. As Leach has remarked (1972) in com-mentary on van Hooff's taxonomy of smiles and laughs, the social meanings which can be attached to such a basic repertoire may be both contradictory and exceedingly elaborate.

If one is prepared to accept the neoteny theory in a general way it is clear that the opportunity exists in the extero-uterine first year for a great deal of learning to occur. It is our contention that this opportunity is to be understood as the source both of the necessity

for social learning and for its possibility. It is a central doctrine
of ethogenics that the causes of action are not to be sought in the
cognitive or emotive conditions of such action. Rather we contend
that the stream of human activity has its source in a degree of
physiological arousal which remains far above the minimal perceptual and appetitive necessities. That is, there are a series of bio-
genic need-states which have no fixed connection to specific sequences
of appetitive or consummatory behaviour patterns, nor to specific
perceptual structures. As a consequence, the powers of perception
are no longer selectively subordinate to the necessities of immediate
action, nor indeed are any other human powers so subordinated. Thus
there remains a redundancy upon which skills may be developed.
We are far from wishing to deny that this feature of development is
present in other animals than ourselves. However, it is our contention that among humans, neoteny is so extreme as to make the
exploitation of relatively redundant powers the main feature of the
human maturational process, redundant that is with respect to the
primary needs of organic survival, *both* individual and specific.

If the problems of the general direction of human development
are illuminated by the idea of an unspecific and relatively redundant
'activation energy', and a correspondingly 'redundant' neurological
elaboration, then certain consequences follow. The first concerns
the gap between a 'need-state' and consummatory action. If, as we
suppose, it is characteristic of the first year of life for there to be a
disconnection between need-state and action, then the opportunity
arises for a labelling of the need-state via some cognitive process
initiated through the labelling by the mother of what she attributes to
a child as his intentions, the processes identified by Richards. Then
once labelling starts, the labels themselves become items in cognitive
processes. The possibility for the origin of semantic grouping seems
to derive from this general situation. It also seems likely that some
such explanation is proper for all those activities that human beings
and other complex animals exhibit which have been called play.
Furthermore, not only does an autonomous structure of labels
appear as the basis of semantic competence, but it may also be the
case that the surplus 'activation energy' may be the basis of a
secondary system of intentions which, of course, are much more
difficult for a mother to label. These could be the source of the
enormously potent and sometimes florid fantasies with which human
beings often prepare for action, and of the crucially human pro-

cesses of self-intervention based upon what Frankfurt has called second-order desires (cf. Taylor, 1976).

Thus, encephalization and its correlate neoteny can be seen to result in two conjugate and central properties of human life, the great plasticity of non-specific activation and the cognitive and linguistic competences which develop initially for its mastery. If human beings are as we have so briefly sketched them to be, then it is plain that the organization of social action must be both elaborate and centred on cognitive capacities. Thus the cognitive processes which lie behind human modes of social interaction can be seen as imposing a range of specific forms on the stream of undifferentiated action, dividing it in time, locating it in place, qualifying it in manner, and providing it with intentional objects. From whence do these forms emerge?

Our answer would be that they are the products of a history of cognitive and symbolic processes among human beings, in the course of which we apply to our own offspring the very same kind of techniques we apply to the animals incorporated in our social order. Human social development then has the form of general domestication. It is to the biology and ethology of domestic animals that we would look for animal analogues.

The effects of domestication upon animals are quite clear (Fox, 1967). They acquire a greater tolerance for novelty than their feral relatives and a complementarily more active exploratory behaviour, perhaps in search of the stimulus of novelty. Their learning ability is correspondingly enhanced (Thorpe, 1963). At the same time the routines of feral life disintegrate into separable elements, so that appetitive behaviour is emancipated from consummatory behaviour, and the acquisition of all sorts of routines not founded in inherited patterns becomes possible (Eibl-Eibelsfeldt, 1970). In all these respects, domestication and neoteny seem closely analogous, and the one may provide a model for the other (Bruner, 1972).

The acquisition of culture as the learning process which a highly cephalized being, devoid of adaptive instinct mechanisms, has to undergo, presupposes the existence of a source from which the patterns which have to be learnt emanate. This source cannot be anything but socially organized man himself. Considering that 'domestication' may be defined as the intentional control through several generations of breeding, feeding and training (Boice, 1973), it follows that in substituting culturally defined modes of conduct for the almost non-existent instinctive behaviour patterns, human life as a stable form of relationship with self-created social and natural environments is the product of self-domestication, *and a doubly reflexive process*. Both the necessity for and possibility of 'self-dom-estication' derive from but are not resolved by human biological history. Finally, it would not be unreasonable to expect some of the adaptability, degree of neoteny and variability of the human popula-tion to derive from initial and rudimentary self-domestication in response to the beginnings of human evolution.

The Occasions for the Manifestation of Personas

The immensely complex nature of the social world and the corresponding complexity of the problems which it continually presents to us, problems such as the difficulty of determining the attitude of another person, the difficulty of determining the nature of the situation in which one finds oneself and the appropriate form of action to adopt, the difficulty of managing a situation to one's own advantage, or at the very least maintaining its stability and preserving the dignity of all involved, and so on—these problems are so complex that we shall discuss the growth and development of what we shall take to be the human personality in terms of some extremely simple, archetypal problem situations.

Imagine a narrow mountain-path: two people are approaching a bend, each unaware of the presence of the other: they meet. A solution to a problem has to be found, that is, it has to be decided who will give way, by how much, and in what manner, to facilitate the free passage of each person. This is a fairly simple problem structurally and yet it generates an extremely complex hierarchy of social problems. First of all no problem would exist were it not for the fixed structure of the relatively permanent physical environment. Secondly, restrictive environments are generally not problematic for someone in the absence of other human beings or their traces (Goff-man, 1971). And lastly, had both travellers been going in the same direction, namely up or down the mountain, then the situation would have been problematic no longer. However, the aims of the two walkers can be imagined to be in conflict, each wishing to travel in a direction contrary to the other.

For such a situation two possibilities exist. It may be that the travellers are already parties to a set of conventions by which, for example, the man coming up stands aside to allow the downward passenger to descend, each recognizes the autonomy and integrity of the other with a series of gestures by which the courteous act of the one is acknowledged and deference is shown by the other. It may be that on this mountain such a solution is standard. However, it could also be the case that the travellers meeting have no common set of conventions by which such a problematic situation can be resolved. They have to create a solution for this particular case and this particular occasion. Such a solution will, by the nature of the case, be improvised within some shared conventions of civility. We shall argue that the repertoire of standard solutions which a person has at his command constitutes a kind of substitute for the instinctive systems by which animals operate their lives. By 'instinctive systems' we mean those sorts of processes which ethologists have uncovered. Part of what constitutes the human personality of a social being is the set of standard solutions of which he or she is master.

But it is clear from simple examples such as the problem of the mountain path, that quite frequently we are in situations in which we have no prepared solution to hand. In those cases we must create a solution. We must operate in such a way as to preserve a social order and yet achieve the solution which we want. It is to the resources and techniques required for this kind of problem-solving that we wish to direct our attention, and we shall argue that the human personality must also be conceived as including resources for the successful construction of improvised solutions to problems of a social kind.

What then differentiates a social solution to a problem from any other? We shall argue that a solution is social only if it recognizes the autonomy and cognitive status of all the parties to the problem, so that, to return to the simple example of the mountain path, were one of the travellers to push the other over the brink and so pursue his way unimpeded, this would not constitute a social solution. However, it is unwise to *identify* the non-social with the exercise of physical causality. It might be well to distinguish between those kinds of physical causality which are meaningless socially and those to which a meaning has been, or is being given, in the course of the interaction. Where physical causality is given a meaning, the exercise of it is part of a social solution. This follows from the fact that if the meaning is to be perceived by victim and actor it is necessary that the actor recognizes the autonomy and cognitive status of the other, otherwise his meaningful physical causality falls, as it were, upon deaf ears.

The archetypal situation which we have described leads us to say in general that there are both standard and improvised situation-dependent and ceremonially potent means of solving the problems with which a social being is continually beset. Within a standard solution lies a standard persona. We wish to emphasize the many orders of creative possibilities for humans in the presentation of personas. The higher-order organization of human cognitive resources allows a person not only to employ a standard solution and qualify his actions in a standard way, thus manifesting a standard social self, but he may at the same time qualify that qualification so as, for example, to indicate his resentment of the presence of the other in the freezing way he politely ushers the other by. Politeness and resentment are joint possibilities of an encounter though they are manifested at a different semantic order.

Each socially competent person then must be capable of the convention bound performance that is called for in standard situations and, as we have pointed out, must also have the resources to cope with situations where the standard devices are not obviously appropriate. In such cases the doublet situation/persona is up for negotiation. A mutual definition of the situation may be achieved by a process in which personas are themselves benefited; and of course a situation having been defined, the identity or persona of the person as interactant in that and that situation only is complementarily fixed. It is our view that the markedly different capability for this kind of activity which differentiates human beings is a reflection in part of differences in the cognitive resources available to them.

In order to make this the subject of an empirical investigation some structural hypothesis must be proffered for the organization of the material We suggest that the resources which are manifested by a human being, either in an observer's accounts of actions and their qualifications or in his own accounts in which his actions are justified or explained, can be organized into a matrix, each element of which may be exceedingly complex. The matrix would recognize four major components of the basis of social competence: namely, knowledge of situations, knowledge of personas, recognition of the possibility of a judgement of the propriety of performance, and a set of rules or conventions which might or might not be capable of explicit statement. The cognitive matrix of a socially competent individual would be made up of rows each of which contained knowledge of situation, persona, the conventions of propriety in that situation, and the set of rules by which the conventions operative in it could be expressed in action-sequences and their stylistic qualifications likely to be thought proper. The columns would then represent the diversity of situations which a person could recognize, create or define; the diversity of personas which he could manifest; the diversity of judgements of propriety which he would recognize, usually personified in an image of some actual individual whose imagined reactions are consulted; and the divers sets of rules appropriate to each situation.

We would like to draw attention to the remarkable similarity between the structure and content we attribute to the cognitive matrix and the rather misleadingly described 'basic components of social action' proposed by Smelser (1963). He recognizes quite 'generalized ends or *values*' which correspond to the imagined reactions of the person or persons to whom our social actor refers the priority of his acts; 'the regulatory rules governing the pursuit of these goals . . . , norms', which correspond to our sets of rules; how, 'if we move to the social system level . . . motivated individuals are organized into roles . . .' corresponding to that part of an individual's ensembles of personas that are institutionally or otherwise formally defined, the usual referent of the term 'role' . . . ; and finally, 'the available *situational* facilities which the actor utilizes as means . . .' which we would regard not so much as 'come across' and utilized, but in more problematic situations as created by negotiations or definitions.

Smelser suggests that the four components of what we would regard as the cognitive resources of social competence form a hierarchy. Values are, for him, the most general components of these resources, acquiring specific form or realization through the application of norms, which can only be displayed in action by appropriately defined agents, whose knowledge of their social (and physical) environment enables them to recognize and so utilize the situation appropriate for action.

The sociological concept of 'role', though extending somewhat into the territory we wish to examine, has certain drawbacks as a social psychological concept. A role performance, as doctor, mother, or managing director, may indeed involve the display of a distinct persona, but role is, in general, defined complementarily with an institution; and indeed has been regarded by some as completely definable as the intersection of certain institutional relations. It seems clear that human social performance involves a considerable number of typologies, only some of which are institutionally defined. Many personas find their definitions in dramaturgical sources, for example.

A cognitive matrix, such as the one we propose, would allow the definition of an ideal competence, deviance from which would lead one to expect breakdowns in performance, and perhaps allow the identification of the situations in which this might occur. In general, we would regard the concept of social incompetence as analysable in terms of inappropriateness of presentational performance, so that a mis-match between elements of a cognitive matrix could be offered as an explanation of inappropriate behaviour in a well-defined situation. From this theoretical position we would offer a number of empirical hypotheses as to the cognitive structures of various categories of deviant. For example, there might be a category which would derive from a short-fall in the range of personas so that inappropriate ways of behaving would be manifested by the actor in a situation which he was able to see called for something other than his form of style of action though he would not know what. There is some evidence from criminological studies to suggest that a certain category of young violent criminals exemplifies that structure.

We have then the theory of social action as a mode of intelligent action, not, as Argyle has suggested (Argyle, 1969), analogous to a motor skill but instead a species of the kind of intellectual skill that is displayed, say, in solving crossword puzzles or rehearsing a play. In our view, we have sufficient evidence from the ethnomethodology of everyday life to say already that human beings can be differentiated along a continuum. At one pole are those to whom perhaps the image of a mechanism whose reactions are wholly automatic is appropriate, at the other those whose social skills, degree of self-awareness and capacity for bodily and verbal self-control are such that they can properly be given the honorific title of Machiavellians. We have yet to discuss any theory of the causation of social action and its qualification to generate personas. As we shall show, the new ethogenic method in social psychology with concentrates on the analysis of accounts does not lead to any simple causal theory. Instead it is concerned with something more fundamental. What is the mode of action of the cognitive resources of a human being in generating behaviour?

Personality as the Set of Formal Causes of Action

We have already repudiated the idea that persona and personality are to be identified. For us, the personality is the basis of the social competence of an adequate human being while his personas are the coherent presentations of social self which appear in the 'adverbial' or stylistic qualifications of his actions. However, we have still to explain how the personality, that is, the set of resources, works its way into action. In order to clear the ground for specific empirical work one must see that one's conceptual system is in order. We must pause, then, to say a word about the variety of notions of causality and to identify that which we believe to be appropriate to this branch of empirical science.

Much the same modes of causality are used in the psychological and social sciences as appear to be appropriate in the physical sciences. The concept of causality that is employed in the physical sciences is generative. Physical science analyses the world into *powerful individuals*, such as magnetic fields. The task of the physical scientist is a twofold investigation of such entities. In pursuit of some knowledge of their natures and of the conditions under which they act, physical scientists have developed a two-tier structure of knowledge, with overt behaviour as the subject-matter of one tier and the mechanism explanatory of that behaviour of another. For example, Boyle's Law would be in one tier and the molecular hypothesis of the nature of gases in the other. If a gas is conceived as a swarm of molecules, the behaviour of the molecules is the cause of, or explains, the behaviour of the gas. Or the magnetic field may be offered in the second tier as the explanation of the way magnetic compasses behave when they are moved from place to place around the earth—the magnetic field and its differentiated structure are the cause of the form of behaviour of the compasses. The magnetic field is a powerful individual, or agent.

In order to find our way about in this conceptual system it might be helpful to reintroduce some traditional terminology, in particular, the distinction between efficient and formal cause. The efficient cause of some action is that particular change in the standing conditions which leads directly or indirectly to the new situation. An efficient cause does not persist; it is like the pressing of a trigger. But no efficient cause could trigger action unless a powerful individual were present to generate it. Thus, pressing the trigger of an unloaded gun will not produce a bang. Gunpowder must be present in the chamber.

The formal cause of an action is that feature of the conditions which generate it which endows the action with its structure or form. In practice, a formal cause is often a synchronic structure which is manifested in the diachronic structure of a process, as, for example, a musical score is the source of the structure of a musical performance.

In a similar spirit, we would be prepared to countenance 'final' or teleological causes, not as some mysterious forces drawing the present towards the future, but as the representation of the goals, the awareness of the acts, the meanings of the actions, within the plan whose unfolding in a diachronic process is the action, and which as a pre-existing structure is the formal cause of the action.

In the psychological sciences it is our belief that progress will best be made by locating the source of action in the person, seeing that action as structured by preformed templates. We would be prepared to go as far as to say that efficient causes may not be part psychology at all, and we shall show in the course of this section what we mean by such a radical proposal. We conceive of the generation of social action as the transformation of a cognitive structure into a linear or more complex sequence of overt actions which may be both behavioural and verbal. In general, the entity which serves as the template for the forms of action will be of the general character of a plan or rule though it may find its actual psychological reality as something more in the nature of an image. Derivatively it may function as a powerful individual having the special property of being a formal cause, the source of the structure of the action sequence generated in accordance with it. It is our contention that human social life can be conceived (as one among several valuable conceptions) as the imposition of form on a basic activity whose ultimate origins are to be found in physiology. Furthermore, the labelling as emotions of certain physiological states as they enter our awareness, can be explained by reference to the meanings of the action-sequence which those feelings accompany. The idea is that it is the running through of the 'template', transformed into a diachronic sequence of real or imagined actions, which explains the reality of the emotions that accompany imagined action, and so explains the effectiveness of certain forms of desensitization.

The characteristic scientific problem for a psychologist, in our view, is the question of the origin of the forms of action, rather than the attempts to find the efficient causes of actions, as particular but unstructured events. In the context of our distinction between standard and non-standard solutions to problematic situations the idea of the formal cause as a derivative source of activity appears in the distinction between those routines which have become habitual or standard and those cases where, though action is plainly called for, the structure must be prepared carefully either in advance of the action or during it at a second order of consciousness. Psychologists have been much confused on this point. Just as Aristotle confusedly supposed that the causal question could be asked about each step or stage of an inertial motion, so psychologists have sometimes thought that we must ask the efficient cause question of each step of a complex routine. Instead, we suppose that in very many cases, and in particular in the genesis of social action, the question of the efficient cause of each component is seriously misplaced. Instead we must ask what structured entity is serving as the template for this organized form of behaviour. Thus, from the point of view of the science of psychology, the *occurrence* of some action or other must be conceived to be spontaneous unless otherwise explained. This distinction is very clearly marked in the relation between syllabic babbling and language. Both babbling and language are forms of the same stream of spontaneously produced behaviour, the former being formless and the latter having form imposed upon it. (Compare the carrier wave and its frequency and amplitude modulations in wireless telegraphy.)

There are several consequences of the adoption of the point of view of agent acting in accordance with structured templates. One ought perhaps to re-emphasize the fact that moving to this conceptualization of action provides the basis for a kind of empirical study that is perhaps ironically much more in the pattern of the established natural sciences than is the now traditional pattern of psychological research which is frequently no more than the search for the conditions that will trigger an action without any attention to the form of the action that ensues. But there are more important consequences than that. The adoption of this set of concepts removes the need for the postulation of any mysterious driving-force such as motive. Motives become part of accounts which are proffered by actors in explanation of their actions. Explanations of actions are more often offered in a context of justification than as hypothetical efficient causes. And it is the set of available explanations that determines, we believe, the range of actions any individual conceives as possible in a situation (Blum and McHugh, 1971). Similarly, statements of wants can be reconstrued as statements of the hoped-for outcome of plans rather than as the descriptions of psychological states which are the causes of actions. These moves eliminate the need for the postulation of any mysterious physiologico-psychological forces such as drives. Finally, intentions become construable as the first phases of plans, goal settings which may never be elaborated into fully implementable plans by the selection of means. This construal fits an observation first made by Lewin that intention vanishes when the goal is achieved, since the plan is no longer active when its outcome is reached; the plan, by transformation, has become the action. It remains for us to ask how, given this conceptual system, we suppose that the content and structure of plans and rules are related to what actually happens.

The simplest and most economical hypothesis is to suppose that a plan or rule is simply related to a sequence of actions by a straightforward transformation; that is, that the content and structure of the plan are identical with the content and structure of the sequence of actions, and that there are certain higher-order rules by which this transformation is effected.

Finally, in this general account of the ethogenic conception of the genesis of social action, we would like to draw attention to the fact that it is characteristic of human beings to produce their own action—structure—generating plans, for example, for the solution of non-standard problematic situations. Thus a quite elaborate structure may be envisaged and carried through in such a short interaction as the problematic situation on the mountain-path.

In the unfolding of these structures in action lies the possibility of the creation and presentation to others of social selves or personas. The actions may be carried out in a variety of ways; the adverbial qualifications fitting together into coherent indicators of a recognized social persona type. To continue our metaphor of the plan as a formal cause or template which is transformed into a diachronic action sequence, we notice that stylistic flourishes are, as one might say, normal to the general line of the development of the action. At least in our cultures the manifestation of a persona in first-order action in what we do or what we say is thought to be unacceptable. One must first try implication, and that is as much as to say that if one wishes to present an attractive persona, or an unattractive one for that matter, one must do it not by overt statement or action but by the manner in which other actions are performed or statements made.

Looking at the means of persona-presentation in this way leads to a further problem-area for psychological investigation. How is the persona presented matched to the action, the 'how' to the 'what'? Not only must there be a coherence between the sequence of adverbial qualifications, in order for there to be anything recognizable presented, but there must also be a coherence between the invariants of meaning in that sequence and the meaning of the actions so qualified. Going through a marriage-service solemnly has one kind of hypermeaning, while doing it flippantly another. So there must be a higher-order set of rules of propriety matching personas to situations. In terms of our conception of the cognitive matrix those rules must be principles according to which the internal organization of any given matrix would be justified and, say, the matches between situations and personas defended. The cognitive resources of a socially competent person must include what Gottschaldt has called 'principles of homology between action and expression' (Gottschaldt, 1956).

How then are we to proceed to the empirical study of personality?

Single Case Studies

It is apparent that the theoretical position we have advocated brings into prominence the individual resources of particular human beings in the creation and maintenance of a social order. The matrix of knowledge and skill in which our social competences can be represented is a structure which we would expect to find in individual human beings, and in very various forms. General facts about personality would appear only indirectly; that is, we might find various meaning relations which were a general feature of that

H

part of language which is used to express and comment upon social selves. Similarly, we might expect to find a fairly standard typology related to fairly standard situations and probably culturally determined.

How far these features can be generalized from one language and culture is a matter for empirical investigation. There does seem to be some case to be made out both from studies in Britain (Argyle and Little, 1972), and of Japan (Benedict, 1967), for a rather general but quite well-articulated fivefold system of types of situation/persona by which certain fairly standard interactions are managed. It is worth pausing for a moment to look at the results of these investigations. The situations are defined in a very broad fashion. They are, for example, interaction with a close relative, interaction with a stranger, etc . . . Five such general situations can be identified and in them five distinct qualificatory styles of action appear, each of which adds up, as it were, to a personal style, a social persona. Among the Japanese these five standard general situations are reflected in distinct forms of language, each appropriate to a certain type of situation.

This kind of differentiation of situations and personas is at a very high level of generality. There are clearly other typologies which cut across this almost certainly universal system. There are personas such as, for example, 'big spender', which are clearly identifiable in consistent ensembles of qualifications to actions to be seen in such resorts as Reno, Nevada. These may be taken on in various states of self-awareness and may prove to be a dominant qualification of wide varieties of social actions. It is our hypothesis that we must seek the origin of such typologies as include 'big spender' in cultural features of the society in which they are found, and their explanation in the history of that society. An interesting cross-cultural investigation of this sort of persona differentiation could be made using, say, the Japanese or the participants in the Kula Ring as one pole of the investigation, and, say, Californians as the other.

It is plain, therefore, that at both levels of generality typologies must emerge from very thorough investigations of individuals. It is to the methodology of the single case study that we now turn.

We begin by pointing out some weaknesses in the so-called 'extensive' design, and identifying the severe difficulties it produces for the attempt to apply its products to individual cases, even to those cases which were part of the material actually investigated. This problem is quite central to an adequate methodology since it is only in individuals that the causal mechanisms which generate such extensively identified conditions as are not artefactual, really exist.

The extensive design involves a criterion of validity which demands the use of as representative a sample as possible in order that putative correlations be properly tested while the process of identifying a representative sample requires that the characteristics by which an individual becomes a member of the sample should be as few as possible. This has been expressed in the logical adage that extension is inversely proportional to intention; that is, the greater the number of members of a class, the less specific their defining characteristics. This relationship is forced on the extensive design by the necessity that the groups to be studied and compared be homogeneous with respect to the parameters to be used for admission to the sample. For example, an extensive design study on the efficacy of a treatment for schizophrenics depends upon the groups 'schizophrenics' and 'normals' being homogeneous. But in order for significant differences to become prominent the groups must also be large. The variability of a human group, or any other non-fundamental natural kind, is such that as the size of a group increases, it becomes less homogeneous, and its notional homogeneity can be restored only by taking into account fewer and fewer properties. And of course this increases the chances that real differences will be obscured.

The problems of the interpretation of the results of using the extensive design are exacerbated by the tendency of practising psychologists to fall into the elementary fallacy of inferring from a statistical fact about the distribution of a property in a class to a degree of support for a hypothesis about the relationship of the relevant properties in individual members of that class. For example, if we find that in 70 per cent of group tasks, democratically led groups are more effective than others, we are not entitled to infer that it is 70 per cent certain that in an individual group democratic leadership produces high task performance.

Nothing can be inferred about individual cases from the statistics. All that can be inferred is the distribution of types of cases in the population. Indeed the population relative to a statistical sample may not even be real. The restriction on defining properties that is forced upon the design by the incompatible demands of homogeneity and largeness of sample means that any particular sample may be different in all kinds of unknown ways from any other. Thus to treat two samples as of the same population can be justified only if that population is an artefact, that is, a fictional projection of the restricted defining properties of the samples. There is no pre-existing population that can be identified before the sample is used, so the inference from the sample to 'the' population is illusory. The inference is a mere tautology.

If, as we believe, the personality is *prima facie* an individual property of great individual complexity, then the extensive design is useless as a method for investigating it. Of course, after a thorough study of a number of individual cases we may be in a position to generalize but the traditional methodology which leaps immediately to the general, in the sense that it seeks directly for valid correlational properties, is bound to produce in the end the most empty conjectures.

We do not deny, of course, that the possibility of analysis of individual cases depends upon the use of *concepts* which are of general application, but it does not at all follow from that necessity that the results of using concepts in a description which are applicable to more than one case should yield a generalizable description of an individual. The issue has been considerably clarified by Bakan's distinction between general and aggregate propositions (Bakan, 1955). He shows that the statistical method tends to identify only those properties which can be applied to a class considered as an aggregate, whereas the aim of the investigator is to discover the relationships between properties which can be claimed in general to be true of each individual. Thus a general proposition requires a population to enable it to be tested, but an aggregate proposition requires a population in order for it to have any sense. This distinction is not new and has been much discussed by logicians. It is the distinction between those properties which are properties of classes and those which are properties of individual members, the distinction which prompted the invention of the theory of types.

We can locate our point of view more exactly in terms of the much-abused and misunderstood distinction between the nomothetic and the idiographic. This distinction, introduced by Windelbrand in 1894, marks out two complementary approaches to the investigation of the behaviour of concrete individual objects. The nomothetic approach moves from the particular to the general, the particular becoming an instance of the generic concept. A nomothetic study moves from the concrete to the abstract. The complementary idiographic approach investigates an individual in greater and greater detail and tends to a more and more concrete form of representation.

The exact relationship between nomothesis and idiograph has been much illuminated by Du Mas (1955). Du Mas proposes that we should examine all possible domains of data collected according to the principle that an observation is made of a particular property of a particular individual at a particular time. He identifies an explicitly idiographic domain, that is, one in which the properties of an individual are determined at all identifiably different times during its existence. Such an idiographic domain can provide us with a characteristic type of information showing how the properties of the individual change with time. Such is the domain of biography. The study of the biographical domain is the study of a single case and there are indeed statistical methods—the so-called O and P factor analyses—by means of which the problems of adequate reliability of profiles can be checked (Edgington, 1972).

What, then, is the specific contribution of the idiographic domain? First of all, information gathered and oraganized around a single individual enables us to conceive of a person as a process in time. We may see him develop as he is surrounded by conditions which he creates and which in turn affect him. Furthermore, we are free to order the relationships between the various components of the idiographic domain in other than temporal ways, looking perhaps for certain relationships of meaning which may bring order to an account of a life course. It is also possible for us to examine internal processes of causation by which, relative to an environment, 'spontaneous' changes occur in the properties of an individual. Indeed, it may be possible for such a study to lead to the formulation of laws of individual behaviour which are quite different from those which would be obtained by the use of nomothetic methods using extensive designs. It would not be implausible to suggest that there are certain regularities, sometimes self-imposed, which are unique to an individual.

There might also be a case to be made for the identification of idiographic 'variables'. The nomothetic method assumes that the properties in terms of which an individual is described for scientific purposes must be the same for each individual. It is yet to be determined whether there are not particular properties unique to each individual, and indeed whether such idiographic properties may not themselves change with time, in some lawful manner. The resolution of the question as to the identity of the properties referred to by idiographic and nomothetic variables cannot be made *a priori*. Therefore it is impossible to validate a nomothetic study, that is show how its *conclusions* would be applied to individuals, unless it is grounded upon a prior idiographic investigation of each of those individuals to see whether the patterns which characterize their behaviour and the generative mechanisms which explain it have any unique properties. Similarily, the transition from the idiographic to nomothetic properties upon which the generalization move of a nomothetic study depends, is far from simple. Before a characteristic can be considered to be universally present in the members of a class, and used inter-individually, one first has also to ascertain whether it represents a consistent form of description during the history of that person. That is, the person has to manifest the same characteristic in sufficiently similar circumstances. Then, the degree of specificity or generality of this property has to be ascertained with respect to the range of variance of variable situations. Only then can the final step of nomothesis be taken. That is, if the characteristic has sufficient generality one still must investigate whether it can be used interpersonally and therefore be considered as the conceptual basis of a nomothetic investigation. Clearly, the first two steps of this process involve intrapersonal analysis, that is, the study of single cases.

While making it possible to ascertain what properties are relevant in each case and what relationships exist between them, idiographic methods are also the only ones which are suited to investigate the meaning of patterns of conduct from the point of view of the individual actor, and thus to begin the process of negotiating an interpretation with the investigator. One must hope that social psychologists have now been sufficiently warned of the dangers of imposing a common-sense or naïve interpretation upon the activities of their 'subjects', or simply taking a common-sense or naïve interpretation for granted (Mixon, 1971).

Is it possible to say any more about the structure of the design of single case studies? We believe that the process can be made yet more explicit.

(a) INDUCTIVE ELIMINATIVE ANALYSIS

This is the name we choose for that kind of investigative process which is characteristic of anatomy. Anatomical knowledge is produced by a succession of detailed dissections and descriptions of individual animals or plants. The product is a detailed scheme of a type. This kind of investigation does not produce predictive functional laws, but rather knowledge of such features of individual organisms as their structure. Formally speaking, the method involves the sequential study of particular cases. The intensive study of the first case leads to the setting up of a hypothetical schema which is then tested by an intensive study of the second case, and so on. Because of its intensity, this method yields hypothetical schema which are extremely sensitive to counter-instances. The schema would be corrected and/or a feature abandoned should it not appear in any successive case. Eventually, the process will have continued long enough for the schema arrived at to be frozen as a type, defining, for example, the anatomy of a species. The method is complicated by the fact that the apparently deviant case may be the central case of another schema, the resources of the man 'marching to a different drum'.

It may even be the case that from the start a somewhat idealized schema is generated which is not exactly reproduced in any particular case. The cases, then, are regarded as successive approximations to the ideal type and, of course, the ideal type is not capable of yielding fine-grained predictions of the structure of particular cases beyond the degree of approximation complementary to the idealization by which it is generated.

We can sum up the discussion by comparing the statistical and idiographic methods item by item (see Table on p. 224).

(b) THE REPRESENTATIVE CASE METHOD (SCHOUTZ, 1965)

In the method described under (a) Inductive Eliminative Analysis, we were presented with individuals and required to generate an adequate 'anatomical' schema for them. In the Representative Case Method we are presented with a problem with an associated schema and we are required to find an individual who fits that schema and thus can form the empirical basis of a solution to the problem.

Unlike the individuals who appear before the inductive, eliminative analyst, the individuals involved in the representative case method are not randomly selected but are the result of preliminary investigation to find a *prima facie* appropriate case. For example, in order to investigate the dynamics of some particularly striking life form such as homosexuality, an investigator using this method would select a particular person who seemed to exemplify in certain key matters the highlights of the representative schema and subject him to intensive investigation.

SYSTEMATIC DIFFERENCES

Enumerative or Statistical	*Eliminative or Idiographic*
A great number of cases with few characteristics	Few cases with many characteristics
Sampling problems	No sampling problem
Only probability statements	No probability statements
More general	Less General

Extensional	*Intentional*
The class is well defined, the problem is to look for characters common to and distinctive of the class which are not explained or included in the definition.	Particular cases are intensively investigated and the problem is to define the class of which they are members, i.e. to select an adequate minimal set to form the *definiens*
Abstraction by generalization	Generalization by abstraction

PRAGMATIC DIFFERENCES

Rapid	Slow
Rigid (fixed categories)	Flexible
Low Risk. Some result, even if not significant, can be announced	High risk. The total elimination of a schema is possible
Adequate publication facilities	Extreme difficulty in publication

The pragmatic differences between the methods seem to provide a sufficient explanation of the absence of idiographic studies from the work of most academic institutions. They are slow, difficult, and of uncertain outcome. It is our view that the temptations to undertake only nomothetic investigations must be resisted since the rapidity with which they produce some kind of results seems to us directly proportional to the triviality of those results.

We do not believe that it is advisable to assume in advance that the scientific study of such topics as human personality will yield inter-individual trans-specific laws by means of which predictions of the outcome of specific treatments can be made. We are convinced that the attempt to investigate personality under the trait or any similar theory is doomed to triviality. It must pay the price for over-hasty assumptions of generality. However, we do not wish to disguise our belief that the adoption of the idiographic method as the essential preliminary to study of the human social performance and the competences upon which it is based is likely to be difficult, time-consuming and, on occasion, disappointing for those who hope for laws of personality and its manifestation comparable to the laws of the behaviour of the ideal gases. Ironically, even in the field of gas physics, so different does the behaviour of each gas turn out to be that idiographic studies of gases have, in contemporary physics, displaced the simple nomothetic methods used by Robert Boyle and his contemporaries.

Constraints on the Empirical Study of Personality

It would no doubt be widely acknowledged at present that the study of personality, the investigation of the processes of person perception, and so on, have generated more data than they have light. We are now in the position, we believe, to identify certain constraints on this empirical study and to mark out certain traps into which earlier investigators fell.

One of the more striking points which has emerged from reviews of the work so far undertaken in this field, is how much more successful a person is in giving an account of himself than he is in giving an account of others (Mischel, 1968). This result is very readily explicable on our theory since the actual behaviour of an individual in some situations will be determined not so much by the stimuli to which he is subjected on that occasion but by the resources that he can bring to bear upon the solution of the problems that this occasion presents. Individual social knowledge is represented both in how the situation is identified and the subsequent actions.

Where investigations have shown some measure of success this has been perhaps for the rather subtle reason that the judgement of the personalities of others is made through a typology of personas.

Provided that the situation in which the actor being investigated is supposed or imagined to act is such as to evoke that persona, then the prediction of his actions would not present much difficulty. The real problem consists in the identification in advance of the situation/persona complex. A further consequence of this constraint is the not unexpected discovery that the judgements that people make of the personas and indeed the personalities of others are independent of the 'reality' of the individual being assessed (Muliak, 1964). It has been suggested that the traits or personality characters which are ascribed to people are not empirically identifiable qualities of those people so much as dimensions of meaning in the vocabulary of person assessment. Thus we both project upon and project to the world of our conspecifics a systematic performance built around our repertoire of recognizable selves. It has even been shown that clinical diagnosis in many cases reflects the semantic structure of language at least as much as it identifies distinct personas or personalities in the people upon whom that diagnosis is exercised (Chapman and Chapman, 1969).

Finally, and very significantly, there does seem to be a very great difference between the alleged discoveries of those using impersonal investigator techniques from those in which actual interaction between real people occurs. The relative neatness and consistency of the results of studying personality through questionnaires and verbal rating scales suggests the reflection of *a priori* linguistic categories, while the highly variable and often bizarre results of personal interaction suggests the difficulty which the analysis of a non-linear dyadic interaction presents to one who supposes there is a simple one-way relationship between the members of the pair. In short, if an investigator did not understand that the persona manifested in his presence is a construct which derives both from his reading of a series of action qualifications and the actor's sometimes deliberate, sometimes habitual, systematic presentations called into being by what he takes to be the perception of the other, then no way out of this potentially infinite regress will be found.

It is clear that there are no simple qualities which distinguish individual human beings as belonging to this or that personality category. One might follow Simmons and McCall (1966) in going so far as to suggest that all the people in a society have, in more or less potential form, the capacity, given the situation, to manifest any of that society's personas. Personality difference then would lie in their readiness to produce them and general capacity to manage them.

Thus, to use a conventional distinction, personas are manifested in processes and are not themselves products. In spite of the warnings of Lewin, the blindness of many practitioners in the field of personality assessment, as well as in the field of aptitude testing, concerning the product-process distinction, seems to be a case of what Max Black has called the product-process fallacy (Black, 1952). In psychology this fallacy derives its importance from the fact that it is precisely at the point where knowledge about process manifests a gap that language-induced abstractions creep in to fill it. In short, the conception of a person derives from our experience of the persona which some human individual feels is appropriate to show to us, and is the reification of an entity which has no real existence, apart from the stylistic unities of his actions.

On the basis of these points a diagnosis of the present plight in which personality assessment finds itself can be attempted. If we take together the failure of sophisticated techniques of the assessment of personality and its attempted projection, with the enormous success of the social skills of ordinary people in this matter, the often overriding effect of the *a priori* structure of language on what we seem to see in the world, coupled with the illusory correlations which result from our own set of common-sense personality theories, the wide range of personas manifested under different conditions of investigation with, finally, the neglect of action sequences as the ground for the presentation of personas, the general conclusion seems to be forced upon us that personality assessment is largely of an artefactual nature. This means that most findings can be interpreted as being much more a reflection of the various procedural ingredients of the approaches used by psycho-diagnosticians than of the real characteristics of a person studied. In a way, contemporary personality assessment teaches us a lot more about the assessing agents than about the assessed person. Whereas a sociologist might see in this conclusion a starting-point for an analysis of the ideological function of present-day personality assessment conceived as a process of cultural self-interpretation, the urgent task of psychologists is to free personality assessment from the artefactual products it has generated and in which it has been trapped. It is our contention that in the complex theory involving personas as the relatively free creative products of dyadic interactions and of the personality as the resources upon which social competence is based, we can resolve the difficulties that the traditional methods have left us.

For an empirical programme, the unravelling of this set of problems can be achieved only by turning our attention to the observation of action sequences and their expressive elements, coupled with the retrospective and anticipatory accounts given about them by individuals from their biographically determined situations, and in the analysis of which we can find the structure of the resource matrices upon which their social competence is based. It should be noticed that in advocating a direct observational and communicative approach in personality assessment we imply a concentration on individual people and on a systematic comparative study of them. This of course would be coupled with an attempt to discover the typology of personas available in the community, say through the stage, television and so on, upon which any individual draws for his knowledge of the locally authentic personas.

The Exploration of Personality Methods of Assessment

The traditional experimental study, designed to elicit the correlations between treatments and responses, makes sense only on some form of 'trait' theory. With the abandonment of that theory the rationale for the old methodology disappears, while on the basis of the new theory new empirical methods can be devised and justified.

Systematic Personality Assessment requires the convergent use of four approaches which up to now have mostly been considered only auxiliary methods. These are:

(a) the setting out of an autobiography;
(b) direct observation of action patterns in various institutional or social settings;
(c) the social inquiry;
(d) the use of deliberately contrived problem and conflict situations.

These four sources provide homogeneous data because: (a) they have to do with common everyday behaviour and situations; and (b) belonging to a world of meanings shared by the person and by the investigator they are accessible to both, and expressible in the same ordinary language. For these reasons the data obtained lead to accounts (justifications, excuses, and various commentaries upon actions) whose authenticity can be checked by negotiating them with the focal person, and other informants. They can also be compared with other accounts by field study as well as by the use of documentary evidence.

However, to be coordinated with each other, these four sources of data must be linked to a common frame of reference, and must, at least as far as 'first-order constructs' are concerned, be integrated within the more or less unified system of cognitive structures manifested by the person in each type of encounter, or moment of action as a part of a situated dyad. It is at this point that more traditional techniques of personality investigation may be used in view of their capacity to solve some specific problems, solutions, of course, limited to contributing to accounts of *that* action sequence for that momentarily situated dyad.

In order to reach these two objectives, use has to be made of a double-faced, Janus-like technique, the Biographical Inventory. This is a systematically organized collection of open questions, questionnaires and ratings which are to be used by the investigators and by the investigated person alike, and are systematically linked up with the four sources of data mentioned above. The Inventory creates justificatory contexts so organized that multiple cross-references and comparisons are made possible. Once they have been analysed, the accounts so generated become the starting-point for detailed interviews oriented towards discovering situational and interactional meaning structures, and can be compared with other accounts from other sources.

The aim of Biographical Inventory is both to make the reconstruction of the whole life-course possible on a presumed and negotiable factual basis within an interactional framework, and to link *in the present*, in terms of actual current meanings and perspectives, present conceptions to current perceptions and accounts of past processes that have led up to them, so as to bring together synchronic and diachronic aspects of personality (Dollard, 1949).

The structure and content of the Biographical Inventory cannot be adequately summarized here. Let it only be said that the systematic development of this technique has led us far beyond the current schemes for 'case studies' (Young, 1952). As it stands now, the Biographical Inventory comprises about 1000 typewritten pages.

The Autobiography is the indispensable first step in Personality Assessment without which the Person cannot give *his* definitions and accounts of his present and past situations and his self and other conceptions within his own time-perspective. The analysis of autobiographical material is not a self-contained technique. Its usefulness lies in its subordination to the more encompassing goal of biographical reconstruction.

Only on condition that it be integrated with other conceptually homogeneous data will it be possible to perform the comparisons and checks that are necessary to establish the import of the information contained in an autobiography.

The problem of the reliability or consistency of autobiographies is a pseudo-problem (Bonnard, 1961). Autobiographical data do not have a fixed reliability. They are *made* reliable by interviews designed to help the person make his typifications and 'first-order constructs' more explicit, and by the use of the Biographical Inventory which invites the person to 'zoom' on various aspects of his autobiography in a relatively homogeneous context of justification (Schutz, 1962).

Another pseudo-problem concerns certain distinctions that have been introduced between comprehensive versus topical autobiographies, structured versus unstructured autobiographies and the four combinations resulting from these two polar dimensions (Annis, 1967). In fact, the successive use of interviews on the Autobiography, the Biographical Inventory and interviews on the data obtained by the latter technique leads the investigator from the unstructured comprehensive biography, through structured topical autobiography, to a structured comprehensive autobiography. Consequently, inducing structure or letting the person give free descriptions as well as restraining or widening the scope of the Autobiography must be conceived as successive phases of an ordered process.

As a corollary it must be emphasized that in personality assessment, as distinct from literary or historical studies, the use of autobiographies is limited to documents produced by individuals to whom the investigators have direct access. Only in this way can the meaning of the writing of an Autobiography be properly evaluated. Moreover it should be noted that the motivational situation in which an Autobiography is being written and its contents are mutually interdependent so that an analysis of the assessment situation can hardly be performed without the context furnished by an autobiographical account.

Most forms of content analysis—whether computerized or not—that have been used up to now on autobiographical material are not only exceedingly time-consuming (Gottschalk and Gleser, 1969); they also seem to us to be fundamentally inadequate for the following reasons: (i) coding of isolated units does not take into account either the hierarchical structure of temporal processes or the contextual determinants of the communicated content; (ii) the usual form of content analysis ignores the *various* uses of language that can be found in autobiographical documents, that is the multiplicity of speech-acts that can be performed by making statements about oneself; (iii) the choice of categories is made by the investigator who imposes his own typifications on those of the person being studied whereas it is one of the Autobiography's specific functions to provide a starting-point for making explicit the kind of 'first-order constructs' a person uses as well as the background expectancies which underlie them (Scheff, 1968).

The kind of analysis that does most to preserve the individuality of an Autobiography consists of four successive steps:

(a) Identifying the topics mentioned by the author: considering that what is lacking in an Autobiography is as important as what is explicitly formulated, use has to be made of a general scheme against which initial themes may be compared. This general scheme is in fact a modification of the table of contents of the Biographical Inventory. The application of this empirically derived scheme required about ten successive readings of the same Autobiography which each time is being considered from a different point of view;

(b) once the elements that are either present or absent have been identified, they have to be regrouped in thematic units composed of coexisting or sequential elements;

(c) the third step consists in the chronological ordering of the thematic units and their constituents. It also involves a formal process analysis according to the method of episoding, developed by Barker and Wright (1955);

(d) finally, thematic units and formal process analysis are brought into correspondence with each other by means of interviews in which the person is encouraged to explicate the meanings he attaches to them. Interpretation can then proceed according to a specified model of the person as a goal-oriented, rule-following, meaning-endowing agent.

Treated in this way the analysed autobiographical material is ready for a deepened analysis by means of the Biographical Inventory and for an integration with the three other sources of data mentioned above. Explicitness of meanings and definiteness of conceptualization in the last phase of the analysis can be stepped up by having the person programme his Autobiography according to the method of programmed cases (De Waele, 1971); and by applying to the autobiographical material the 'scenario method', in which the authenticity of total episodes as possible social realities is tested (Mixon, 1972).

Direct Observation and Social Enquiry

To be consistent with the general principle that all human behaviour is socially situated and with the general view that personality is to be conceived of as a set of social competences, the social situation of the individual who is being studied in personality assessment and the assessment procedures themselves must be considered objects of study of first-rate importance.

It is astonishing to see personality studies being conducted within the confines of an office or a laboratory as if such highly specific ecological conditions could be considered to be representative of the various situations in which an individual will display the whole gamut of more or less standardized solutions he has at his disposal. To be sure, such a conception of assessment can only be based on the explicit or tacit assumption that personality is made up of 'traits', or 'dispositions', or once and for all fixed 'defence mechanisms' which are impermeable to situational definitions and determinants. But then one should not be surprised either at the low predictive value of classical personality assessment methods, or at the enormous difficulties besetting attempts at replication, or at the difficulties resulting from so-called 'method variance'.

On the ethogenic view, however, situation definitions being an integral part of the cognitive matrix through which interactive performance and problem-solving express themselves, the study of situations, their possible requirement and meanings are inseparable from the study of an individual personality. This is not only a theoretical principle but also a methodological one, which means that in the assessment of an individual personality, generalizations of social performances over situations and their storing in the individual's cognitive matrix as a standardized solution can never be taken for granted, but has to be proved and investigated inductively in each case. So, the personality investigation always has to start from the largest possible sample of social situations in order to discover which ones are particularly relevant to that individual and how they can be grouped in more general situation schemata. One of the functions of the autobiography and of the biographical reconstruction consists precisely in making such a study of situations possible, and reciprocally the various situations which can be studied at the time of the assessment will inevitably shed some light on those that were significant in an individual's past history, as currently conceived by him.

A first kind of contemporaneous situational analysis that has to be performed concerns the assessment situation itself and the wider context in which it takes place. Two extreme cases can be distinguished according to the degree to which the assessed person inhabits his daily 'natural' social environment. At one extreme the assessment situation, which may consist of a series of occurrences, is limited to the personal encounter with the investigators, e.g. in the case of a consultation. At the other extreme assessment may be embedded within the highly complex social structure of institutions like the army, a prison, or a hospital. In the latter case the assessment situation is directly influenced by the institutional structure of which it is but a subordinate part, so that the investigations have to include every possible aspect of the conduct-in-situation which the individual may exhibit while residing in the institution. While this kind of day-to-day observation by trained participant observers can be organized without too great difficulties, its interpretation has to face the difficult task of having an institution studying itself from within.

When the assessment situation is not integrated within the framework of an institution, there still remain important contextual features to be analysed such as the referral agencies, and there is still the reception and waiting-room situation to be considered. There are good reasons to believe that the observation of the waiting-room may yield information at least as important as that gathered by the use of usual methods.

Whatever the kind of background of the assessment situation, it has to be carefully observed and analysed in a Goffmanesque way, if the meaning attributed to it by the individual is to be properly understood.

As to the global life situation, it calls for detailed social investigations which will best be carried out by participant observation. The various aspects that have to be taken into account are numerous. They range from income, budget, neighbourhood, housing, internal arrangements of houses and flats, to professional career and working conditions, family organization and functioning, leisure activities, group participation etc., as these are perceived by those taking part. In spite of its obvious importance for personality investigation, social enquiries have been sadly neglected by social psychologists. Still, it is the only way to acquire some knowledge about the social situation and the persons an individual has to deal with in his daily life, and the meaning he gives to those interactions. In Murray's well-known book, *Exploration of Personality* (1938), where dozens of very ingenious methods of personality investigation are presented, and discussed, the social enquiry is not even alluded to. This is probably due to the fact that on the one hand the social enquiry is considered to be the reserved hunting-ground of social workers, and on the other hand very few sociologists have shown interest in the development of a clinical idiographic sociology. So it happens that the requirements of ethogenic social enquiries remain unsatisfied as well by the one-sided pragmatic orientation of social workers as by the neglect of sociologists. Still, it is to be expected that the present wave of interest in participant observation will sooner or later draw the attention of sociologists to the methodological and technical problems raised by the necessity of elaborating the ethnography of our own tribes. Already two important points should be noted. First of all, a social enquiry has to make use in a systematic way of various techniques covering all the discriminable aspects of social life—documents and how they are generated, local authorities, various kinds of informants, direct observations, 'in situ', etc. —these are the sources of information for the various account systems interlocking around the ambiguous encounters of social life and giving them substance as episodes. These must be compared with each other and checked as to their meanings. It is also necessary to have the official, or professional, or private informants negotiate their accounts one with another. Secondly, before it is carried out, the social enquiry has to work from the descriptions and commentaries furnished by the individual who is being studied and when it has been completed he has once again to be confronted with its results, since their social reality consists only in the meanings he gives to them and which can be negotiated with those with whom he is presently interacting.

Situational Tests Redefined

Up to now, situational tests have been conceived as a supplement to psychometric tests. It was thought that because of their apparent similarity to the predictive tests of naïve trait theory they might shed light on the influence of personality and social variables of which pure aptitude measures do not take account. However, if they are to serve new functions in personality assessment, situational tests must be freed from such restrictions. As we are not primarily interested in some specialized performance and its end result, but instead want to concentrate on the temporal articulation of action and expression processes through which various personality characteristics so abundantly reveal themselves, there is no need for the situations that are staged to simulate narrowly 'real' tasks. Also, if the aim is description, comparison and interpretation rather than prediction, situation tests will have to be judged by other criteria than those defined by psychometric theory.

In advocating this point of view we are not, in fact, being so very revolutionary. Rather, we are taking up again a line of research which was started by W. Koehler, K. Lewin and K. Gottschaldt. Following the suggestions of the last-named author, as well as making use of the formal process analysis developed by R. Barker and H. F. Wright, we are making use of various problem situations in order to arrive by systematic intra-individual comparisons at formulations of descriptions of individual personalities based on direct observation and communication. We are simply trying out some Gestalt-psychological ideas in the field of Personality Assessment. This is the reason why, being desirous to profit as much as possible from the results accumulated by general psychological research, our most promising techniques consist in various levels of aspiration situations, soluble or insoluble problem situations requiring the use of tools or conceptual restructuring, and also group tasks which are far from being completely unknown. And these are *formal* analogues of 'real-world' occasions.

The issue of 'realism' which has mostly been considered to be a distinctive feature of situation tests is another problem which is in need of reformulation. The authors who have written about situation tests generally seem to consider 'realism' and 'similarity to a task executed in daily life' to be synonymous. In fact, 'similarity' defined as structural identity (be it isomorphism or homeomorphism) between the components of task and test does not imply realism. A situational test may very well be a model of a task without eliciting behaviour which would necessarily be 'realistic'. Moreover, even if the behaviour in a situational test looks similar to the one observed in 'real life' this phenotypic resemblance does not allow any inference as to their genotypic identity. As a matter of fact 'realism' admits of all degrees, from 'stubborn' reality to dream fantasies, and depends on the subject and on his 'definition of the situation' (Thomas, 1966; Schutz, 1956). This is a problem which cannot simply be brought under control by attending to the similarity between test and criterion task. If there often are good reasons to contrast behaviour in a testing or experimental situation with the kind of actions performed in real life, it is because the latter are characterized by self-initiated goal-setting and task involvement and by the activation of central layers of the personality system, and by the momentary situation being an integral part of a larger meaningful whole of the individual life-world. Quite opposite states of affairs may obtain in taking tests or being the subject for an experiment. Thus it is not sufficient to justify the use of situation tests by appealing to the principles of consistency (Murray, 1938). To admit as a matter of principle that 'a given subject will respond to similar environmental situations in a similar manner' is one thing, and to show that he actually has done so is quite another. In fact, whether a person's behaviour in a contrived situation is more or less 'real', and whether his conduct is similar to the one he manifests in other circumstances, are questions to which the answer cannot be taken for granted and must be settled empirically. The real problem is to stage situations in such a way and of such a kind that the degree of realism of action and expression processes as well as their eventual similarity whith analogous ones may be established by a comparative analysis of direct observations and the accounts furnished by the subjects, a problem largely solved by Mixon, for at least one class of cases (Mixon, 1972).

To avoid ambiguity of meanings which Mixon has shown to be the central problem in social psychological research in this method, problem situations are developed as far as possible by an interaction method, the person being studied identifying real problems he once faced which, so he defines, are like the problem situations *as he conceives them*.

Having taken so much critical distance from the current opinion of situational tests, it seems advisable, in order to prevent confusion of aims and means, to choose another name for the methods of personality assessment on which our research bears. To keep things simple, we would suggest calling them 'problem and conflict situations'—abbreviated to 'PCS'. Of course, this is not sufficient to characterize them positively. In order to differentiate the method of PCS from other methods like psychometric tests, field work, naturalistic methods or systematic experimentation, the two dimensions used by E. P. Willems (1969) to locate various research activities provide a useful framework. The first dimension describes the degree of the investigator's influence upon, or manipulation of, antecedent conditions of the behaviour studied. The second dimension describes the degree to which units are imposed by the investigator upon the behaviour studied. Whereas psychometric testing and classical experimental designs would be considered to be high on both dimensions, with field work medium and naturalistic investigation low on both dimensions, there are still other combinations which will not be considered here. The PCS method could be described as being medium in the degree of manipulation of antecedent conditions, while being low on the degree of impositions of units of meaning. When confronting a person with PCS's the investigator defines by means of the instructions only a few of the necessary conditions of the situation.

The others are, as it were, 'filled in' by the person's interpretative construction of the situation. It is indeed essential to the method of PCS that the observed person should have the opportunity gradually to structure the problem situation in which he has been placed. The emergence of active or reactive attitudes like suspiciousness of the investigator's intent, various modes of responsiveness to the demand characteristics of the task or evaluation apprehension, which might, with other methods, be considered to be the source of disturbing artefacts, belong to the kind of fundamental data the method of PCSs is explicitly designed to elicit. On the other hand, as the observations and recordings are concentrated on action and expressive processes with their verbal accompaniments and stylistic qualifications, it is essential that the lowest degree of imposition of meanings on the ensuing behaviour and the surrounding situation should be used.

At first sight, it might look as if the method of PCS's were an analogue of projective methods in the field of action and expression. While this cannot be judged to be altogether false, there is another aspect of PCS's that considerably weakens this analogy. The action and expression process has also to be taken into account as such. Previous research by Gottschaldt and his collaborators, as well as our own findings, demonstrates that the richest and most revealing data are obtained when the initial conditions are so defined that they develop into one or more conflict situations. It is when the individual whose personality is being investigated has to come to terms with a conflict of *growing* intensity that the unfolding processes take on their most fascinating individual qualities. Thus it is not only essential that the problem situations should lead to more or less soluble or insoluble conflicts but also that the task and the means at the disposal of the subject for its execution should be such that as much as possible of the action and expression processes may be directly observed and recorded. The context of justification is itself a kind of conflict situation.

A few words should be added concerning the staging of the PCS's. Great care must be taken to enrich the action field appropriately. This means that the environmental background against which various means–end structures can emerge as figures must have a carefully organized content destined to favour the appearance of a great variety of meaning attributions, restructurings of the situation, adaptive and defensive moves. For example, it is quite obvious that if no perceptible substrate is provided for them, no substitute actions will ever appear. It is for this reason that it may be important that the specific task used in a PCS should be embedded in the context of familiar objects and of some kind of a daily life environment.

Setting aside end-effect registration and other achievement scores as well as global ratings, we are left with the difficult problem of analysing the directly observed and recorded stream of behaviour. The task consists in devising an analytical tool that will enable us to decipher what may be called the syntax of action. The concept of the temporal Gestalt is present everywhere in Lewin's work. In his well-known work on the structure of action of mentally deficient children, K. Gottschaldt (1933) has touched explicitly upon this subject from a diagnostic point of view. But it is the great merit of R. Barker and H. F. Wright (1955) to have explicitly formulated in the course of their ecological studies a method of process analysis. The fundamental elements of this analytical method are molar, goal-oriented behaviour and situation units which are called episodes and phases. The definition of their various relationship like different types of direction, temporal inclusion, overlapping, inter-ruption. etc. . . . make it possible to give a detailed formal analysis of the temporal integration of action processes as they can be directly observed and recorded. Besides the coding of formal characteristics, coding of the content of episodes as to goals, instrumental actions, expressive behaviour, social interaction and verbal exchanges can be carried out. It is to this method that we have resorted to analyse the protocols of PCS's. Although it has been devised for the study of naturalistic ecological data concerning the behaviour of children, research that is being carried out in our laboratory has shown that it is also applicable with considerable reliability to the behaviour of adults in group PCS's.

Whereas formal process-analysis seems to be applicable to any kind of PCS protocol provided it is sufficiently detailed, and may even be used with biographical material, the content categories that are to be used for the coding of each formally defined action unit have to be adapted to the specific characteristics of each PCS. The objective towards which we are now heading consists in the develop-ment of a set of content categories that are at the same time specifically adapted to each PCS in use and applicable to them all. This means that they will have to be related from PCS to PCS as 'determinates' under the same 'determinable'. It is only if this con-dition is fulfilled that a comparative analysis will be possible and that the problem of the consistency of personality characteristics will receive the adequate treatment for which it has so long been waiting. However, comparative formal and content analysis of directly observable action and expression processes is not the only outcome of the method of PCS. As Murray has noted in his 'guiding rules for designing situational tests', '. . . the [subjects] should be given an opportunity either in the course of the task or immediately afterward to discuss their performance. Much can be gained from the subject's own account of how he would, or of how he did, handle the assigned problem. He is usually capable of giving the most plausible explanation of his own behaviour.' (Murray, 1938).

Like many other interesting suggestions formulated by H. A. Murray, it is far from clear how much of it has ever been realized, for no published data are available on this question. However, on the basis of our first findings, it can be confidently asserted that the systematic exploration of the form and content of the retrospective accounts given by a person subjected to a PCS so strikingly supplement direct observations and are so revealing that they are to be considered an integral part of the whole procedure. After all, we have good reasons for considering a man as a purposively acting, rule-selecting, inventing and conforming being who is able to monitor consciously his behaviour and the way he displays himself to others. Only behaviourists or psychonanalysts have not yet learned that people know a lot more about the causes and reasons of their conduct than is commonly supposed by presumptuous psychologists. The real problem is to persuade and help them to express the accounts they otherwise keep to themselves.

In order to attend to this essential aspect of the method of PCS's a standardized 'focused interview' in the sense of Kendall and Merton (1956) has been developed and put to use. Based on previous clinical explorations concerning PCS's a detailed set of topics covering 'all possible' cognitive and affective processes that are not directly observable and which may occur in any of the PCS's has been defined. Of course coding of the data which are obtained by means of this focused interview requires taking into account the corresponding observational data and vice versa, and the person for whom this kind of account is given.

It would be a fundamental mistake to look upon the method of PCS's which we are trying to develop as a closed and self-contained whole exclusively devoted to the analysis of momentary situations extending over a few hours. First of all, it is essential that observational as well as interview data obtained from individual and group PCS's should be systematically compared among themselves. This, as has already been noted, requires the elaboration of various kinds of content categories in order to make comparison possible. Second, the use of standardized focused interviews has shown that, after PCS's, the accounts of the subject very easily and frequently go beyond the limits of the immediate situation and, by assimilation or contrast, mention other relevant life-situations. Instead then of focusing on immediate past situations it becomes possible to widen the scope of the interview so as to include the comparisons the subject is induced to formulate concerning biographically determined situations. This transition will be considerably facilitated if, previous to the application of the PCS's, subjects have been asked to answer a set of open questions about various goal-setting, frustration and conflict situations they have previously experienced. As these questions are so phrased as to elicit the description of biographical situations that are formally analogous to the PCS's they can easily be compared with them within the same conceptual framework. But it is also possible to ask the subjects to make their own comparisons. If biographical situation and a summary of the PCS's are typed on separate cards, these can be used to have the subjects sort all possible triads in their dichotomous categories so as to make use of a modified version of Kelly's Role Repertory Test. The difference with the latter technique is that, instead of comparing persons, the subjects compare biographical data and PCS's. Here again appears a fundamental difference that separates our conception of PCS's as a point of departure and once we are in possession of all relevant data we search for analogous situations as these are defined by the subjects in their own terms, rather than imposing *our* conception of similarity of situations.

There are, of course, still a lot of technical problems that confront us when we make use of PCS's as they have just been defined. Foremost among them is the training of observers and analysts. These have first to be made familiar with the kind of action and expression processes which are to be observed. This means that, without trying to report anything, they have to acquire a sufficient degree of sensitiveness and perceptual differentiation towards the extraordinary richness of behaviour processes that unfold themselves in PCS's. Witnessing a certain number of PCS's and discussing the data with trained observers after having served as a subject is the first step that can be recommended for training. Then comes the learning of an adequate language. By means of specially programmed video-tape recordings, the use of an adequate terminology can be taught in a standardized way. Although the analytical treatment of the observers' account stops short of an analysis of the molecular components of action it is necessary that future observers should acquire a standardized terminology and the verbal skill for the reporting of the *therbligs* of action processes. At the same time they should be taught to look for goal-oriented molar behaviour units by comparing their own reports with those made by experienced

observers. Most difficult of all, however, is the teaching of standardized, but at the same time flexible descriptions of the expressive and
stylistic aspects of behaviour processes. A method for this kind of
training is still to be found. Probably it will require that the observers
should pass through an 'analytical' stage during which they would
learn the use of a set of specially devised symbols to depict the
observed expressions before they can again make use of normal
language.

All four sources of information, when taken together, enable us
to ascribe a set of cognitive resources to the person involved which
are the basis of his social competence, and the source of the personas
he presents in action. We can also tell how he sees his past and
perhaps his future. And by these methods we too may share in his
knowledge of himself, and add our own educated guesses to his
about his future. It will be a very long time indeed before we can
tell whether there is anyone else like him.

REFERENCES

Annis, A. P. The Autobiography: Its Uses and Value. *Professional Psychology*, 1967, 14, 9–17.

Argyle, M. *Social Interaction*. London: Methuen, 1969, pp. 179ff.

Argyle, M. & Little, B. R. *J. Theory Soc. Behaviour*, 1972, 2, 1–35.

Baken, D. *Perceptual and Motor Skills*, 1955, 5, 211–12.

Barker, R. & Wright, H. F. *Midwest and its Children*. New York: Harper & Row, 1955.

Benedict, R. *The Chrysanthemum and the Sword*. London: Routledge & Kegan Paul, 1967, Ch. 3.

Black, M. *Critical Thinking*. Englewood Cliffs, N. J.: Prentice-Hall, 1952.

Blum, A. F. & McHugh, P. The Social Ascription of Motives. *American Soc. Rev.* 1971, 36, 98–109.

Boice, R. Domestication, *Psych. Bulletin*, 1973, 3, 215–30.

Bolk, L. *Das Problem der Menschwendung*. Jena, 1926.

Bonnes, H. *Psychology of Personality*. New York: Ronald, 1961.

Bower, K. S. Situationism in Psychology, *Psych. Rev.*, 1973, 80, 307–36.

Bruner, J. S. The organization of early skilled action. *The Integration of a Child in a Social World*. In Richards (ed.). Cambridge: Cambridge University Press, 1974, Ch. 9.

Bruner, J. S. The Nature and Uses of Immaturity. *American Psychologist*, 1972, 27, 687–708.

Carus, C. G. *Symbolik der menschlichen Gestalt. Ein Handbuch zur Menschenkenntnis* (Lrg. Th. Lessing) 3. Auflage. Celle, 1925.

Chapman, L. J. & Chapman, J. P. Illusory correlations as an obstacle to the use of valid psychodiagnostic signs, *J. Abnormal Psych.*, 1969, 74, 271–80.

Conrad, K. *Der Konstitutionstypus*, Zweite Veränderte Auflage, Springer, 1963.

De Waele, J. P. *La Méthode des Cas Programmés*. Bruxelles: Dessart, 1971.

Dollard, J. *Criteria for the Life History*, New York: Peter Smith, 1949.

Du Mas, F. M. *Psychological Reports*, 1955, 1, 68–75.

Edgington, E. *Canadian Psychologist*, 1972, 13, 121–34.

Eibl-Eibelsfeldt, I. *Ethology*, Holt-Rinehart-Winston, 1970.

Fox, M. W. The Influence of domestication upon animals. *Veterinary Record*, 1967, 80, 696–702.

Gehlen, A. *Der Mensch*. Bonn: Athenäum-Verlag, 1955, pp. 91–139.

Goffman, E. *Relations in Public*, London: Allen Lane The Penguin Press, 1971, Ch. 6, Part One.

Goodall, J. *In the Shadow of Man*. Collins, London, 1971.

Gottschaldt, K. *Die Struktur des Kindlichen Handelns*, Ambrosia Barth, 1933.

Gottschaldt, K. Hundlung und Ausdruck. In *der Psychologie der Persönlichkeit. Revista di Psichologia Anno L*, Fascicolo IV, 1956, pp. 161–75.

Gottschalk, L. A. & Fleser, G. C. *The Measurement of Psychological States through the Content Analysis of Verbal Behaviour*. University of California Press, 1969.

Hardy, Sir A. Escape from Specialization. In Huxley, Hardy & Ford (eds.), *Evolution as a Process*, London: Allen & Unwin, 1954, p. 125.

Harré, R. The conditions for a social psychology of childhood. *The Integration of a Child into a Social World*. In Richards (ed.), Cambridge: Cambridge University Press, 1974, Ch. 12.

Harré, R. & Secord, P. F. *The Explanation of Social Behaviour*. Oxford: Blackwell, 1972.

Hofstätter, P. R. The rate of maturation and the cephalization coefficient = a hypothesis. *J. Psychology*, 1951, 31, 271–80.

Keith, Sir A. *A New Theory of Human Evolution*. London: Watts, 1948.

Kretschmer, E. *Körperban und Charakter*. 21/22 Auflage. Springer, 1955.

Lashley, K. S. *The problems of Serial Order in Behaviour in Cerebral Mechanisms in Behaviour. The Hixon Symposian* (L. A. Jeffress, ed.), 1951.

Leach, E. The Influence of Cultural Context on non-verbal behaviour in Man. In R. A. Hinde (ed.), *Non-Verbal Communication*, Cambridge: Cambridge University Press, 1972, pp. 315–44.

McKinnon, D. W. The Structure of Personality. In Hunt (ed.), *Personality and Personality Disorders*. New York: Ronald, 1944, Vol. I, Ch. I.

Merton, R. K., Fiske, M. & Kendall, P. L. *The Focused Interview.*, Free Press, 1956.

MISCHEL, W. *Personality and Assessment*, New York: 1968.

MISCHEL, W. Towards a Cognitive Social Learning Reconceptualization of Personality. *Psych. Rev.*, 1973, 80, 252–83.

MIXON, D. Actors rather than Subjects. *J. Theory Soc. Behaviour*, 1971, 1, 19–31.

MIXON, D. Instead of Deception. *J. Theory Soc. Behaviour*, 1972, 2, 145–77.

MONTAGU, A. *The Human Revolution*. Cleveland and New York: World Publishing Co., 1965, pp. 114–31.

MORGAN, E. *The Descent of Woman*. Souvenir Press, London, 1972.

MULIAK, S. A. Are Personality factors rater's conceptual factors? *J. of Consulting Psych.*, 1964, 28, 506–11.

MURRAY, H. A. *Explorations in Personality:* a clinical and experimental study of fifty men of college age. New York: Oxford University Press, 1938.

PORTMANN, A. Zoologie und des neue Bild des Menschen, *Rowohlts dentsche enzyklopädie*, Hamburg, 1951.

REES, W. L. & EYSENCK, H. J. A factorial study of some morphological and psychological aspects of human constitution. *J. Mental Science*, 1945, 91, 8–21.

RICHARDS, M. *The Integration of a Child into a Social World*. Cambridge: Cambridge University Press, 1974.

ROHEIM, G. *Psychoanalysis and Anthropology*. International University Press, 1950.

SCHEFF, T. J. Negotiating Reality. Notes on Power in the Assessment of Responsibility, *Social Problems*, 1968, 16, 3–17.

SCHOUTZ, F. C. *Research Methods in Personality*. Century Psychology Series, Appleton-Century-Crofts, 1965.

SCHUTZ, A. *Collected Papers*, Vol. I. The Hague: Martinus Nijholt, 1962.

SCHUTZ, A. *The Phenomenology of the Social World*. Chicago: Northwestern University Press, 1967, pp. 75–6.

SECORD, P. F. & BACKMAN, C. Personality theory and the problem of stability and change in individual behaviour: an inter-personal approach. *Psych. Rev.* 1961, 68, 21–32.

SHOTTER, J. The transformation of natural into acquired powers. *J. Theory Soc. Behaviour*. 1973, 3, 141–56.

SIMMONS, J. L. & McCALL, G. J. *Identities and Interactions*. New York: Free Press, 1966.

SMELSER, N. *The Theory of Collective Behaviour*. New York: Free Press, 1963.

STORCH, O. *Die Sonderstellung des Menschen in Lebensabspiel und Veverbung*. Wein: Springer-Varlag, 1948.

STRAUSS, A. *Mirrors and Masks*. New York: Free Press, 1959.

TAYLOR, C. The Self in Question. In T. Mischel (ed.), *The Self*. Oxford: Blackwell, 1977.

THOMAS, W. I. Situational analysis. In M. Janowitz (ed.), *W. I. Thomas on Social Organizations and Social Personality*. Chicago: University of Chicago Press, 1966, pp. 154–67.

THORPE, W. H. *Learning and Instinct in Animals*. London: Methuen, 1963.

VAN HOOFF, J. A. R. A. M. A. Comparative approach to the phylogeny of laughter and smiling. In R. A. Hinde (ed.), *Non-Verbal Communication*. Cambridge: Cambridge University Press, 1972, pp. 209–238.

WILLEMS, E. P. & RAUSH, H. L. (eds.), *Naturalistic Viewpoints in Psychological Research*. Holt-Rinehart-Winston, 1969.

YOUNG, K. *Personality and Problems of Adjustment*, New York: Appleton-Century-Crofts, 1952.

ZELLER, E. *Konstitution und Entwicklung*. Göttingen: Verlag für Psychologie, 1957.

Index of Names

Index of Subjects